enier Joe Kirkwood   Jan Stephenson   Hords

Ossie Pickworth   Frank   Phillips

The Black Knight   1904

Australian Open   Kel Nagle   Back Cl

yer   Royal Melbourne

Harry Whitton   Norman Von Nida

ickory Sticks Golf   The Far East Circuit

Sir Bob Charles   Bruce Crampton   Bump and Run

Alan Murky Murray

David Graham   Victoria   Bobby Jones

good   Greg Norman Graham Marsh   Billy Dunk

Ross Perrett

DEDICATION

This book is dedicated to my step-grandfather **Mickey Heald** from Aldeburgh Golf Club in Suffolk, England. Mickey was a fine golfer and a true gentleman. He was also a devoted husband, loyal father, a decorated war veteran and later a successful businessman. When I was aged 12, Mickey spent a few weeks with me in his treasured garden (in Suffolk) teaching me how to hold the golf club, the posture and the rudimentary swing using only plastic practice golf balls with holes in them. After two weeks in the garden I was itching to hit a real golf ball on a golf course. The day came and Mickey took me to the 'River Course' at Aldeburgh Golf Club. On the first tee he said, 'I will take great pride in teeing up this, what I hope is the first of  many golf shots.' When I struck that real golf ball for the first time, using a persimmon head … I was hooked. I have been ever since. My tiny frame, as a 12-year-old, had propelled the golf ball like an arrow about 180 yards straight at the pin. I had a par 4 on my first ever golf hole and three more pars for the nine that we played. Six years later I saw Mickey again, in Suffolk, and I was playing off 3 as an 18-year-old and very keen to make golf my life. Mickey looked at me knowingly and suggested, 'I think you will have a fine amateur career to complement your working life, dear Andrew.' He gave me a hickory shafted putter when I was 18: I still use it to this day, in his honour.

Photo: 1922 Hudson Super Six touring car. NSW State Library (hood_07531)

Bump and Run: At The Feet Of The Masters
Andrew Crockett

First published in Australia in 2013
By Hodaddy, Burringbar NSW

Watercolour art by Robert A. Wade and Jamie Kasdaglis

Illustrations and hand-drawn fonts by Harry Daily

Foreword © Adam Scott

Designed by Andrew Crockett

Layout by Gemini Tiger Creative
www.geminitiger.com

Proofreading by Tim Learner

Cover art & Design by Jamie Kasdaglis

Printed in China.

ISBN 978-0-646-90531-0

Publisher Note : This is not a history of golf.

More information **bumpandrun.com.au**

CONTENTS

FOREWORD

The opportunity to share and celebrate the exploits of our pioneering golf professionals is a privilege.

Pioneers are by definition brave and adventurous, people who prepare the way, who initiate and take part in the establishment of new paths. So it was with many of the great names of Australian golf. Certainly they took their games to the established centres of golf, often with great success, but they were also instrumental in creating the new frontiers of golf - opening the sport to countries and people to whom golf had been a mystery.

These men paved the way for the generations of professionals that followed. Their legacy sees the modern players enjoying golf in all corners of the globe. The growth of golf in the Far East, symbolised by an ever expanding professional tournament schedule, is a direct result of their spirit and love of the game, and their willingness to travel. Their modes of transport are likely incomprehensible to us today. Multi-week boat journeys to exotic places only read about in novels, 4 days of propeller driven aircraft to reach England - such was the golf circuit our professionals undertook. They compiled a lifetime of experiences never felt before, all the while playing their game and sharing it with fledgling newcomers to embrace.

Happy reminders of these times and pioneers abound. I have been fortunate to win the Singapore Open 3 times. When I first held the trophy an elderly long term expatriate in Singapore reminded me that Frank Phillips won the inaugural Singapore Open title in 1961. His name was on the trophy - the first name. Similar reminders can be found in clubhouses and locker rooms across the world and provide glimpses into feats of our travelling pros. Engraved on boards and in silverware I've seen the names Von Nida, Ferrier, Thomson, Nagle, Crampton, Graham and more. Not content to ply their trade in an insular fashion at home, they explored and conquered. When there was nothing to conquer, they created.

It is appropriate to recognise our past golfing heroes. The professionals of the modern era have also had to travel a path away from their homeland in pursuit of golfing success, but because of the men before them that path is paved, the footing secure and the destination known.

We have much to thank them for. Let's celebrate them together, remember their faces and enjoy their words. This is their story.

Adam Scott

Golf was intended to be played along the ground with humps and bumps and 'bad luck' an intricate facet of the intrigue and uniqueness of the sport. Over time golf is becoming more and more sterile with manicured golf courses, cloned swings, equipment and technology that seems bent on trying to make the game easier and easier. Golf was meant to be hard, like life, the game itself becoming a mirror of our internal struggles and it doesn't take a wise man to know that the hard road and the path less trodden is the one that builds character. The elders of golf provide us with some interesting clues and it is my hope that the content in this book not only assists golfers to improve their game, but also provides some historical education for the afflicted and the happily addicted.

Andrew J Crockett (author)

12
questions
with the
elders of
golf

AT THE FEET OF THE MASTERS

AT THE FEET OF THE MASTERS BIOGRAPHIES

Jack Nicklaus (USA)
Born: 1940
Official Professional victories: 120
Triple Grand Slam Champion + most prolific Major Champion with a record 18 professional major championships
British Open Champion 1966, 1970, 1978
US PGA Champion 1963, 1971, 1973, 1975, 1980 (record-tying total)
US Open Champion 1962, 1967, 1972, 1980 (record-tying total)
US Masters Champion 1963, 1965, 1966, 1972, 1975, 1986 (record total)
US Amateur Champion 1959, 1961
Eisenhower Trophy individual 1960
Australian Open Champion 1964, 1968, 1971, 1975, 1976, 1978
19 second-place finishes in the Majors
73 US PGA Tour Victories (3rd all-time)
World Cup 1963, 1964, 1966 (with Arnold Palmer), 1971 (with Lee Trevino), 1973 (with Johnny Miller)
Record 8 Champions Tour (Senior PGA Tour) Major Championships
Authored Golf My Way in 1974, an all-time best selling instructional book. Led to video version of Golf My Way, the best-selling instructional video series.
World Golf Hall Of Fame 1974
Greatest player who ever lived
Named Golfer Of The Century and Golfer of the Millennium
The Golden Bear

Peter Thomson AO, CBE, MBE
Born: 1929
Official Professional victories: 82
British Open Champion 1954, 1955, 1956, 1958, 1965
World Cup (with Kel Nagle) 1954, 1959
Represented Australia 11 times in The World Cup
PGA Senior Championship (Britain) 1988
Open Champion of Australia (3), Germany, Italy, Spain, India (3), Hong Kong (3), Philippines and New Zealand (9).
1956 Texas Open
US Champions Tour - 9 victories in 1985 alone including PGA Seniors Championship
News Of The World British Matchplay 1954, 1961, 1966, 1967
World Golf Hall Of Fame 1988
Peerless Pete - Australia's greatest golfer

Kel Nagle
Born: 1920
Official Professional victories: 80
British Open Champion 1960 (St Andrews)
US Open 1965 - tied with Gary Player, lost playoff
Open Champion of Canada, Australia, France, New Zealand (7), Hong Kong and Switzerland
1961 shot 260 (64-65-66-65) on the par 74 Woodbrook Golf Course to win the Irish Hospitals tournament. Also shot 260 to win Hong Kong Open in 1961.
World Cup Champion (with Peter Thomson) 1954, 1959
Represented Australia 9 times in the World Cup
PGA Senior Championship (Britain) 1971, 1973, 1975
World Golf Hall of Fame 2007
The grandest gentleman of Australian golf

Gary Player (South Africa)
Born: 1935
Official Professional victories: 165 (on six continents)
British Open Champion 1959, 1968, 1974
US PGA Champion 1962, 1972
US Open Champion 1965
US Masters Champion 1961, 1974, 1978
Australian Open Champion 1958, 1962, 1963, 1965, 1969, 1970, 1974
US Champions Tour victories - 19
Senior PGA Championship 1986, 1988, 1990
US Senior Open 1987, 1988
Senior Players Championship 1987
World Cup (with Harold Henning) 1965 + individual honours, 1977 individual honours (represented South Africa 16 times in The World Cup)
The only non-American golfer to achieve a career 'Grand Slam' (others have been Ben Hogan, Gene Sarazen, Jack Nicklaus and Tiger Woods)
Authored 36 books
World Golf Hall Of Fame 1974
One of the greatest golfers of all time
The Black Knight, Mr Fitness, International Ambassador for Golf

AT THE FEET OF THE MASTERS

Norman Von Nida OAM

Born: 1914

Official Professional victories: 43

Philippines Open 1938, 1939

British Open 3rd 1946, 1958

Australian Open Champion 1950, 1952, 1953

Queensland Open Champion 1935, 1936, 1937, 1940, 1949, 1953, 1961

Australian PGA Championship 1946, 1948, 1950, 1951

NSW Open Championship 1939, 1946, 1947, 1948, 1953, 1954

British Masters Championship 1948

Won 7 tournaments in Britain in 1947 and won the Vardon Trophy (71.25)

Represented Australia in the World Cup 1956

Sports Australia Hall Of Fame 1989

Aided the careers of many professional golfers (Peter Thomson, Gary Player, Bruce Crampton and Bruce Devlin)

Pioneer of the Far East Circuit

The best bunker player of his era

Internationally recognised for his coaching

Trailblazer of Australian golf

Bruce Crampton

Born: 1935

Official Professional victories: 42

New Zealand PGA Championship 1954

Australian Open Champion 1956

Far East Open Championship 1959

US PGA Tour wins – 14

Won three consecutive US Tour events in 1965

4 time runner-up to Jack Nicklaus in majors (1972 US Masters, 1972 US Open, 1973 US PGA, 1975 US PGA)

Vardon Trophy winner 1973, 1975

1973 won four times on US PGA tour and runner-up five times

Ten hole-in-ones during his professional career

2 Legends of Golf Titles with Orville Moody

20 US Champions Tour victories

Represented Australia in The World Cup 1963, 1964, 1967, 1972

Member Sport Australia Hall of Fame and Texas Golf Hall Of Fame

First foreign player to win a million dollars in official prizemoney in the USA.

Bill Dunk

Born: 1938

Official Professional victories: 45

Australian PGA Champion 5 times

Australia's most prolific course record breaker (80+ course records)

1963 Malaysian Open

1970 led World Scoring averages (70.21) from Jack Nicklaus

1971 – at Coffs Harbour he surged to 11 under after only 12 holes.

1972 New Zealand Open Champion

1975 Sanpo Classic (Japan)

1976 Sapporo Open (Japan)

Represented Australia 3 times in The World Cup

10 victories on the Senior tours of Australia and Japan

Member Australian Sporting Hall Of Fame

Did not like travelling

'Dunk courts anonymity. If there were a pill to make people invisible, he would take an overdose.' Peter Dobereiner

Graham Marsh MBE

Born: 1944

Official Professional victories: 67

World Matchplay Champion 1977

Dunhill Cup winner in 1985 (representing Australia with Greg Norman and David Graham)

Open Champion of India, Switzerland, Germany, Holland, Malaysia, Thailand and Scotland

Professional victories on the European, Australasian, Japan and US tours

20+ victories in Japan

US rookie of the year 1977

Six victories on US Champions Tour including two majors (1997 US Senior Open) Twice winner of the Japan Senior Open

A demi-god in Japan

Sir Bob Charles ONZ KNZM CBE (New Zealand)

Born: 1936

Official Professional victories: 68

British Open 1963 (Lytham and St Annes)

Twice runner-up in the Open Championship 1968, 1969

New Zealand Open 1954, 1966, 1970, 1973, 1978

New Zealand PGA 1961, 1979, 1980

Houston Classic 1963

Piccadilly World Matchplay Championship 1969

Canadian Open 1968

Swiss Open 1962, 1974

6 US PGA Tour victories

4 European Tour victories

8 Australasian Tour victories

23 Senior PGA Tour wins

Senior British Open 1989, 1993

World Golf Hall Of Fame 2008

First left-handed golfer to win a Major

Frank Phillips

Born: 1932

Official Professional victories: 23

Australian Open Champion 1957, 1961

Philippines Open 1960

Singapore Open 1961, 1965

Malaysian Open 1962

Hong Kong Open 1966, 1973

Far East Circuit pioneer

1965 Yomiuri Open (Japan)

Represented Australia in The World Cup 1958

Life Member of the Australian PGA

Nicknamed 'Choppers'

David Graham

Born: 1946

Official Professional victories: 38

Australian Open champion 1977

US PGA champion 1979

US Open Champion 1981 (first Australian to win US Open)

16 Top-tens in majors

World Cup Champion 1970 (with Bruce Devlin)

Piccadilly World Match Play Champion 1976

Dunhill Cup 1985 (with Graham Marsh and Greg Norman)

Dunhill Cup 1986 (with Rodger Davis and Greg Norman)

Open Champion of Australia, America, Japan, Thailand, France and Mexico

Victorious on six different continents

Five Champions Tour wins

Only Australian to win two different majors

Club making expert

Not yet in the World Golf Hall Of Fame

Played perhaps the finest final round in major golf history with a flawless 67 around Merion (Pennsylvania) in 1981 to win the US Open

Bob Shearer

Born: 1948

Official Professional victories: 28

Australian Amateur 1969

Australian Open 1982

Australian PGA 1983

Madrid Open 1975

Piccadilly Medal 1975

PGA Tour of Australasia order of merit 1974, 1977, 1981, 1982

Led 1976 US PGA Tour qualifying

Won Tallahassee Open on the US Tour 1982

Represented Australia in the World Cup 1975, 1976

Four European Seniors Tour victories

Life Member Australian PGA

One of the great drivers of the golf ball

Ian Stanley

Born: 1948

Official Professional victories: 28

19 PGA Tour of Australia victories

1975 Martini International (European Tour)

Represented Australia in The World Cup 1974, 1975

Senior British Open 2001

The Clown Prince

Jan Stephenson

Born: 1951

Official Professional victories: 26

Won five consecutive NSW Schoolgirls Championships (1964–1968)

1973 Australian Ladies Open

1974 US LPGA Tour Rookie of the Year

Won three ladies major titles: 1981 Peter Jackson Classic, 1982 LPGA Championship, 1983 US Women's Open Championship

1985 French Open

16 LPGA Tour victories

Noted for her short game

Helped establish the Women's Senior Golf Tour

'The sinuous body movements of this sexy kid from Sydney are reminiscent of Marilyn Monroe' The New York Times

Jack Newton OAM

Born: 1950

Official Professional victories: 9

1969 Lake Macquarie Amateur

1972 Dutch Open

1972 Benson & Hedges (European Tour)

1974 British Matchplay

1978 Buick Open (USA)

1979 NSW Open

1979 Australian Open

Won the PGA Tour of Australia Order of Merit 1979

2nd in 1975 Open Championship (Carnoustie, Scotland) – lost 18-hole playoff on the final hole to Tom Watson.

(Jack Nicklaus finished tied 3rd)

Tied 2nd in 1980 US Masters (won by Seve Ballesteros)

1983 during height of his professional career Jack Newton had a near fatal accident on the runway at Sydney Airport. During a rainstorm he accidentally walked into a spinning propeller: he lost his right arm and eye and suffered severe abdominal injuries. He spent the next eight weeks in intensive care. Thanks to the support of his golfing friends and wonderful wife (Jackie), Jack Newton went on to have a successful career as public speaker, radio and television commentator, newspaper reporter and golf course designer.

Chairman of the Junior Jack Newton Golf Foundation

Bruce Devlin

Born: 1937

Official Professional victories: 28

Lake Macquarie Amateur 1958

Eisenhower Trophy 1958

Australian Amateur 1959

Australian Open (as an Amateur) 1960

Dunlop International 1968

French Open 1963

NZ Open 1963, 1983

Australian PGA Championship 1966, 1969, 1970

8-time winner on the US PGA Tour

World Cup 1970 (with David Graham)

Represented Australia five times in the World Cup

16 top ten finishes in the Majors

Successful golf commentator and golf course architect

Peter Toogood (amateur – see pages 208-209)

Question: If you think about professional golf back in the 1950s and 1960s, could you have imagined that it would turn into, what is now, such a lucrative career?

Bruce Crampton: No, I don't believe anyone could have. I have seen so many innovations and advancements happen in my life. For instance we didn't have a telephone in our home until my father (who was a policeman) became an Inspector. I can remember at Slazengers there was a switchboard operator and when a phone call came in she would take a wired plug out and stick it into whatever hole (extension) the call was supposed to go to. Look at what you and I are doing now (Skype video call): who could foresee this? This is just magnificent technology. I just scratch my head and wonder what my little grandchildren are going to see in their lifetime. It is hard to conceive that today's youngsters will see as much advancement in technology, in their lifetime, as my generation has seen in ours.

It applies to more than just electronics. Let us consider the golf industry. Today's players on the PGA Tour, Champion's Tour and LPGA Tour have fitness trailers, nutritionists, sport psychologists, managers and PR people. The players are bigger, stronger and fitter. They are using technically advanced golf balls and golf clubs. I recently became aware of advancements in robotics which are being used to fit players with precise specifications for their clubs. US PGA Tour events are played on courses with hybrid grasses specially developed to produce better surfaces on fairways, tees and greens. Today's mowing equipment options enable grounds' crews to significantly reduce the amount of grain on golf course greens by using mowers incorporating brushes and 'verticut' blades. Machines are being used to roll the greens not only to smooth them out but also to create a desired putting speed. Triplex riding mowers are now commonly used on fairways instead of just tees and fringes.

When I started playing in America most of the tournaments had purses of $15,000 total prize money. I vividly remember the first $50,000 tournament: it was the 1958 Buick Open at Warwick Hills Country Club in Grand Blanc, Michigan. Professionals came out of the woodwork! There were so many entries; Monday's qualifying field was the largest of the year. I'm not sure what Deane Beman's aspirations were when he was the Commissioner, but Tim Finchem [current US PGA Tour Commissioner] told us early on it was his objective to see that the income of the top members of the PGA Tour was in keeping with the top players in the other sports; basketball, football, baseball and tennis.

What a great success story the PGA Tour is. When I first started competing over here the tournaments were run through The Tournament Players' Division of the PGA of America. This is the way it was for several years, but as total prize money increased, and more and more sponsors wanted tournaments, discussions began amongst the tournament-playing pros about breaking away from the PGA and forming a separate organisation. I sat in on many of the meetings. I wasn't one of the ringleaders, but I totally agreed with the concept. The time had come for us to run our own affairs. The new organisation was initially called the 'Tournament Players Association' (TPA); then, when Beman became Commissioner he moved the headquarters office from Bethesda, Maryland, to Ponte Vedra Beach, Florida, and changed the name to the 'PGA Tour'. This organisation now encompasses so much more than just tournament activities. To say it is 'huge' is an understatement.

Bob Shearer: No. When I started to play well and win money, the blokes that had played 10 or 20 years before you had a crack at us: 'Have a look at the money you make!' Fortunately I did a few decades at it, so I passed through a few generations, I guess. You could never foresee what they are doing now, playing for millions.

Jan Stephenson: I always dreamed of going to America and imagined it to be very glamorous and lucrative. I dreamed it exactly as it has become.

Graham Marsh: No, you wouldn't. That would not have even entered into my mind. When I was a youngster at 18, I was following the US tour and the way to follow it was through golf magazines that would arrive in the country a month or more after they were published in the US. There was no golf television coverage in this country other than perhaps a news clip from the British Open if Thomson was doing well. Perhaps you would get a news clip of the Masters or the other majors for about thirty seconds. The major news outlets devoted minimal inches to golf on the sports pages. No golf magazines were published in Australia; we had to rely on Golf Monthly or Golf Digest from the USA. The internet was still just a thought. I used to go to the newsagency and pick up a magazine to see what was happening on the US Tour. One of the milestones of that era was when Arnold Palmer had just gone over $100,000 in prizemoney for the year; everybody thought it was just an incredible achievement. The majority of the better players were making $30,000 to $50,000 a year and that was it. When I started playing professionally I set three major goals for myself. Win 50 golf tournaments, win a major and aim to win a million dollars in prizemoney. A million dollars was considered a lifetime's earnings at that stage. Who could have imagined that I would go back to the USA at 50 years of age and win close to nine million dollars on the Senior Tour?

Television is what gave the advertisers the exposure and brought the big money to golf.

Bill Dunk: No, I couldn't. There is no way. When I first went to America we thought $20,000 was a lot of money. The Americans were playing for $20,000 to $50,000 a week and we thought 'God, there is a lot of money in this country'. That is a drop in the bucket compared to what they play for now. When a fella gets a bonus of ten million for winning a tournament [Fed Ex Cup] it is unbelievable really, isn't it.

I used to run a pro shop and while I played golf my wife ran the shop. In between times I did a bit of property building. So, I made enough money to buy those properties, with my wife's help of course. But it used to take guys like Player and Palmer most of their life to make a million dollars and these days they make it every week. We had enough money for a lifestyle and we could afford to buy a house, but it was nothing like it is these days where you win a couple of tournaments and are set for life.

My parents very much thought it was a mistake to get into pro golf because there wasn't any money in it. Even when I bought a set of units in Gosford, my mother had retired and was living in one of them; she used to save her pension and try and force it on me saying 'you can't make money playing sport'. It was like that right up until she died: that is how adamant she was about the whole thing. We used to fight like hell about it. My old man said 'let him do what he wants to do' but my mother was dead against it.

photo: A young Peter Toogood admiring his father's trophies, from Peter Toogood's archives.

Question: If you think about professional golf back in the 1950s and 1960s, could you have imagined that it would turn into, what is now, such a lucrative career?

Bruce Devlin: We were fortunate to have had a golf tour back then, primarily in the USA, a place that every one of us in those days wanted to play on. If you look at the money that the players of my era made we were not able to win enough money to set ourselves up for life; we were forced to find other things to do. Myself for instance: television, developing golf facilities and of course golf course architecture. It is now a game where if you win a couple of tournaments in a year you can be in a position of taking care of yourself and your family for a lifetime.

David Graham: I don't think anyone could have pin-pointed that accurately but I do think it is wonderful that the game is that popular and sponsors are prepared to put that kind of money into it. It is obviously all, economically, working otherwise it would never have happened. You can just go down the list from the Snead-Hogan-Palmer-Nicklaus days and certainly this generation can thank Tiger Woods. Golf is a drug free sport; other than John Daly it has never had anyone who has brought discredit to the game in that way which has always given it a good reputation that is very appealing. It has always been a sport where people can comfortably take their family and their children. In pro golf you go and watch people perform at a level that most people can only dream of.

There was no money in golf when we started out, we just thought we were living good. We all shared cars and slept rough. We played Pro-Am tournaments and had to put up with five-hour rounds of golf with 20 handicappers to maybe get $500. When I won the Australian Open [1977] I think I got a cheque for three grand or something. We all did that; we all started out grinding, with very few exceptions. In America in the early days we are talking about having a tour pre 'Holiday-Inns'. So the Sneads, the Nelsons and the Hogans – they travelled the country and they did sleep in their cars playing golf tournaments with a $500 first prize.

Frank Phillips: I won tournaments in the Far east. I won the Singapore Open twice and I think I got $1500 and $3000. Adam Scott has won it the last couple of years and he got $1.3 million. It started out as a $20,000 tournament and now it has gone to millions. The growth of the game is just unbelievable. I just can't believe the money they make now. They make more money in one week than I made in a lifetime and I won 45 tournaments around the world. They can make enough money in one tournament to retire and invest the money properly and never need to work again. I would take the $1.3 million, pay the $300,000 in tax and, hello, you've got a million dollars; you put that in the bank at 6% and you're right! It is scary and I don't know where it is going to stop, but when you get those tournaments at the end of the year and they are playing for ten million dollars that is just ludicrous. But golf is a good advertising thing, it is a great medium for that. I could never have imagined it though, not back then; I could never have imagined making millions.

We didn't make fortunes, but we made good livings and we are comfortable. I was joking with Kel Nagle about it I said, 'Geez, Kel, we each won well over 100 tournaments: you could combine all the money we ever won and today's players win more in one tournament than we won in a lifetime.'

The biggest cheque I ever got was in the Philippines and it was $7500. I didn't even win the tournament: they used to give 1000 pound bonus for the best round each day and I won it twice. Ran third in the tournament. Everything is pro-rata: you could buy a house for 5000 pounds. In 1957 when I won the Australian Open, the Lakes Open, NSW Open and about 25 Pro-Ams the headline at the end of the year was 'Phillips wins 3800 pounds'. That was almost a house, although I paid pretty good tax in those days. We used to play in Pro-Ams where first prize was $100.

Ian Stanley: No. In those days we only had one main tournament that was on the television and that was the British Open. We only saw that in black and white. Today, every tournament is televised and it has opened up a whole new ballgame. I think it took guys like Arnold Palmer, and his charisma, which really got people interested in watching. These days they are playing for so much more money, but there is so much more money in sponsorship for golf equipment and logo placements on bags, shirts and visors … it has completely changed.

Arnold Palmer's manager at that time (Mark McCormack) set up IMG. IMG is such a big company now – it is in all parts of sport all around the world. I think Arnold was Mark's first client, then Gary [Player], Jack [Nicklaus] and Peter Thomson. In those days they wanted Peter to make it part of 'the big four' and they had those exhibition matches all over the world, but Peter knocked it back. I don't think he agreed with the way golf was going to go … he was more the old style.

Kel Nagle: I had no idea. We were lucky to get 200 pound purses. It is television. Television and advertising have developed it. The advent of Arnold Palmer in the 1960 British Open – he went across to England and it really got fired up from then. More and more people went across for the British Open after 'Arnie' made his first trip. Arnie appealed to the people; they love an all-American boy. He didn't have a copybook swing, but he was very strong and could hit the ball out of the rough. He was a good putter. He appealed to the people and he had 'Arnie's army' behind him and it all sort of developed from there. Then Jack Nicklaus came along and Gary Player and it was 'the big three' which really got the whole setup going. Plus the fact that the American PGA, Deane Beman and others handled it all pretty well to get the sponsorships happening.

Peter Toogood: No, not really. I suppose you would blame television … that gave it the impetus. I remember my father ... he didn't stop me turning pro but he wasn't very keen on it because there wasn't much money in it back then. My father encouraged me to get education qualifications first and I did all of that, got my teaching degree and he told me that after that I could do what I liked. By the time I finished my degree I was very keen on teaching and I never turned pro.

There will always be interest in the top amateurs. Most of the top amateurs have to work and don't have the time to play golf that a professional has. It's the constant play, daily practice and competitive play that gives the professionals the extra edge on their ability.

Sir Bob Charles: We had no idea professional golf would turn into such a lucrative profession. The early '60s for me were having a round-the-world air ticket and when the £1000 you had saved ran out, you came home. Fortunately for me I started my pro career [1961] with two second place finishes in South Africa and won a Bowmaker Tournament on the European Tour to keep me going. However I continued sharing rooms and cars with fellow pros, staying in bed & breakfast for a few pounds a night, forever conscious of minimising expenses. You must remember: there were only 25 to 30 'money spots' in those days.

photo: John W Fischer III archives — location unknown

Jack Newton: I certainly wasn't expecting the deluge of money that came into the game not long after I had my accident. When I won the Buick Open [1978] I think I got $30,000; when I lost the playoff for the British Open [1975] I think I got 5,000 pounds and Tom Watson got 7,500 for winning the bloody thing. So, I had the accident in 1983 and by 1987/88 it was already starting to soar. I guess I always had faith that golf is a world game, a massive game, but yes, I was surprised it changed so radically and so quickly.

I think Arnold Palmer and Jack Nicklaus had a massive influence on the commercial elements of the game, then along came Watson. At that time when I was playing over there in the US there was a lot of really good players, like Raymond Floyd and Lee Trevino, Johnny Miller, Hale Irwin, Tom Kite, Craig Stadler and others. The biggest expansion, to me, has been in Europe. When I first went to Europe there were limited events first of all – but most of them were played in the British Isles. There was the French, German, Italian and Dutch and also the Spanish Opens but that was all there really was in continental Europe. With the advent of the European Tour, per se, which John Jacobs was instrumental in starting – Jacobs was a pro who played Ryder Cup and later became a famous coach – it was John Jacobs who recommended that Ken Schofield run the European Tour. These days you have some of the communist countries staging a National Open as part of the European Tour. I don't agree that the European Tour should be in Asia because I don't think that is their place. Potentially, if they haven't already I think the European Tour is going to surpass America, particularly because they are going to different countries, whereas the Yanks are dipping into the same well all the time. There are good players now in Europe and they are coming from all sorts of countries, cultures and backgrounds.

When I was a young bloke a lot of good young American players used to come here to Australia to play because they had heard about the golf courses. I remember a great friend of mine, Ed Snead [USA], who had never won in America came out here and won the NSW Open [1973] at The Australian Golf Club and then he went straight back to America and won there [Kaiser International, October 1973]. This is where a lot of the young American players today are not developing into the type of players that the media and everyone else wants, because they haven't got enough variety in their game. They are used to playing on greens that are cut at this, the rough is cut at that, the fairways are at this and usually on soft greens and it is the same every week. I have a bit of doubt as to whether that is going to get them to the level they need to attain unless they do travel. It is well recorded that if it is not 75 degrees with the wind blowing out of the north-east at not more than 15 kilometres an hour, they want to pack up and go home. You see some of these golfers declining to play in some of the majors, for whatever the reason. I suppose the attitude is 'Oh well, I will miss this week and go down the road next week and play for $5 million'. Whereas we had to play every bloody week because there wasn't enough money.

Jack Nicklaus, Palmer, Floyd, Gary Player, Miller, Watson, Trevino: they all travelled. I think you have to play a variety of courses and that is what worries me about our young players today: they all want to rush off over to play college golf in America and I think they would do better to stay here and get tournament experience. Jason Day and Steve Elkington are the only ones I can think of who went straight to America and have done all right. In all the years I have been involved in junior golf in this country Jason has been the best technically, plus he had all the other ingredients you need. I just felt like this kid really has something special.

Jack Nicklaus: I always looked at golf as a game. I never looked at it as a means to a lucrative career. I always looked at golf as: if you played well and you won, the money would come. Today, they seem to play for money. I mean, there are a lot of guys who play the game for the game, but unfortunately, many today play golf for money rather than the love of the game. I played for the love of the game, and the money came secondary.

Scott Tolley: So you see these stories about guys sleeping in their car to win $50 in exhibition matches …

Jack Nicklaus: They probably needed the $50. No, it's true. There was a time when you couldn't make a living playing golf.

Scott Tolley: So you didn't get into golf because you were getting rich?

Jack Nicklaus: No, that was never even a thought.

Norman Von Nida (from Neil Bennett's tape): The money in those days was nothing compared to what it is today; I think the first tournament that I won in New South Wales was what we call a professional purse, a club purse, and the first prize was five pounds, roughly round about ten dollars. The Australian Open: the first one that I won, I think, was seventy-five pounds first prize. Last Sunday Greg Norman's first prize was thirty-five thousand dollars and roughly 3 years prior to that, when Kerry Packer was sponsoring the tournament, the first prize was over fifty thousand dollars. So, you can see that the prize money has escalated enormously since I first started to play golf.

In retrospect, from the beginning of my career as a golf player, one could sort of never envisage the enormous potential that there was in becoming a tournament golf player today, as against what it was when I was young. Very early on in my career the World War became fact; in 1939 I was in America and war was declared and I had to come home

Scotland

and I was a member of the First Armoured Brigade, ASC, for around four years. After the cessation of the conflict I took up my profession again, as a golf player, and also again there was practically no money involved in being a tournament player, so I had to sort of compete against the amateurs and play them for money and most of the people that I used to play for money were professional gamblers, bookmakers, people who were making their profession out of gambling. It was a very precarious and very difficult way to earn a living, but fortunately for me my skill was such that I was able to earn a good living at it. After about eighteen months of this I made enough money to afford to go to Great Britain in 1946. I took off for Great Britain [by boat] to try my luck over there and fortunately for me I was successful enough in the first year and again I was successful in the next year. In each succeeding year I was becoming more experienced and fortunately for me my golf was improving. I realised the enormous future there was in golf during these years by going to Great Britain and playing in Europe, England, Scotland, Wales and Ireland and also in America. I took it upon myself to try and help some of the other players, younger persons than myself.

The reason that I went to Great Britain was that there was much more money to win in Great Britain that what there was here in Australia and actually that is the story of professional golf: one plays for money and one plays for where the most money is.

photo:John W Fischer III archives - The Open Championship Scotland

Question: Once you had the fundamentals of the full golf swing in place, what sort of practice routine and practice drills did you focus on during the prime of your career?

Bill Dunk: In the summertime I would hit 600 balls before I started work. Just going through the clubs. In the wintertime I would probably hit 200 balls. I used to be a weak long-iron player. When I was the assistant at Ryde Parramatta Golf Club there used to be a church where the motel is now. The boss used to come down in the morning and we would do nothing but hit 2-irons. He used to say, 'I want you to hit it over the corner of that tree there by the 18th green.' When I started out I was no chance, but slowly I got it right up near the top branches but I could never get it over. It didn't matter how long I practised there, I could never get it over and the main reason for that was the bloody tree kept growing. But it made me stronger with my long irons.

Jack Nicklaus: You don't ever have the fundamentals down. First of all, you don't ever have the fundamentals down and the practice routine was whatever I needed to practice at that time. I never did any drills, and a lot of players do drill. I don't recall every doing a drill in my life.

Sir Bob Charles: Those of my era were all self-taught; there were no coaches to confuse and golf was a game, not a science. Perfecting a swing that repeated and reduced the errors was constant. This together with getting the feel of the course and forming a game plan was the focus of practice.

Bruce Crampton: It would depend on the facility I had access to. Because I am a human and not a machine very little stayed the same for long periods of time. There was always plenty to work on, and improvements to be made. I strived to be the best I could with what I had to work with, and prepare myself as best I could for any eventuality.

For the average golfer playing golf is rest and relaxation and it should be an enjoyable escape from what they do normally. It is not their profession. Therefore treat it as fun and enjoyment. Leave the professionals to stress out about it and worry if they are going to make the cut or not. Another suggestion to the average golfer would be to video their swing and look at it; you are introducing another sense, another perspective and that is a plus. The camera doesn't lie. I would also suggest players getting the V1 software program and uploading their video: the technology is amazing.

Peter Thomson: Just a warm up before we start. That is all.

Bruce Devlin: Problems with the swing always come back to the fundamentals. I was always checking two of the most important things that work together: ball position and alignment. If either were out of kilter then the likelihood of a bad shot increased greatly.

David Graham: As long as the sun was up I'd be hitting balls.

Graham Marsh: The better we become, like anything in life, if you want to get to the next level at something it is the law of diminishing returns. It takes that much extra effort to get there to produce that little last result. You have to be self-analytical and be able to turn around and say 'I have a problem with my short game' or 'I hit it in the rough three times during the course of the round with my driver and I lose a stroke every time' or 'I get on the green and I three-putt five times and that is costing me 5 strokes during the course of the round'. You have to

critically analyse your own game and try and understand what your real weakness are and what you find difficulty with on the golf course on a day-by-day basis ... then just go out and work on those. There is no point going to the practice fairway if you have hit the ball well but three-putted 5 times. Understand your weaknesses and aim your practice towards your weaknesses so they can become your strengths.

Frank Phillips: Start with a 9-iron, put an umbrella out on the fairway about a 125–130 yards and I would hit a couple of bags at it. Once I had that right I would hit 20 or 30 drivers and then go and practise chipping and putting. After a round I would work out which shots I had not hit like I wanted to; next time I would practise, I would practise that shot until I thought I had it right. My stock shot was a draw, but I would practise the cut shot too so I had it in the bag if I needed it. People used to say 'you are practising so hard you are wasting all your good shots', but you are not practising too hard: you are building your confidence up. Golf is a great game of confidence.

When I first went to England I then spent twelve months practising how to hit the ball low, out of the wind. Then I could play both shots, target golf flying it in high and stopping it or the older way of running it in. The secret to hitting it low was all in the left hand, take the club back a little bit sharper than normal but I would drive my left hand back through the ball very hard and didn't let my hand turn over. If you are young player coming through and this bloke over here is better than you and he hits 500 balls a day, go out and hit 600 a day. I went from a handicap of 22 to 2 in 12 months.

Photo: John W Fischer III archives

Sir Bob Charles

Question: Once you had the fundamentals of the full golf swing in place, what sort of practice routine and practice drills did you focus on during the prime of your career?

Gary Player: once I felt like I had the swing, I spent most of my time on the short game. Putting is what wins the golf tournament. Tiger Woods has shown that. Tiger Woods and Phil Mickelson are not great drivers of the golf ball, yet they have been number one and number two because they are great putters. I take my hat off to anybody who can do that.

Jack Newton: When you are going to a tournament it is not a place to be toying with your swing thoughts and sorting new moves out. You should have done your homework before you get there. At tournaments I predominantly worked on rhythm. The first thing you do when you are nervous or you don't like a club/shot is that you swing too fast. That throws everything out. If you keep a swing thought that gives you good rhythm then you will get away with a lot more than if you haven't got that rhythm. Talking about the juniors again: the trouble we have now is this lob wedge phenomenon going on. I have nothing against lob wedges but they are being played because it is probably one of their favourite clubs; but when they sit down and think about it the low percentage shot they are trying to play with a lob wedge, they may have a better chance of a good result by playing it with an 8-iron or a putter. Get the ball on the green and chasing up to the hole, rather than using the lob wedge; if the lob wedge doesn't spin you are over the back, if it spins too much you are way short. There is no consistency to it. Kids are spending way too much time bashing 300-metre drives and not enough on the short game. We have some good coaches in this country but we don't really have anyone who specialises in short game coaching – whereas the Yanks have probably got half a dozen.

I learnt to pitch by chipping over my old man's sweet pea line (about 6 foot high) in the back yard at Epping. I got that good at it that I could chip the ball over the sweet pea line with any club, from a sand wedge to an 8-iron, and I could get it to stop on the grass before it broke a window. The average high-handicap golfer could wipe strokes off their game if they learnt to get on the green from 50 metres out and two putting every time. That would make a massive inroad into improving their golf.

Ian Stanley: You never had your swing down, it always changed. You might have slept badly the night before and you might be stiff down one side. I would always start on the practice range with a wedge and just slowly warm up. I would pick a target and work towards that target: it might be a three-quarter 8-iron … then step it up to a full 8-iron. Try and move a couple right to left, then left to right and just get a feeling of moving the golf ball. If it just felt like I had the fade going, then I would go with the fade for that day and work on my swing after the round – I wouldn't fight the fade and try to iron it out before tee-off. If I had the draw going on the practice fairway I would go with the draw for the day. Once warmed up, the rest of the time before tee-off would be spent chipping and putting, then working out how to get away to a good start off the first tee. I used to think 'what would Kel Nagle do?' and the answer was always: go nice and slowly at it. Simplicity is the ultimate sophistication.

Kel Nagle: I think one of the main things is to hit a few shots before you tee off. The majority of amateurs, they will get their clubs out of their car, put the shoes on, go down to the first tee and tee off. We would always go and hit a few balls: start with the short ones, then gradually work through the bag until you are satisfied you are hitting it reasonably well. Then go and have a few putts. You have settled yourself down a little bit before you tee off. Not that I was nervous, but I found I was a little bit keyed up to start off, but once I hit the first shot I was back in the swing of things. I put more time into putting than any other part of my game, so the fact I have enjoyed success with my putter is not only luck. In my younger days I used to think nothing of spending hour upon hour crouched over a pile of golf balls, playing pitch and run shots or putts. It developed my touch. [Via Golf the Australian Way.]

You are given 13 clubs to play 36 shots and you are given one club to play 36 shots. In other words if you hit every hole in regulation figures you would only have 36 strokes and the other 36 strokes comes with your putter. My advice to anyone is to practise putting and get that percentage down on the green.

Question: Once you had the fundamentals of the full golf swing in place, what sort of practice routine and practice drills did you focus on during the prime of your career?

Peter Toogood: When we came to Tasmania we lived in a house that was actually on the golf course. So when I came home from school, apart from fishing on Browns River I had nothing else to do but go and play golf. Although my father didn't stand over me, just watching him play and a few hints here and there all helped. I was very keen on sport; I also played football, cricket and tennis and I was quite competitive. I did want to achieve and do my very best, so naturally I did practise a lot.

I used to enjoy time by myself when I was practising. I would make up little problems. I remember I would go to this one fairway at Kingston Beach when there were very few golfers on the course and I had to achieve hitting twenty balls down the fairway and if I missed one I would have to start again. There was a lot of pressure on when you got to 18 or 19. If you missed a fairway you had to start again. I used to do that quite a lot as a practice routine. I did the same thing with hitting the greens: you know, I had to hit so many in a certain spot and if I missed one, then I started counting again. I have no idea why I had that practice routine but I used it for all sports.

I used to caddie and mind my dad's golf pro shop when he was out teaching. I caddied every Saturday and Sunday for A-grade golfers. Len Nettlefold, who won two Australian Amateurs [1926 & 1928] – I caddied for him regularly and he taught me a lot. One man I caddied for was chairman of the match committee and when I was old enough to join the club (17 was the age a junior had to be to be eligible to join) he played with me in my first competitive round; he took me into the clubhouse, showed me how to behave and all those important things. I had a very good grounding through caddying and playing. On Sunday if one of his playing partners didn't turn up he told me to go and get my clubs and I could play – I still had to carry his bag. They were only small bags in those days. I was very fortunate to learn that side of golf and have that respect for the game.

Norman Von Nida: With regards to practising and things like that, it depends on one's physical structure and one's mental attitude to what it is that they feel is the best way for them to practise. I used to play, when I was in Great Britain, as many as three and four rounds a day in practice and if I wasn't hitting the ball as good as what I felt that I was during that I would go onto the practice tee the following day and hit balls for roughly two or three hours. One would choose a club that one wasn't really confident with to practise with. With regards to playing what we call 'hazard shots' in a bunker I became recognised as probably one of the best bunker players in the world during my career as a player, through the number of hours I used to put into the bunkers. When I would go to practise I would get in a bunker and stay in there for probably two or three hours and through doing this one was able to judge the weight of the sand and the speed of the club contacting the sand at the right position behind the ball, to allow it to come out quite close to the hole, or even sometimes go into the hole. This is an absolute essential in that one must practise like this if one is a tournament player, because if you are in a bunker and you feel that you can get up and down in two, then you have saved a stroke from a bad shot. This is the only way you can save a shot: practice.

Before I went out to play a tournament I would hit 5 balls with a 7-iron to start off with, 5 with a 5-iron, 5 with a 3-iron, 5 with a 3-wood, ten with a driver, ten with a pitching wedge and ten with a sand iron and then go on to the practice putting green. Through doing that, all that you had done is relaxed your muscles and allowed your subconscious brain to get that relaxation in your swing from the time you tee off to the time you finish on the 18th green. You must have that trust in your subconscious brain to perform that movement that you are going to make on every shot that you play relative to the club you actually have to play it with.

Photo: National Archives of Australia A1200, L11987 Norman Von Nida wins, 1949

Question: Who are some of the best <u>putters</u> you have ever seen and can you isolate any of their characteristics, be it a technical or mental trait they possess, that you believe makes them so good at putting?

Graham Marsh: I don't know that I could say there was a best putter. I think what happens in golf is that when players have their best years they go on a streak with the putter. They have the most fantastic run where they make putts from everywhere. And then, for whatever reason, they tend to not make as many putts and they stop winning. I don't like to look at putting as a single entity. For me it is all related to what we describe as the short game. I am much more interested in those players who get the ball into the hole in the least number of strokes from 50 yards. That revolves around your putting, bunker play, chipping and pitching. You can go around a golf course and have 19 or 22 putts; but if the longest putt is 6 foot what does that mean? There have been some great putters out there, there is no question about that; but I see the great putters as great short game players. **Gary Player** was wonderful with the short game, **Billy Casper** was superb, **Arnold Palmer** in his day was sensational, **Tom Watson** was freaky with the putter and with his total short game. **Crenshaw**, **Ballesteros** and **George Archer** all made yards of putts every round they played. **Kel Nagle** was totally reliable from six feet and the New Zealander **Bob Charles** holed more long putts than most. Of the modern day players **Tiger Woods** tops the list as being the most creative. Whilst he was before my time, when you talk with the living legends of the game, it is hard to have a discussion about putting without **Bobby Locke**'s name being mentioned. Perhaps he was the greatest of all time as he made as many putts on greens that were prepared marginally better than the teeing grounds we see on modern day courses. You have to look at the big picture and see how they managed their short game because they all had bad runs with the putter at certain stages throughout their careers. Even the best putters in the world go through phases where they can't get the ball in the hole. **Johnny Miller** – when he was winning was making putts from everywhere, but that went pear-shaped on him at one stage. Then there were great players who were never very good with the putter – a name that comes to mind is Roberto de Vincenzo who was a masterful player from Argentina. He won tournaments because he just hit it closer to the hole than everyone else and putted poorly. He won over 100 tournaments including the British Open and was sadly robbed of a US Masters due to a slip up with the score card on the final day.

Bob Shearer: I think that putting was more individual going back through the years. First of all, one of the greatest putters was **Bob Charles**. He was dead-wristed and back and through. He took it back the same distance that he went through and that was for every putt, whether it was from 2 foot or 40 foot. Just using shoulders and arms and the club was linked to them: it never moved. Another guy in the States who was regarded as one of the best putters was **Ben Crenshaw** … and he was the opposite [of Charles]: he opened the putter on the backswing and then closed it on the way through, which was like a door that was opening and closing … and he was quite wristy. They call it 'tap putting now' but he wasn't tap-putting because he had long backswings and long follow-throughs, but he just made the ball roll beautifully. He was probably the best putter I have seen from 30 foot and out, he always used to roll it dead – very rarely had to worry rolling a three- or four-footer coming back.

I was very fortunate in my early days to have a few rounds with **Bobby Locke**. He was probably the best putter, but he aimed ten feet right of the hole and pulled everything. His action was very individual. He was one of those blokes who would have a 25-foot putt: he would hit the putt and not even look at it – he would stand and look at the gallery and tip the peak of his cap, he knew where it was going. The last time I played with Bobby Locke was the Australian Open at Royal Queensland [1973] and on the 18th I hit a driver and a wedge to the hole and by that stage I think he hit two woods, but he holed a 60 footer on that last green. He made 3, I made 4. Bobby Locke pulled the crowds in. It was the year Jesse Snead won; we had all the crowds following our group (Bobby Locke, Bob Shearer, Bill Dunk) and I tell you who was caddying for me: it was Wayne Grady. Also, one of our great putters, **Kel Nagle**. He was a very good putter and he was a tap-putter. **Brad Faxon** was a great putter; he wasn't a 'tap-putter', he was a feel putter – he used to roll it so good that you would think 'it can't miss'.

If you watch the players on the US Tour, the guys with the short putter, they are basically doing the same thing. When I first started you had Thomson who ended up forward, just broke the wrist and tapped it. You had **Nagle** who had the ball further away from the body, took it back and tapped it, **Charles** doing the pendulum thing. The first one to really try anything different was Sam Snead with the croquet between the legs action; they banned that and then he went side-saddle. I think the people teaching today are probably more learned in the game and they stick to particular techniques.

Photo: Bobby Locke October 1938 The Lakes Golf Club. NSW State Library (hood_18357)

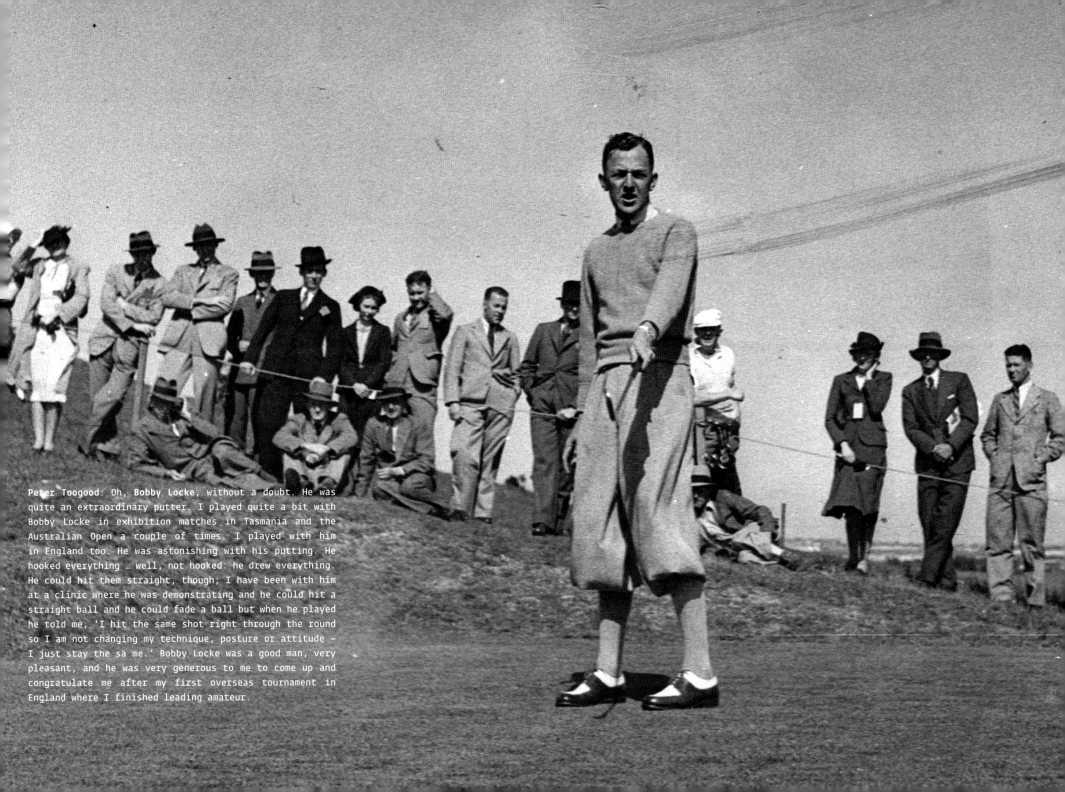

Peter Toogood: Oh, **Bobby Locke**, without a doubt. He was quite an extraordinary putter. I played quite a bit with Bobby Locke in exhibition matches in Tasmania and the Australian Open a couple of times. I played with him in England too. He was astonishing with his putting. He hooked everything … well, not hooked: he drew everything. He could hit them straight, though; I have been with him at a clinic where he was demonstrating and he could hit a straight ball and he could fade a ball but when he played he told me, 'I hit the same shot right through the round so I am not changing my technique, posture or attitude – I just stay the sa me.' Bobby Locke was a good man, very pleasant, and he was very generous to me to come up and congratulate me after my first overseas tournament in England where I finished leading amateur.

Question: Who are some of the best <u>putters</u> you have ever seen and can you isolate any of their characteristics, be it a technical or mental trait they possess, that you believe makes them so good at putting?

Bruce Crampton: We are all different. We are all human beings. I am no different to you or anybody else, I put my pants on one leg at a time just like you do. There is no right or wrong way to putt, just like there is no right and wrong way to swing a golf club. Some have better fundamentals, which will stand up better under pressure, or stand up for a greater length of time.

I saw some excellent putting. **Eric Cremin** was an excellent putter and he putted purely with his wrists. **Billy Casper** was a terrific putter with his own method. **Jack Nicklaus** is a great putter, bent over the ball in his easily recognisable posture. He certainly has his own style.

One has to include **Bobby Locke**. He was indeed a great putter. Bobby Locke hooked everything from right to left with his woods and irons and there is a great story about one particular Tam O'Shanter Tournament in Chicago. The story is told that the cups were set on the right side of every green for all four rounds of the tournament. Even that didn't stop Bobby from winning the tournament. Bobby had a habit of calling everyone 'Cap'. He putted with a closed stance and used a sort of hooking motion with his right shoulder. After holing a makeable putt he would often say, 'Boy, that one tried hard to get out, Cap.' I talked to him about why he hooked his shots so much. He told me if you aim down the middle of the fairway and try and hit the perfect shot, you only have 50% margin of error on each side, but if you aim to one side of the fairway and work your golf ball across it, you have better odds of keeping the ball in the fairway ... or on the green. Most modern day players like to move their shots from left to right, the reason being that when a player gets under pressure/stress the tendency is to fight the golf club with one's left hand in an attempt to guide the shot. Lee Trevino is a great example. He would aim down the left and actually block-cut everything towards his target. When he got under stress coming down the stretch during the last nine holes of an event, no problem – he just continued to do what he was doing: move the ball from left to right across the fairway or across the green.

Dave Stockton has always been an excellent putter. I really like his method of keeping the back of his left hand moving squarely down his target line. Dave is working with **Rory McIlroy**, so in my opinion Rory is getting first class advice, and it's obviously working. For Rory to have accomplished what he already has, at such a young age, he must also be added to the list of excellent putters. His putting stroke, along with other parts of his game, sure impressed me when he won the US Open at Congressional Country Club. A few years ago **Tiger Woods** was the best putter in the world. Look at **Jim Furyk**: he is a terrific putter with his cross-handed style, although I've seen him miss a few crucial putts this year. Bottom line is there is no right or wrong way to putt. I just tell anyone who asks, 'it is all about confidence: if one feels like one can put it in the hole with a broomstick then that is what one needs to use'. So much depends on what is going on between one's ears. If a golfer starts missing putts the hole starts looking like a thimble, but when things are going well, one's confidence builds, it's easier to see the correct line and the hole starts looking as big as a bucket. Remember, you don't have to roll the ball down a line as narrow as a thread of cotton to make putts, there is a margin for error because the cup is four and a quarter inches [108 mm] in diameter, which is roughly the width of the yellow lines on highways. Provided the ball is rolling at the right speed, it should fall in if it touches any part of the hole.

Norman Von Nida: I've seen them all, but as far as I'm concerned no one ever came close to the big Australian **Jim Ferrier**, the former US PGA champ and two times winner of the Australian Open. Jim averaged no more than 24 putts per round. It was just unreal. In 1938 at Royal Adelaide in the Australian Open, Ferrier had about 20 putts in the morning round and 21 in the afternoon to beat me for the title. In the 1939 Australian Open at Royal Melbourne, Ferrier did it to me again with 19 putts in the morning round, including two chip-ins, and 21 putts in the afternoon to beat me by two shots. [from Robertson's book]

Ferrier was a big man, but I could outdrive him by 30 or 40 yards from the tee. But he knew he was the best putter. He had a dominating personality. I borrowed one of his putters and used it for about two years; I started putting well with it and wouldn't give it back, so he had Donny Rodgers get it out of my bag to get it back to him. From 150 yards in, he was as good as anyone I have ever seen, his putting was so good. After he went to America he became a very good player, but when he was in Australia from tee to green he was about a 4 or 5 handicapper. After the war he had gained something like 70 yards on how he was driving the ball.

The next best putter was South African **Bobby Locke**, who many other judges consider the best putter who ever lived. Bobby Locke uses an ancient hickory-shafted putter and a style that violates all principles, ancient and modern, except one: confidence in his ability to put the ball in the hole. His stance is unorthodox – feet close together with the ball opposite the left foot. Locke ignores the almost sacred rule that the club should be taken back with the face at right angles to the direction of the putt, and swings the club in an arc, turning the face and rolling his wrists. What does this prove?

To me it proves conclusively that putting is 99 percent mental and one percent mechanical. [from Golf is my business]

To beat Bobby Locke in matchplay was very very difficult because you had to watch him hole these putts all the time. He played Sam Snead in a series of exhibitions in South Africa. Sam Snead told me that Bobby Locke was never inside him on the green more than once in any of the rounds, yet Sam only won two of the 18 matches they played. He said Bobby beat him 16 times, just holing a lot of putts. I played Locke in a 144-hole exhibition match in South Africa and he beat me 1-up. I played as good as I could play. He would average 6 putts less than me every round.

Sam Snead once told me that Kel Nagle had the best putting action he'd seen. Also Eric Cremin: the late Eric Cremin was a marvellous player, probably one of the best putters on fast greens that I ever had the pleasure of playing with.

Putting is one percent method – 99% confidence.

Photo; Jim Ferrier (putting) during the State Open Championships at Kensington (Australian) Golf Club Sydney NSW 6th-10th September 1937. Norman Von Nida looking on.
NSW State Library (hood_15877)

Question: Who are some of the best <u>putters</u> you have ever seen and can you isolate any of their characteristics, be it a technical or mental trait they possess, that you believe makes them so good at putting?

Bill Dunk: Any one of those guys that use those long putters, they have always been good putters. They only believe that they are bad. If they can putt with one of those long bloody things they could putt with anything. They could putt with a broom. I hate those long putters and I think they are just a crutch. But if I told Peter Senior that he wouldn't believe me. Confidence is a wonderful thing, isn't it? None of the guys who win tournaments can't putt, even Adam Scott. When he wins he putts as good as anybody. I think he is better with the short putter than he is with the long one. **Ben Crenshaw** was a super putter. It is basically rhythm and staying very still: that is the mechanics of it. It is a hit, not a push. You have to make a release, that is what it amounts to.

Kel Nagle had entirely his own putting style and pre-shot routine with a wonderful rhythm. Sometimes after I had played a couple of rounds with Kel I would start to get that feeling and I would think 'God, this is how Nagle feels' then I would play like God for a couple of weeks until I lost the rhythm. [Laughs] Then I would have to go back and play with him again. I will never forget playing in the Watties Tournament in New Zealand with him. Kel is about six shots in front and I am playing in the last round with him. I'd hole a birdie and he would say 'that's more like it, you can do it – just hole a few more and you can win this tournament' ... [Starts laughing … then continues] ... and I beat him by a shot. He was encouraging me all the way until the last few holes.

Jan Stephenson: The greens have become so consistent. We never knew how the speed would be from week to week. Now they keep them so similar and are in far better condition. The putters are better designed and manufactured. Also, because of the competition, they expect to make more putts. I see a huge difference in confidence - consequently aggressive nature - of the new professional golfers. They hit them in firmer, and look surprised when they don't make putts that we were happy to make. **Nancy Lopez** used to be very aggressive and I believe that was why she made so many putts. She was so intimidating when she was around 15-30 feet. Our greens were slower and she was so sure that she was going to make them. In my era there were a lot of good putters. **Bradley**, **Sheehan** and **King** stand out … as do **Carner** and **Inkster**.

Jack Newton: Putting is very much a mental thing. Yes, technique does come into it, but I have seen some horrible techniques that work very well. **Bobby Locke** comes to mind straight away. He aimed to the right of the hole, as he did on all his golf shots, and he sort of shouldered it in – and he was an incredible putter. **Kel Nagle** was a great putter. He had a good routine: he put his putter in front of the ball and didn't stand over it forever; then it was a one, two, three, bang - in. He was a kind of 'pop putter': shortish backswing, but accelerated the putter head through the ball. **Bob Charles**, the Kiwi, was an incredible putter. Once again, fairly good technique but those guys just don't think about missing from 8-10 feet. **Ben Crenshaw**: you would play with him and he would hit it all over the show and hole 3 thirty-footers a round! It must be nice standing on the first tee knowing you are going to hole 3 thirty-footers today. That is the positive side of being a good putter: that is the way they think. **Tom Watson**: when I played him off in the British Open he never looked like missing one – he was a genius putter, but he was a very aggressive putter and if he missed and it went two metres past, he would crash it back in. So there are all sorts of different ways to play and be a good putter; but if I had to give someone a 4-metre putt to save my life I would give it to **Jack Nicklaus**. The number of times Jack Nicklaus had to hole a putt at a crucial stage of the tournament … he would usually make it. I remember once he told me that he didn't draw the putter back until he had imagined the ball going into the hole. I have always thought: to be a good putter you have to have a good imagination, particularly on fast greens, like Royal Melbourne, where some putts can break off the world and you have to use your imagination and if you don't get it right you may end up with a putt almost as long as the one you started with, coming back. I also think that is one of the reasons **Tiger Woods** has been so dominant: when he was on with the putter he was unbeatable.

Jack Nicklaus: There are putters who are renowned for having a great stroke and are said to be a great putter. There are bunker players who are great bunker players. There are drivers who are great drivers. There are golfers who are great golfers. But the great, great golfers and great, great putters, and great, great sand players do it when it means something. To me, the ones who do it when it means something are the ones who are remembered as great putters. You think of a **Tiger Woods**, an **Arnold Palmer**, a **Gary Player**, a **Tom Waston**, and if you want to be kind, I suppose I could be included in that list. Because we did it when we had to do it. That, to me, is what makes you a great putter. Of all the aspects of the game of golf, I think this is particularly true with putting. It is interesting when you hear people talk about someone being a great putter and then when it gets down to the end of a tournament, where is that great putter? The one thing about a putter that makes him or her great is being able to do it when they have to do it. Every one of these great

players has to be a great putter, or they would never win anything. So in the end, I would say it is the mental outlook, the positive ability to be able to make a putt when you have to make it, and to do it consistently.

Bruce Devlin: The record speaks for itself. I know of no player who was that much better than the competition that putted badly. **Palmer** made more long putts than most, **Nicklaus** was one of the best as well as Player. All the great putters were the mentally strong individuals. **Casper** was as good as any of those cited above.

David Graham: I think **Nicklaus** was the best putter I ever saw because he won more majors than anybody else. Nicklaus was by far the best putter inside of 6 feet that has ever played. **Ben Crenshaw** was a phenomenal putter. People talk of **Bobby Locke**, but I never saw him putt. There are a few players on tour now that are fantastic but they haven't won a lot of tournaments. **Steve Stricker** is a fabulous putter. **Lee Trevino** was fantastic. **Tom Watson** was the best aggressive putter. The most graceful putting stroke was most probably **Ben Crenshaw**. In the last twenty years nobody has putted better than Tiger Woods.

Usually the guys who win the most tournaments turn out to be awfully good drivers, awfully good iron players and exceptionally good putters. Some of the best putters are the guys who aren't very good players but they still make a living out of the game because of their ability to putt, rather than their ball striking.

Photo: Johnny Fischer putting in the Quarterfinal match of the 1932 US Amateur against Francis Ouimet. From John W Fischer III archives.

AT THE FEET OF THE MASTERS

Question: Who are some of the best <u>putters</u> you have ever seen and can you isolate any of their characteristics, be it a technical or mental trait they possess, that you believe makes them so good at putting?

Frank Phillips: Kel Nagle was one of the best putters I have ever seen. **Gary Player** was brilliant. **Bill Dunk** and **Bobby Locke** were brilliant, but **Kel Nagle** was a very consistent putter. He didn't miss many short ones, I will tell you. He was a really good player too. You have to be able to get it on the green and you have to be able to putt. You will find that most of the good putters are good players too.

I class **Ben Hogan** the best ball striker I have ever seen, **Jack Nicklaus** the best player I have ever played with and I class **Gary Player** as the best competitor I have ever seen. I knew Gary Player when he was 19 and he didn't have much natural ability, but through sheer determination and dedicated practice he became a great player. He won 9 majors. That was one thing about Gary Player: he was the toughest player I ever played against but he could still enjoy himself. He could get away from golf and forget about it.

Gary Player: Best putters … confidence. I listen to these TV commentators say 'he hit a bad putt because he jabbed it'. Two of the best putters that ever lived, **Bobby Locke** and **Billy Casper**, were both jabbers of the ball. I also jabbed the ball when I putted and I still do today and I think I holed as many putts as almost anybody. **Arnold Palmer** jabbed his putts as well; they all jabbed in our time because the greens were so slow. There is not one particular stroke that makes you a good putter. I believe good putters have got better eyes and better feel.

Bobby Locke had very good manners on the golf course, he was very relaxed and he was the best putter that I ever saw. He obviously set the bar in South Africa for me to try and beat. That was a great bar for me to try and beat. I've seen them all, and there was never a putter like him.

Ian Stanley: I was very fortunate that when I did my apprenticeship under Geoff Flanagan at Huntingdale he had me chipping and putting a lot. He used to say, 'Half the game is tee to green, the other half is around the green'. We used to spend hours upon hours … I would be playing bunker shots with an 8-iron, so that when I did eventually go in there with a sand iron, it was easy. He taught me how to pitch it and how to run it. With putting he always said, 'You never hole a putt by being short, so make sure you hit it at least 18 inches past the hole'. That stuck in my brain.

When I went out to play, all the good putters, such as **Kel Nagle**, were very aggressive. With his short putts he was very aggressive and with his long putts he always lagged them, so they were only little tap-ins. The man who was probably the best putter and a man I was fortunate to play a lot of golf with was **Bob Charles**. Bob's action was all shoulders and arms and he used to rock it back and through, there was no wrist action … his backswing was as long as his follow through. When he hit the ball, at the point of impact the club was travelling at its maximum speed. He was never decelerating into it and he always hit it firmly. **Jack Nicklaus** was a great putter: he was never short, he always got it past the hole. All the great putters are aggressive with putts ten foot and under – they are always at the hole or past it if they miss. They just have no fear – just bang and knock it in. **Tom Watson** was one: he would ram them in.

Kel Nagle: Bob Charles was a great putter. **Player** was pretty good. Arnold was a good putter, but a very bold putter. **Bobby Locke** was a great putter. **Sam Snead** must have been a very good putter early in the piece because he won a lot of tournaments and you can't win unless you putt. All those top players must have been good putters,

otherwise they wouldn't have won. I just developed my own technique that felt good for me and it might have been a little bit unusual, but it worked.

Peter Thomson: Kel Nagle and **Bob Charles** were outstanding … **Arnold Palmer** … **Gary Player**. They were the ones who got them in the hole. Holing 30-foot putts was like breaking the four-minute mile when that was done. No one thought it was possible prior to that. When Arnold came into the picture he started taking aim from thirty feet! We all thought 'well, you can't hole a putt from thirty feet'. But he did; he holed a couple every round for a few years. Once he started holing these long putts, then everybody did, because they took aim, whereas prior to that time you rolled the ball up near the hole so that you put the next one in.

Sir Bob Charles: No question **Bobby Locke** was the best putter ever; day in, day out on fast, slow, grainy and bumpy surfaces. He beat the Americans on their tour and annihilated **Sam Snead** on a tour of South Africa where they played exhibition matches. Putting is all about reading the greens, having confidence and believing you can hole the putt.

Tom Watson: Ben Crenshaw was probably the best putter I ever saw, in my era. I call him 'Doc' –the doctor of the greens.

Question: Aside from yourself, who is the greatest ball striker you have ever seen?

Bill Dunk: There is a hundred of them. Thousands of them better than me.

Bruce Crampton: Ben Hogan. Tommy Bolt was a great ball striker too. In America most of the time it's best to hit high shots that land softly. The caddies used to have some sayings about Tommy Bolt; 'Bolt had the ball come down like a butterfly with sore feet' or 'Bolt could have the ball go in the water and land on a lily pad and it wouldn't move because it came down so soft.'

Peter Thomson: Oh, I think **Snead** – I would have to give that to Sam Snead. Sam Snead brought a grace, an artistry to golf that lifted it out of the tradesman's craft – to see Sam Snead perform was to see poetry in motion.

Jack Nicklaus: I wouldn't put myself in that category. I think I was a good ball-striker, but I think that the two best ball-strikers I ever saw were **Ben Hogan** and **Lee Trevino.**

Jack Newton: Trevino is the best; he could make a golf ball talk. I just loved the way Trevino played golf. If he had been as good a putter as the other guys, they would never have beaten him. Sure he didn't fly it through the air as far as some of the others but he could hit any shot he wanted to. Some people thought all he could hit was a fade, but he could do anything. His shots with a wedge in his hands were exceptional. I see the kids today and they get anywhere near the green and out comes the lob wedge – whereas I could see Trevino playing the same shot with an 8-iron. The 8-iron would be far less risky than playing a lob wedge. Trevino could make that 8-iron spin on the third bounce, the second bounce, whatever. **Greg Norman** and **Brett Ogle** were probably the best drivers I had seen, for guys who hit it that far they were incredibly accurate. I would say Jack Nicklaus had the best course management I have ever seen; he never seemed to pick the wrong club and if he missed his target it was never by much.

Frank Phillips: Oh, **Hogan**. The first US Masters I went to, I sat behind Hogan for an hour and it was so pure … that 'click' … he used to get that 'click' with the iron shots. **Norman Von Nida** got me invited down to Houston and Ben Hogan said, 'I remember you; you sat behind me at the Masters watching me hit practice balls.' I said, 'Yes, Mister Hogan.' He said, 'Did you learn anything?' I said, 'Mister Hogan, I learned that you don't fade the ball like they reckon' (because the ball used to look like it was going to fade, but then it would come back. It used to fade away and then come back with a hook). That was the impression of Hogan I had: just a fantastic ball striker. Hogan was quite abrupt when he took the club back, he was rather quick on the takeaway, but the best striker I have ever seen in my life. I have never seen anybody hit the ball like Hogan did. Hogan used to drive it 260 yards back then. Imagine him today with the modern equipment … he would beat them all.

Gary Player: Ben Hogan. There is nobody who ever hit the ball as well as Ben Hogan. He was the best golfer I ever saw in my life. He hit the ball so much better than everybody else. He didn't have all these beautiful greens to play on, the manicured fairways and modern equipment … what would happen if you had Ben Hogan around today with all the modern equipment, beautiful condition golf courses and prize money? I don't think he won $300,000 in his whole life.

Jan Stephenson: Mickey Wright was very impressive. I had the opportunity to play with her before the end of her career. Also, one of my biggest thrills was spending time watching **Ben Hogan** hit it. All those stories that you hear about his caddy not moving were true. On Mondays after a tournament I would go out to Shady Oaks. After lunch, I would be with him when he went through his practice routine. It was amazing! When **Peter Lonard** was working with Gary Edwin, and at his peak, I saw him hit shots that reminded me of how Hogan hit it.

Annika Sorenstam was the best I have ever seen on the LPGA tour. She could hit her ball so straight, with no curve. I loved her work ethic, and how she dissected the golf course with such precision. Very Hogan-like. With the modern PGA, there are some great golf swings, and none on either tour that standout. They are all so close, with short game and long game technique. I love **Louis Oosthuizen** and **Jason Dufner.**

Sir Bob Charles: Ben Hogan was the best striker of the ball and his record proves that statement. However, it did not come easily for him and he achieved results by dedication and hard work. I did not see **Bobby Jones** play but I would rate him together with **Byron Nelson** and **Sam Snead** as the next best ball strikers.

Norman Von Nida: Before the war **Hogan** used to hook the ball, so big and so far he couldn't keep it in play. After his accident he reconstructed and reshaped his swing to become the great Hogan that he became. **Sam Snead** was a wonderful player. He had the most rhythmic and beautiful swing of anyone who has played the game. If he had of been able to putt like **Jim Ferrier, Bobby Locke, Hogan** or them fellas, nobody would have ever beaten him he was so good.

Ian Stanley: Trevino was amazing. He could do anything with it. He could nominate the shot before he hit it.

David Graham: Lee Trevino.

Kel Nagle: I used to love watching **Sam Snead**: lovely big flowing swing. Hogan was a good placement player, always in position to hit the greens. **Billy Casper** was a good player, good putter too.

Bruce Devlin: Ben Hogan controlled the height of his shots, and therefore the length the ball goes, better than anyone else. **Lee Trevino** was a close second.

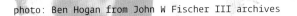

photo: Ben Hogan from John W Fischer III archives

Question: Aside from yourself, who is the greatest ball striker you have ever seen?

Graham Marsh: Ball striking is much easier to rate; it is just the purity of the golf shot and the consistency of the golf swing. How many times you drive the ball on the fairway and how often you hit it close to the hole. Of the pure strikers of the golf ball, perhaps the only one I didn't see was **Ben Hogan**. Categorically, I would say a guy like **Roberto De Vincenzo** was a wonderful ball striker. I would place **Sam Snead** up there as a superb ball striker and manoeuvrer of the ball and I would certainly put **Lee Trevino** into that class. Trevino could do a tremendous amount with the golf ball with every club in his bag. His ability to control his shape and trajectory on his shots was quite amazing. It also helped that he never lacked in confidence. They say, though I saw little of him, that the Canadian **George Knudson** was a terrific ball striker. In fact, Hogan, I believe, is on record as saying that apart from himself George Knudson was the best striker of the golf ball on the PGA tour. When you have 18 majors behind your name it is hard not to recognise **Jack Nicklaus** as being one of the best all time ball strikers. There always seemed to be a different sound when Jack hit his shots and I guess the same can be said of **Tiger** today. You cannot win Majors without controlling your golf ball. [George Knudson (1937–1989) won the World Cup Individual in 1966 and the World Cup team event in 1968 with Al Balding.]

Peter Toogood: Von Nida for precision, **Peter Thomson** for economy (he did it so easily), **Dai Rees** [Wales] was a very good striker. My father came out when I was practising one day and he said 'if you want to be any good you need to do this, this and this'. I was about 16 at the time and thought I was pretty good. This was the year that **Byron Nelson**'s book came out with all the photos in it. We had the photos all around the fireplace at home and of course there was no television in those days so I spent most evenings around the fire looking at the wonderful **Byron Nelson** swing. When I was at St Andrews in the Australian team for the Eisenhower Cup in 1958, after the third round I was sitting in the locker room and Bobby Jones had sent a man down to fetch me for a cup of tea. I was up in talking to Bobby Jones for about two hours and he asked 'how come you have an American type swing'? I told him the story of the Byron Nelson book and that I had copied his swing from looking at his photo.

Bobby Jones told me 'you don't play the game to impress people'. We talked mostly about course management and how we go about playing the game. A lot of the ideas that he explained that he used when playing a round of golf in competition I passed onto the juniors I used to look after in Tasmania. Play the shot that you want to play, not the shot that people might expect. Concentrate and keep your own technique; don't go around trying to copy everybody else. Attack the game, but don't try and overkill it and put yourself in positions that can cost you. Don't change your mind, stay with your initial thoughts.

Bobby Jones was following the American that I was playing against and he remarked about my accuracy off the tee – in fact they are still talking about it today: 'do I ever miss the middle of the fairway?'. One bloke got up in the clubhouse the other day and said, 'If we all hit the ball like Tooey we wouldn't need all the greenstaff we've got on the course – we'd just mow the centrepiece up the fairway.' I think what impressed Bobby Jones was when I played the 14th, 15th, 16th at St Andrews: I drove it straight down the fairway by the out of bounds wall while most of the other players hit their tee shots inland to avoid the out of bounds. He thought that was pretty clever.

Bob Shearer: I can't go past **Jack Nicklaus**. Also, I think **Greg Norman**. There was a bloke I always used to enjoy watching was **Tom Weiskopf**; he was the first bloke I saw who had that long slow swing and just belted it miles. He was about six foot 3, mind you. I am only saying people I saw or played with, I never saw Hogan. I actually played with **Sam Snead** at Augusta [1979]; he was way past it at that stage, but you were allowed to play the Masters if you had won it before. On the par 3 the 4th hole played quite long in those days and he had to hit a 3-wood and I hit a 4-iron. He gave me a full mouthful about 'young blokes hitting it too far, you little bastards'. He was a bit like **Thomson**, he was older and didn't hit it far, but it went exactly the same height, same shape, same everything. Thomson was like that; he lost the distance but the same ball flight was there.

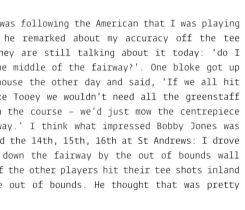

Question: Most amateur golfers have a 'favourite club' and they seem to associate that with hitting good shots. Conversely some players have clubs in their bag that they 'hate'. How important is it to look down and see a golf club you like the look of, if you are going to hit a good shot?

Ian Stanley: I think it is quite amazing when I play my home course, Huntingdale; I get to the 13th – it is a lovely little par 4 with a water hazard on the left hand side – and I see players pull out their drivers and say 'I always hit it in the water' then they go bang and hit it in the water. I say to them, 'Why don't you hit a rescue club or a 3-wood up the right hand side and then approach the green with say a 5-iron instead of trying to thread the magical drive up there and hit a wedge in?' But they continue to hit it in the water. The next hole there is no water on the left and they pull out the driver and hit it perfectly down the middle. So, it is all in the head. Whether they have got their favourite club or they haven't, it is all in the head.

You should be playing a shot that suits the hole, but also what you're thinking. There might be a hole on your course that causes you trouble every time you play it. We have a member at my home course who hits it in the front bunker on the par 3 3rd hole and takes three shots to get out, every time. These days he hits a 9-iron short of the bunker, chips it onto the green and walks off with a 4 and is quite happy because he gets a shot there. It gets pretty frustrating playing with guys who have a high handicap and have the shots to spare, but they are trying to play the hole like a pro. Why not play the hole like you have that shot? You might be playing a hole where the fairway bunker comes into play with the driver; why not hit a 3-wood off the tee, take the bunker out of play and leave yourself with a longer shot to the green?

Jack Newton: Given the game is a psychological game, it is very important. If a bloke I am playing with says that to me, that they hate the club in their hands, I would say 'get rid of it, replace it'. But the same person may go and hit balls once a week at the driving range but they never practice with that club – they will get their favourite club out. If you have got a club that is a bit like pulling out a death adder, then you won't pull it out, so you had better get rid of it because you are carrying a legacy in your golf bag.

Bob Shearer: I liked all my clubs. I didn't mind if I had a 3-iron or a wedge to the green, as long as I had that shot at the green. OK, maybe not 3-iron, maybe 4-iron up. 4-iron just felt the same as a 7-iron or an 8-iron; it will just go that distance. You have got to put the same swing on it. It is very easy to say that, but it is all up between the ears again. As I am getting older it is not worrying me that it might be a 5-iron and not an 8-iron. I am not worried that the 5-iron is more difficult to hit; I am just pissed off that I am not far enough down there to pull the 8-iron! I actually didn't have a favourite club: I liked them all. Everybody loses the plot at different times – some blokes get to 65 and they can still play and compete, others don't even get to 54 and they are gone. Some are even earlier – major champions one year and can't hit it the next. I would have loved to have been the bloke who got **Ian Baker-Finch** or **David Duval** going again; I would be a billionaire by now.

Bill Dunk: It is amazing how you can look down on a club and think 'this is the best-looking club I have ever seen: perfect'. I still hit all sort of shots with it though, same as anybody else. I think everybody has a situation where they find it difficult on certain holes. I think the worst feeling is when you stand over a shot and you think 'have I got the right club in my hand?'.

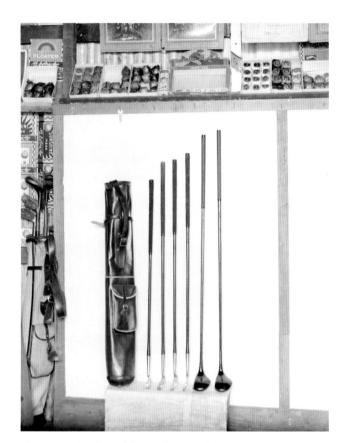

photo: National Archives of Australia A3560, 4528

Graham Marsh: The only contact between you and your clubs is through your hands. If you look down and see something you do not like the shot is already over and the result will not be pleasing. The game is hard enough without having to fight the equipment on every shot. Much also

42

depends upon your ability. A 27-handicapper is probably not too concerned about the minor details of what he is playing with. A reasonably balanced starter set matched to height will suffice to learn the basic fundamentals of the game. When you progress to playing reasonable golf, it becomes important to have equipment that suits you. If you have a club in your bag that you don't like, my advice is to get rid of it because it's the kiss of death every time it comes out of the bag. It is worth remembering on a bad day probably nothing feels or looks right. At least give the club a fair chance.

Bruce Devlin: You shouldn't have a club in the bag that looks bad especially with all the equipment trailers that are available today. Most golf professionals have the ability today to personally fit their members with clubs. Manufacturers have many different models to choose from so I see no reason why you would have a club you don't like the look of.

Frank Phillips: There is always one club in the set you don't like. I always had one. For me it was the 7-iron; I could not hit the right thing with the 7-iron. It just didn't look right. So I got there with the old club designer at PGF and I said, 'I love the 6-iron; let's take a 6-iron blade and make it into a 7-iron.' That solved the problem. It looked like the 6-iron, but it had the loft of a 7-iron. Of course I started hitting it better! If you have a club in your bag you don't like, you will avoid it, so you are minus a club.

You find people who get a good putter and they putt well with it, it's a lifetime thing. **Gary Player:** we are up in Tokyo and he walks into this little sports shop and picked up this bloody blade putter, black. 'Shit, that looks good,' he said. That's the one he won all his tournaments with. Cheap putter, cost him $3, looked like a toy putter. He used it all his life.

Gary Player: It is very important. Sometimes you have a club that you don't like the look of and there is usually a reason: it doesn't have the right lie, the right shaft, the grip is too thick or too thin. There is usually a reason, so get it checked with your local pro and get it fixed so you like the look of it.

Peter Toogood: Make sure that you have shafts that suit you. A lot of people play with shafts that are too stiff or too whippy. A lot of people look at the shape of irons and heads and think 'oh, that's nice', but the shaft is the most important bit to take notice of.

Sir Bob Charles: Every club in the bag had to look good, feel good and perform well. If the club does not have all three components I would make a change.

Bruce Crampton: Very, very important. Any tradesman is only as good as his tools. I had the luxury, when I was playing, to go to the factory where my clubs were being built and spend two or three days there. I would closely examine every club and make sure it looked exactly how I wanted it to look. I didn't want to be on the last hole on a Sunday afternoon needing to hit a 6-iron onto the green, look down and start thinking 'you are the ugliest club I have ever seen'. I made sure I loved every club in my bag. To my way of thinking that got me half way to

hitting good shots. The average golfer doesn't have that luxury. The best advice I can give them is to go with something they like the look of - it doesn't have to be what the top tour players are using. If you are looking down at the club and thinking 'I don't like the look of this club', then your subconscious cannot work properly. It's in their best interest to eliminate this kind of thinking from their mind.

Question: If you were standing over a golf shot and you were entertaining a negative thought, did you have any simple techniques/methods you would apply to get back to 100% confidence?

Bob Shearer: I would step away from it for a start. If I had a shot I was thinking 'shit, there is water left', I'd step away. Noel Blundell and his work with sports psychology – he helped a lot of sports. What he was teaching, I was doing automatically but I didn't know I did it. He noticed that I had changed my routine just a touch and I worked at getting it all right again, then I had two really good years. When I am playing with an amateur and he is chopping it a bit I just tell them to focus on the pin and get all the other thoughts out of their head. Everyone, who plays golf regularly, will hit a good shot when they take out all these other thoughts.

Jack Newton: The scariest shot in golf is the first tee at Augusta, particularly the first time you play there. It is very much a matter of 'please, God, just let me hit it'. I always found a couple of deep breaths and to trust your swing. If you are not happy on a tee with a driver, go and get your 3-wood. You have to trust your action and keep it simple with your swing thought.

Bill Dunk: I never rushed. I would like to feel the top of the swing. That is about all I ever did. I am not one of the academics, you see. I also figured that if I didn't hit a good one, I could chip and putt well enough to get out of it.

You've got to be confident you've got the right yardage, the right club in your hand. You know how far you are from the hole but it just doesn't look right. The yardage you have in your head doesn't seem right: you have humps in the ground, it might be downhill/uphill or maybe hitting across some water. If you walk forward a bit (I used to count it out) say ten of fifteen yards it can make you realise that yes I do have the right yardage. Now you are

confident and you can go ahead and hit the shot. Sometimes the flag on the green might be taller or shorter than the other holes – that can mess up your feel, too.

Bruce Devlin: Put the golf club back in the bag and go through my regular routine again. Visualise the shot and then make it.

Graham Marsh: As a professional you train yourself to concentrate and you have your own mechanisms to deal with it. Of course, once a poor thought enters your head the first thing you have to do is back off. You simply must come away from the shot, regroup, re-visualise the shot then go back and attempt to play it again.

People forget that golfers are not machines. They go out there, they still have emotions ... whether it be dealings with family, or business ... some days are better than others. We all have those emotions and it is a question of focus: you just have to find a way that works for you. I always found getting to the golf course an hour before and warming up helped – it wasn't that I need to hit balls for an hour; it was that I needed to be alone for an hour and concentrate on getting in the right frame of mind and getting myself up, so that when I went to the first tee I was focused. I would try not to look at people when I was playing golf and just try to keep myself in the confines of the course and try not to get distracted. Try to relax but not get distracted. You cannot be up for the whole five hours – that level of concentration isn't possible – so you have to be able to relax, without being distracted. Understand what you are there for and what the moment is all about. It is not an easy thing to do. When you have two players tied going head to head the one that has that better self-control is normally the one who will finish up winning.

Frank Phillips: When I got under severe pressure I would think about the golf swing and what I was going to do then I would go ahead and do it. I wouldn't try and hit the ball on the green: you swing the golf club and the ball will fly on the green. There are so many players you see under pressure and they try to hit it on the green and they miss. To me, that is a very basic rule that a lot of young kids don't know. You can't hit that ball on the green, you have to trust your swing and that is what you practise for. It becomes automation.

Gary Player: I didn't have negative thoughts. I just believed there were only two things; you could either hit it well or badly … I'm going with the well.

Ian Stanley: If you look at all the great players today, when they go to hit a shot they go through the same routine. They do the same thing every time, but if that routine is messed up, or you have a negative thought, go back to the start of your routine. I think that is one of the reasons golf is getting slower: someone might back away from a shot because someone has made a noise in the crowd. In the old days if someone made a noise in the crowd and you hit a bad shot you had someone to blame, but you can't do that anymore.

Peter Toogood: I just believed in tempo and in all sports keep your head still at impact and keep your rhythm through your legs. I know it's different nowadays – they have all these gurus who coach different techniques – but like all sports if you see a batsmen in cricket hit a lovely off-drive there is no effort in it: the feet are in the right position, the head is still and it is a nice smooth calm stroke.

Sir Bob Charles: One can only shut out negative thoughts by concentrating on the target whether it be the fairway, the green or the hole.

Norman Von Nida: If a competitor tees off with a negative attitude – that is, that he doesn't think he's got any chance of winning – nine hundred and ninety nine times out of a thousand he is not going to win. The most essential ingredient for anybody winning is to have confidence in his or her ability to win it, otherwise they shouldn't tee off. 90% of all winners in golf are confident they can win. If they are not confident they may as well not tee off. Unless you believe you can win and have confidence in your own swing ... this is how and why I don't agree with all these gurus that teach this theoretical crap about what you've got to do here and what you've got to do there. To me, if you watch Faldo, Price, Norman … the simplicity factor in the movements they make in their swing and the knowledge that the conscious brain can't compute what is happening as it is happening so fast. If you watch Elkington, it is just a simple easy swing: take it back, move your knee, swing and watch the ball fly.

When you are out on the golf course if you're trying to think about the theoretical factors and trying to determine how you are going to hit this ball with all this theory … there is no way at all you can do it. So many people tend to think that because it's a longer shaft you have to make a different swing. You don't. All you can do is trust your physical movement that allows the club to be swung the way it should be swung. Your conscious brain can never intrude on the physical execution of the stroke when you swing at the correct tempo.

David Graham: Yes. Don't think negatively.

Jan Stephenson: I believe that I have had some pretty negative thoughts when I was standing over a putt to win. People would say I was very calm looking and confident, but inside I was shaking and thinking there was no way I was going to make it. I believe that pre-shot routine is important at that moment. If I didn't change my pre-shot routine, then my subconscious did not know that I was negative. If I had changed my pre-shot, then that would have woken up my subconscious that something was wrong. I believe that subconscious is 95% at that point.

photo: Jan Stephenson from Golf Australia's archives

Question: If you were standing over a golf shot and you were entertaining a negative thought, did you have any simple techniques/methods you would apply to get back to 100% confidence?

Bruce Crampton: Everything begins with a thought. At the level that I was fortunate to reach, golf is played subconsciously. The only contact one has with the golf club is with one's fingers. I believe the thought transference from one's fingers to the subconscious part of one's mind is what one plays with.

I played 'picture golf' … I would visualise and compute, taking into consideration: the lie the ball is in, the stance, the way the ball is going to come out, the trajectory of the ball flight, what the wind is likely to do to the ball flight, what the ball is going to do when it hits the fairway or green, how soon the ball is going to stop … after considering all these aspects of a given shot. I'd then select the club I felt gave me the best chance of 'painting' that imaginary 'picture'. From that point on, the more one is able to get one's conscious mind blank, and let one's subconscious take over, the more likely one is going to consistently produce satisfying golf shots. This is commonly referred to as 'getting in the zone'.

As human beings we don't dream when we are consciously awake. We dream when we are asleep and the conscious mind is at rest. The dreams are in our subconscious. The subconscious doesn't know right from wrong, left from right, up or down – it just knows. Therefore if one is standing over a golf shot and notices a camera aimed in their direction, the fact that one is conscious of that camera detracts from one's subconscious to work as effectively. The most important thing that needs to take place at that particular moment is the golf shot and the camera can detract from that. Being aware of the camera can take on an egotistical approach where one starts thinking, 'Have I got the right grip, am I going to hold a pretty follow through for this picture?', or it can take on the thought of 'When is he going to click it?'

and one starts listening for the click. The fact you are listening for the click takes away from the shot. It could be a leaf that one notices and immediately begins wondering, 'Is it going to blow during my swing?' It could be a pair of white shoes being worn by a member of the gallery standing behind one's shot, which can be seen out of one's peripheral vision, and during one's backswing the person moves their feet. The fact that one is aware of this type of thing means that one has lost that imaginary picture one had.

Good rest is so important; a rested mind doesn't wander as much. One hears a lot of talk in golf about 'muscle memory'; it is my opinion that muscles do not have memory. I believe we practice in order to train our brain to fire our muscles in the correct order. Jimmy Demaret used to have a Macgregor Jumbo driver and on the top of it was inscribed 'LFF'. Do you have any idea what that stood for? 'Let the Fucker Fly.'

If one is thinking 'don't hit it left', 'don't hit it fat', 'don't blade it', 'don't chilli-dip it', don't whatever – hell, everything begins with a thought and all one is doing is manifesting for that to happen. One needs to have only ONE picture, and a positive one at that; this is what I am going to LET happen.

If one is working on swing mechanics and thinking of one thing on one's backswing and one thing on one downswing as an example, by the time you think of what you are actually trying to do and transfer that to your reflexes, the club head is somewhere else in that swing and it's all been a waste of time.

Under tournament conditions, the reason that the top players pull off the shots they do – I am talking about

the amazing shots when they only have one chance to do it – is because their adrenalin is flowing, all their senses are heightened, they're seeing better, hearing better, feeling better. Their whole nervous system is keyed up. It's OK to get one's motor revved up to the red-line but not go over it. Another way of saying that is, 'It is all right to have butterflies; the key is to get all the butterflies flying in formation.'

I seldom slept well when I was close to or actually leading a tournament. The night following a victory was also a restless one for me. I realised how important it was to 'wallow' in that victory. I replayed in my mind all the good shots and all the good things that happened. Part of the reason was that it was fun to do and it never happened often enough for me to get used to it, but I was also reinforcing my subconscious so I could pull on that if I got in a similar situation downstream.

There were occasions when my adrenalin was flowing for a couple of weeks or more. Eventually 'Mother Nature' decided 'that's enough' and I abruptly came back down to Earth.

I certainly didn't play super every day, but experienced peaks and valleys, like most folk do. Golf is so much like the game of life: it picks you up and puts you down. One day you miss the cut and the next week you win the tournament.

The same principles apply to be successful in any endeavour or profession. One has to be a hard worker, dedicated, make sacrifices, believe in oneself and be willing to go the extra mile. 'The game is just played in a different arena.'

photo: National Archives of Australia A1200, L36356. Royal Canberra Golf Course 1st hole. Photographer W Pedersen. Players (left to right) Stan Leonard (Canada), Mike Souchak (US), Peter Thomson (Australia), Gary Player (South Africa).

Question: Can you think of some players who were outstanding golfers but they didn't really get the kudos they deserved in the media ... a player who was under-rated, but had the game?

David Graham: There are thousands of them. But you are going to ask me to name names, right? There are literally thousands of them all over the world. There is no guessing as to the calculations as to why they could have or why they didn't; there are a lot of explanations. Maybe they weren't good enough in the first place, maybe they didn't have good nerves, maybe they didn't have the right heart, the right application, the right desire, maybe they wanted to be a better father than a better golfer, maybe they didn't like to fly on aeroplanes, maybe they didn't like the Chinese food.

Bob Shearer: I can think of them, but I don't want to say them because they might read the book!

Bill Dunk: Most of the characters I met on the tour had all won something. One fella that impressed me was the American who had a withered left arm. **Ed Furgol** he couldn't bend his left arm so he used to just crank it with his right arm and the left hand would just hold on anyway. He could really play.

Dan Cullen was a hell of a player in Australia, but he never had the opportunity to do anything because first of all the Second World War got in the way. He was a bomber pilot and we all know the story about how he had only been to Germany 'at night'. That really rattled his nerves sitting in one of those things dropping bombs on people. He can still play, at 90 years old; he has the best rhythm you will ever see ... except maybe for **Nagle**.

I believe that the really top players would do well at anything they tried. They are usually bright people and they can control their mind better than most. If you take **Gary Player** ... he could talk the leg off an iron pot and have you believe what he wants you to believe. If you take a fella like **Arnold Palmer** he would do well at anything – he has an aura about him: he walks into the room and people know he is there. **Nicklaus** is the same – he has that something about him that people take notice of. That is why **Greg Norman** has done so well – he is the same type of character. Most of us aren't like that. We are lurking in the shadows.

Bruce Crampton: Players may under-rate themselves in their own mind, or the press may under-rate them because they are not colourful and flamboyant, or they don't toady up to the press with a PR person etc. But if they score well enough to become a champion they will be treated accordingly.

One player who comes to mind is **Jon Guston**. You may never have heard of him. Jon had the most beautiful golf swing one could ever wish to see. Unfortunately he was not able to record enough low scores to become a consistent winner. Of course, becoming successful in professional golf tournaments is by no means the only way to achieve success during one's lifetime.

Bruce Devlin: Not sure if you mean only Australian golfers or not, but one American golfer that had a fantastic game was **Paul Bondeson** (passed away this year [2012]). He was leading the Doral Open in 1964 by 3 shots with 6 to play and lost to **Billy Casper**; he was never the same after that.

Jack Newton: I'd have to put **Peter Senior** in that category. **Greg Norman** was getting all the kudos, all the newsprint. One year I remember Peter Senior had won about nine tournaments and Norman had won about three but you never heard about Peter Senior. Norman was great for the game, but I believe the media spin was incorrect.

Gary Player: I think if you spoke to young people today they don't realise how great **Sam Snead** was. The most natural golfer that ever lived.

Ian Stanley: I used to love watching the guys hitting balls on the practice fairway. When I was an amateur I used to like watching **Kevin Hartley**: he was a terrific amateur but he was also an engineer and I don't think he wanted to take that step into pro golf. Also a guy at my home golf club, Huntingdale, a guy called **Alan Reiter**. He has won the club championships over twenty times and is a life member of the club.

On the professional side of it, in England I used to love watching **Neil Coles** – great player. He never travelled much. He hated flying. He played a lot of Ryder Cup matches and he could hit all types of shots and that is what I used to love watching. **Lee Trevino** hit the ball with so much control, left to right, right to left, high or low.

Most of the tournaments I won were on links courses where you have to learn to pitch and run the ball ... you have to fiddle with the ball and that is what I love about the game. When I first turned pro and we used to go out and have practice rounds, I used to wait every Tuesday morning for the great **Kel Nagle** to come down for his practice round. Then I would go and ask him, 'Excuse me, Mister Nagle, have you got a four for your practice round?' I would go and play with him and watch him, watch his manner on the golf course ... how he walked, how he kept his pace going – he wasn't fast or slow: he kept a good rhythm and his golf swing was the same. Watching him chip and putt, you know it is not all hitting the golf ball through the air – it is how to score and he was the master at it. Also, playing within yourself and not getting out of your rhythm by trying to hit it too hard. **Peter Thomson** was the master of that – he would just get up there, put a nice easy swing on it and get it into play.

Kel Nagle: In Australia … **Sam Richardson** had a great swing and lovely hands on the golf club. **Dan Cullen** came along about the same time as I did; he also did time in the war. Richardson was the same. 'Slammin' Sam' Richardson, he was the professional at Moore Park in Sydney. **Billy Holder**, **Billy Bolger**: they were great players. Dan Cullen. You had to play well to win in Australia at the time. There were about eight or ten pros in Australia that you had to compete against really. The top players were the fellas like **The Von**, **Eric Cremin** and **Ossie Pickworth** and if you finished up beating them or getting up in the first ten, you picked up a little bit of prizemoney. It was a hard road to hoe in those days! We used to go all over the place for 100/150/200-pound purses. Then it gradually got up to 1000-pound purses in tournaments like 'The Advertiser' in Adelaide, then Ampol came in with a bit bigger tournaments. Then there was McWilliams Wines 5000 at the Australian Golf Club that I won. You didn't win the whole 5000 but, you know, I won more for that than I did for winning the British Open!

Peter Toogood: Roberto de Vincenzo [Argentina] was a beautiful golfer. I played with him in the Australian Open at The Australian Golf Club. The short hole there, the 6th, was playing into a strong wind and most players couldn't get there with a driver. Roberto hit a 4-iron over the green. He was very strong with a nice quiet swing – he didn't bash it. **Matthew Goggin** is under-rated.

Sir Bob Charles: Two players come to mind: Bobby Cole of South Africa and John Lister of New Zealand. John did win Quad Cities on the US tour but had his heart ripped out, as you say, by missing cuts week after week and losing exempt status. **Bobby Cole** had plenty of talent but not the mental toughness to succeed.

Frank Phillips: Well … it is amazing, but you hardly ever hear my name mentioned. When they had the Australian Open or the NSW Open they would always mention everybody else but they would hardly ever mention my name in the lead-up to the tournaments. I won 5 NSW Opens and 2 Australian Opens and plenty of others when they were big tournaments, but it was always somebody else that they put in the media – they rarely put me in there.

Was that because you were not very friendly with the magazines of the era?

It might have had something to do with Tom Ramsey, yes. I was very good friends with Tom Ramsey and we fell out. He wrote a book on the Far East and he didn't mention me once. I was a bit feisty in my time. I could get pretty stroppy when I wanted to. He did apologise later in life and so it goes. [Tom Ramsey died in 2011 as one of Australia's greatest sports journalists.]

Randall Vines was a very good player who never really got the write-up. I don't really know why. The others I can think of are **Brett Ogle** and **Bob Stanton** – they were very good players, both won events in America but then things happened and they just faded out.

I've seen kids coming through and I have thought, 'well, you have got everything' – they can hit the ball and have fabulous short games – but when they get under pressure they just can't seem to produce what they can ordinarily do. I think that is the main thing at the top end of the game: it is toughness of mind and being able to perform under all that tournament pressure.

You look through history and you see people have won 14, 11, 18 Majors and all these players who have won 7 or 5 and you see Greg Norman – 2. People will look through the history books and think 'he wasn't that good'. He was World number one for two or three years, for god's sake. There was something in his make-up … I don't know what it was … maybe it was because he just couldn't play safe, maybe it was that which cost him two or three Majors.

I saw **David Graham** when he was 21 and he had very little ability, but he worked and worked and worked at it and he won 2 majors and had a great career. I see a lot of the young players today and I don't think they practise hard enough. I have been telling this young man, who wants to be a professional, that he should be hitting 500–1000 balls a day, because when you hit that many balls you start to get the strength of hand and the strength in your arms and your shoulders. I saw him the other day and he said 'I can't hit 500 balls a day'. So I said 'shake my hand' and honestly I could have broken his hand off and I am 80 years old and about a third as strong as I used to be.

Hitting practice balls strengthens the hands and when you get under pressure your hands don't let you down. I say if you want to be a great player, hit 500 balls in the morning and play 18 holes in the afternoon.

Question: What are some elements of the game that you think are disappearing from the modern game?

Bob Shearer: My short game. In my heyday if I was 60 to 120 yards out and I hit it to ten foot I was pissed off. Now I am absolutely delighted if it goes to ten foot. These days they just seem to come up short or go long, the depth perception and feel is not what it once was.

Jack Newton: The bump and run. That is why I always tell the young blokes to go and play in Asia, play in Britain and learn to play all the shots. In Britain the lob wedge in certain conditions is just useless; you have to get the ball on the ground. That is one of the reasons the Europeans are doing so well, playing a variety of different courses, different grasses and having to play all the shots. That prepares them well for the major tournaments.

Bill Dunk: More the manoeuvrability of the golf ball than anything else. That has been lost. They don't seem to have to do that any more because they hit it so far. Although you do see 'Woodsie' (**Tiger**) get it out of trouble every once in a while – that is the style of character he is.

Bruce Crampton: Certainly one is how much more the little ball sat down … the little 1.62 inch diameter golf ball … it really used to nestle down. Before there were watering systems and all the modern grasses, we used to have to handle all sorts of indifferent lies and work out how to manufacture a shot. The modern tournament courses are groomed to perfection. Certainly hiring a caddie and walking are things of the past for most average amateur golfers now that golf carts are readily available.

Bruce Devlin: Being careful of where you missed your shot to the green. With clubs now having up to 64 degrees, players no longer care whether they miss left or right. One thing that would help is limit the maximum loft a club can have. I would suggest that it be no more than 56 degrees, the same loft that Gene Sarazen had on his first sand iron.

Jan Stephenson: The one element that I am sad is being lost is the lack of emotion. I realise that focus, and controlling your emotions, is important. One shot can make such a difference now. However, I think of the times that **Nancy** would beam, **Carner** would jump up or I would get mad. Now the modern LPGA player is lacking in sharing their emotions with their fans. I think that is one of the reasons that **Bubba Watson**, **Keegan Bradley** and **Tiger Woods** are so popular. They wear their emotions on their sleeve.

Frank Phillips: The golf swing has changed because of the equipment. It is more upper body instead of lower body. In the old days with the golf balls we had and the persimmon heads, everything had to be pure or the golf ball wouldn't fly. These days they don't change their swing much, they just change their golf club.

Now, of course, they have got the lob wedge. We did not have the lob wedge and there were shots we could not play. If you had to go over a bunker to a sloping green, you could not stop the ball. You had to work it back onto the green, then try and two-putt it. Made missing the green on the wrong side a penalty. The problem with the lob wedge is, watching the young kids around here, they get just off the green and they play a lob wedge. When I was taught, I was taught to get the ball on the ground as quickly as possible. If you are just off the green take a little

7-iron or a 6-iron: it's just like a putter. The young kids get there, on the fringe, and they pull out the lob wedge. It looks great when it comes off, but they have lost the art of the 'pitch and run' shot. I didn't see one player pitch and run here at the NSW PGA tournament.

Gary Player: The belly putter and the long putter is a tragedy. Golf is at least 30% nerves. These long putters and belly putters are really eliminating the nerve angle and that is a shame. Golf – the man who is the best player teaches himself to have good nerves.

Ian Stanley: After watching the Ryder Cup this year, I think you could say that it is becoming more of a football match at times with the crowd yelling chants and things like that supporting their team or player to the detriment of the other players in the group. The respect and etiquette seems to go out the window from the crowds. It is coming from America. You play in the British Open – the crowds over there are fantastic: they give you warm applause when you walk onto the green and when you hole out. They really give you the accolades when you hit a good shot, but they don't get down on you when you hit a bad shot.

America changed the golf ball: it is now going high through the air with all the dimples. They have added extras – sand irons and whatever – and everyone gets up and hits it so hard. Golf, when it first started, was played on a links golf course. You played through the sandhills and you played through the environment. You go to America and most of the courses are in old swampland. To get the soil to build the fairways they have got to put water hazards in. Consequently the game of golf has completely changed: you are hitting the golf ball through the air and the 'bump and run' and the 'pitch and run' shot are taken out of it. They are putting bunkers at the front of greens now, whereas in the old days you had a bunker either side of the green so you could roll the ball on. Courses like Royal Melbourne, Barwon Heads and The National make you play a variety of golf shots whereas many of the modern designs dictate hitting a high ball at a target.

Peter Toogood: Judgement of distance. In my early days we had to learn how to judge distance by the use of mounds or bunkers. Now they have everything: markers on the fairways, markers everywhere else and these days they even have those distance things on their buggies or even on their watches! I think that takes a very important element, a skill, out of the game. It wouldn't matter if you knew the distance down to the last inch, you still have to hit it that distance.

Sir Bob Charles: Distance is King. The element of accuracy and hitting fairways and greens is not so important as it used to be.

Jack Nicklaus: I think there are a couple of elements of the game that are disappearing. Course management has disappeared, simply because of equipment. You haven't had to manage, because the ball doesn't curve as much. Plus, the fact that the golf balls we played in those days were not very consistent. Particularly the ones that I played. (Jack chuckles) You never knew whether they were going to hook or slice, so I had to be repetitive in what I did. And today they can be far more aggressive because the reliability of the equipment is far better. But I think the element of shot-making comes because the ball doesn't move and the reliability of what it's going to do is pretty obvious.

Scott Tolley: This is interesting, this part about the Bump and Run, because I know you don't carry a lob wedge. You carry a pitching wedge and a sand wedge.

Jack Nicklaus: I've never used a lob wedge. I always felt like I had a 58-degree wedge and if I opened the face, I had a lob wedge. I had enough trouble learning how to use one wedge rather than learning how to use two, and figuring out which one to play. That's why I don't do it. I never did do it. It was never the strength of my game. I felt like all it would do is make a weakness more of a weakness.

Question: Do you find it sad that the <u>technological</u> advancements in equipment and golf balls have basically made the history books obsolete? How can we compare a round of 64 at St Andrews in 1960 to the same score today? Do you believe technology is taking some of the magic out of golf?

Graham Marsh: Whether it is taking magic out of the game is a question that is good to ask my generation, because the next generations that have only grown up with high-tech equipment can probably not understand what could have been done with the older equipment and smaller <u>golf ball</u>.

There are a number of questions to be asked about the huge technological advances that have been made with equipment in recent years. Has technology moved us too far away from the grass roots of the game? Are we in danger of destroying the history of the game by making many of the greatest golf courses in the world obsolete? It would appear that the materials being used to improve golf clubs is totally out of control. This only leaves the <u>golf ball</u>. Are the governing authorities prepared to tackle this matter? The history books will never become obsolete; however, the way the game is headed will never be able to make comparisons in the future as we will be talking about a game none of us are familiar with.

Bob Shearer: Possibly. But it has gone that way since golf started. It went from the feathery <u>ball</u> to the rubber one and it went 50–80 yards further than the feathery. Most of the changes have come with the <u>ball</u>, but in this day and age the pro's actions are better and they are stronger. They are fitter. If you don't go to the gym these days you may as well not even play. I am not against the modern <u>ball</u>, although it has made our great old golf courses obsolete. Ever since I started playing, golf clubs didn't like it if you shot a really low score on their course during a tournament.

The <u>ball</u> is a lot different to what it was, I can tell you that now. The <u>ball</u> is minimum 40 yards longer. When I was playing we could use the small <u>ball</u> too – you could use either the small or the big <u>ball</u>. When we had the transition I found I could get a lot more spin with the small <u>ball</u> for some reason. The small <u>ball</u> definitely went further into the wind and the big <u>ball</u> went further downwind, which is logical. 1.62 to 1.68 doesn't sound like much, but there was quite a difference when you looked at them. When the big <u>ball</u> first came out they looked like tennis balls to us! With putting it makes sense that the small <u>ball</u> ... the hole doesn't change size so it would be easier to hole the putt, but they said the big <u>ball</u> rolled better and I must say I found it rolled beautifully – past the hole.

Most of the swings you see these days seem a bit mechanical. If something goes wrong they have got nothing to fall back on. In our day you felt the shot and if it wasn't feeling right you would change it mid-round. Some of these young blokes look like they have one way of swinging it and they can't change it – if their swing is off they are stuffed. I am not talking about the top fellas: they know how to do it.

Bill Dunk: I don't really believe that it has helped that much. It has helped in that it has made the club lighter, you can have it longer, so you can hit it further but I can't make the bloody things go any better than the old clubs. I don't think the technology makes that much difference; there are just bigger and stronger people playing and there are a lot more of them. They are more athletic than they have ever been – they even work out in gyms and things – they have coaches and whatever, head doctors, dietitians. We never had any of that. I don't know how I ever played.

With a steel head and graphite shaft I could hit it, probably, 20 yards further. I believe it is more the fact that there is a lot more money in the whole deal, there are a lot more athletes in the whole deal, not just ordinary characters that were drop-outs from other sports. On the other hand, I think they have lost a bit of playing talent as far as being able to manoeuvre the <u>ball</u>. They can give it a deadly hook or they can give it a deadly cut, but they can't finesse it. At one time we used to be able to finesse it in the wind, hit it with a fade or a draw, low or high and they don't seem to worry about that these days so much. The clubs don't allow anything other than 'rip it out there'.

I don't know much about the <u>golf balls</u> these days because I haven't played for 12 years. We went through a lot of changes, as far as <u>golf balls</u> are concerned, in our day. I started out using the small <u>ball</u> and the big <u>ball</u> was sort of forced on us – all of a sudden it's a different <u>ball</u> game, particularly in the wind, with the bigger <u>ball</u>.

I went to America to play some event – 'America versus the rest of the world' sort of thing – and I was partnered with **Bruce Devlin** who had these bigheaded things and I was still using the blades. Bruce said, 'I will take all the help I can get', but my way of thinking was that if you hit it out of the middle it didn't make any bloody difference.

Jan Stephenson: Technology is something that you cannot stop. It does not make me sad. It is life! I love all the new technologies with teaching by Skype, email and phones. It means you can improve more quickly. **Hogan** and I would not have had to wear our bodies out trying to figure it out by trial and error. Now one swing, and I can get right back on track. If I have a question, I take my swing with my phone and email it immediately. I usually can get an answer back from my coach before too long. I love that! Any magic that was lost will be returned with the putter not being connected. Other than that, you can never take out the magic in golf ... It is magic ... Always will be!

Jack Nicklaus: Well, you know my feeling on that. I mean, obviously the <u>golf ball</u> has changed all the record books because you no longer have the golf courses that we had then. All the golf courses have been changed because the <u>golf ball</u> goes a different length, so you're comparing apples and oranges. Is it bad that the <u>golf ball</u> goes a long way? Probably not, from the way golf courses are being built today, but you have 'obsoleted' most of the 33,000 golf courses in the world. I think that's the number given to me yesterday. If you shot a 64 at St. Andrews in 1970 and 64 today, St. Andrews hasn't been changed dramatically. But a 64 at St. Andrews would've been several shots better today.

I know the governing bodies are looking at it and they're continuing to look closely at it. What they come up with, I wouldn't venture to guess, but I know they will do what is in the best interest of golf. Right now, golf takes too much land. It takes too much water. It takes too much chemical. It makes the game take too long, and makes the game too hard. If you took a percentage away from what the <u>golf ball</u> does today, all of those factors would reduce and a great many of the 33,000 golf courses in the world would not be obsolete. Because there's only one course for tournament golf that in my opinion isn't obsolete – a course that does not have to be doctored – and that is Augusta National.

'My old man built me a couple of woods when I was about three or four. He was the greenkeeper at the golf club here [Gosford]; my mother did the catering in the clubhouse and we lived in a flat behind the clubhouse. That's how I got into golf. I used to putt around the green with some of the members for a penny a hole. When I lost I didn't have to pay them, but they would pay me if I won. I was there all the time.' **Bill Dunk**

photo: Bill Dunk aged 3 from his personal collection

Question: Do you find it sad that the <u>technological</u> advancements in equipment and golf balls have basically made the history books obsolete? How can we compare a round of 64 at St Andrews in 1960 to the same score today? Do you believe technology is taking some of the magic out of golf?

Bruce Devlin: Technology of both the club and the ball has ruined shot making in my opinion. Players no longer 'work' the <u>ball</u>: they either hit it dead straight or pull or push the <u>ball</u>. The other issue is the old great courses: there are hardly any of them left that have a legitimate par five. Personally, I think there should be two sets of rules, one for the pros and one for the amateurs. Of course all sanctioned tournaments by the governing bodies would be played under the rules of the pros.

David Graham: In some regards technology has brought magic to the game. People pay a lot of money now to go and watch guys hit drives 330/340 yards like **Dustin Johnson**. That is very entertaining. Technology hasn't helped the average player play at all – the game is still incredibly difficult for them whether they play with modern clubs and new <u>balls</u>, or the older equipment.

Clearly the <u>ball</u> goes a long way – there is no question about that – but I think the single biggest thing that has changed golf from a competitive standpoint, for the sport, is the lob wedge. The lob wedge basically obsoleted every bunker in golf and it has had a huge impact on designing golf courses. I think from the pro standpoint, more so than the <u>ball</u> or the square grooves, if the USGA had limited the loft to 58 degrees I think it would have had a much better impact than worrying about any other part of the game.

Frank Phillips: I think it has to a certain extent. We used to play with the little persimmon heads with the driver, which only had a sweet spot about the diameter of a shilling piece. The big technology now is that you have a wood and you hit it almost anywhere on the huge clubface

and it flies just as far! With the persimmon head if you hit it off the heel or the toe it went nowhere. That is the big improvement with golf. The golf swing has also changed with the new technology. Watch the young players these days and they just turn their shoulders, get hardly any body movement, except for **Rory McIlroy** – he has got a wonderful golf swing, but it is old-fashioned and he will wind up with a bad back in time.

Things change. In 1961 or '62 when **Jack Nicklaus** first played the Open he was a course walker and he walked the course with his caddie and marked out the yardages. When he first got to England and walked around the Open, they had a special general meeting as to whether they were going to allow it. The face of golf changed right then when the Secretary, who had the casting vote, allowed it. Of course today the players know exactly how far they have got from there to there: it's marked on the course for them. In the old days we used to walk out from our <u>ball</u> and get a feel and judge the distance taking into account the wind and the slope. Sometimes you would have to hit a three-quarter shot in, or finesse something in there. That is what has changed the golf swing: these days all the shots are full shots. The other one that has changed golf is the long putter.

The <u>golf ball</u> … I remember a conversation I had with **Arnold Palmer** at the Centennial Australian Open [2004] and he agreed with me that they should slow the <u>golf ball</u> down so they cannot hit it as far. Arnold said he built a course in America that was 7900 yards long and the average golfer cannot play it because it is just too long, too tough. So he put a tournament on there and he said they shot 21 under. That is the technology that has made them have to make such a long course and it is OK for the young pros, but the average player can't play the bloody

golf course. They cannot keep making the courses longer and longer. So, unless they do something about the <u>golf ball</u> they are going to keep hitting it enormous distances and making the courses look ordinary. Look at **Adam Scott** around Kingston Heath when he won the Australian Masters (2012): all the bunkers were in the wrong place, there was no decision to be made off the tee, just take out the driver and bomb it over the traps. It made the course look very ordinary. The only way they will bring these great golf courses back is if they slow the <u>golf ball</u> down, but they won't do it. All it needs is to, say, slow the <u>ball</u> down off the clubface from 320 feet per second to about 250 feet per second … all of a sudden they have lost 50 yards. That is all it would take – 50 yards. I have been saying it for 25 years and **Arnold Palmer** is the same, but they won't do it. Everyone loves to see someone hit it out there miles. I was a big hitter in my day and the crowds used to love it.

What amazes me is they hit their iron shots so far. In our day a 6-iron went 160 yards and that was a big hit – these fellas are hitting wedges 150 yards! It is just technology, that is all it is. I had some young fella say to me 'you wouldn't have done any good today because you didn't hit it far enough' and I said 'I used to hit it over 340 yards with a persimmon head' and then I said to these young fellas 'could you have imagined **Ben Hogan** who used to hit it out there 260, all of a sudden hitting it out there 300? He would have bloody murdered ya.' Maybe the way to slow them down is give them persimmon heads and see how far they hit it.

photo: National Archives of Australia A1200, L3186 Spalding Factory

Question: Do you find it sad that the <u>technological</u> advancements in equipment and golf balls have basically made the history books obsolete? How can we compare a round of 64 at St Andrews in 1960 to the same score today? Do you believe technology is taking some of the magic out of golf?

Jack Newton: I always thought the biggest change would come in the form of fitness and the use of more psychology. I under-estimated how much the equipment revolution would take over the game. I don't think they can do much about the golf clubs, aside from what rules are in place, but the <u>golf ball</u>, they can certainly slow it down. **Jack (Nicklaus)** has been spruiking that for years, I have had a crack at the Royal & Ancient, but they don't seem to be listening.

When I was on air during the Australian Open at Moonah Links [2008] we had one of the top dogs from the R&A in the commentary booth for a while; when we were off the air I said to him, 'Mate, when are you going to do something about this <u>golf ball</u> going too far? It is threatening the history of the game; all the great courses are going to be obsolete and look at where we are, playing British Open courses that are 7, 700 yards long. It has no correlation to the average golfer. They wouldn't even get around these championship courses, let alone play any good.' He said, 'We have got it on our agenda to look at it in 2012.' Here we are banning long putters and the golf ball hasn't been tossed up for discussion in any form for review. They slowed the <u>ball</u> down in tennis; why can't we slow it down in golf? When I was playing in America the longest hitter there, **Dan Poll**, averaged 276 yards for the year. That is approximately 250 metres. There are women golfers now who would hit it well over 250 metres and every man and his dog on the tour hits it 300+. We are just going to run out of room, basically, on some of these famous golf courses. I get senior golfers telling me they hit it further now than when they were teenagers.

Gary Player: I think the modern <u>golf ball</u> has done golf an immeasurable amount of harm. I think the technology should be there for the amateurs, who are at the heart of the game. The <u>golf ball</u> has hurt the game with professionals because they have made the golf courses obsolete and everyone is trying to spend money on their existing golf courses around the world to make them tougher. It has hurt the game of golf. The members don't like it. They have made golf too expensive. The clubs have got themselves into debt. They didn't have to change their golf course because their course was absolutely bloody magnificent! They didn't have to change anything at the sandbelt in Victoria, but they have changed many of them. It was unnecessary. They were beautiful, beautiful golf courses for the members and they loved it. Now, they changed them because pro golfers are hitting the <u>golf ball</u> so far. Just cut the <u>ball</u> back 40 or 50 yards with pro golf and you didn't have to spend all that money and levy the members to get out of debt.

You haven't seen it yet, but they are coming. These seven foot guys are coming and they are already hitting the <u>ball</u> 400 yards. They will be hitting the modern ball 420 yards and all the golf courses will be obsolete, then they will have to go back and change the modern <u>golf ball</u>.

Ian Stanley: Technology is not making history obsolete because the guys are still shooting the same scores. The <u>golf ball</u> is going too far. Why don't they, like in tennis ... go to the first tee and they are using the same ball as everyone else in the field. You can't compare a 64 at St Andrews in the '60s to a 64 today for two reasons: the <u>golf ball</u>; and the golf courses today are manicured so much better than what they were in that bygone era. They have got these new mowers – they cut the greens finer, faster and smoother. If you play in America, all the fairways are cut at the same height for each tournament, the rough has got to be a certain height and it is only occasionally like the US Open or the US PGA that they trick the courses up with deeper rough and faster greens. What is sad about the technology is that you have

these world class courses, like Royal Melbourne, that they cannot lengthen because it is surrounded by houses. Why not bring the <u>golf ball</u> back so it doesn't travel so far? In my day a big drive was 275 yards, maybe 280. I just finished designing a golf course in China; it is 7500 yards … an absolute monster with 200-yard water carries. You put an amateur golfer on that and he is buggered – he cannot get across the water. Today I think with what is happening with golf course design and making golf courses so long, it truly has become a power game.

Kel Nagle: It's all changed. I think it can give golfers too much to think about. Keep it simple. The technology is in the <u>golf ball</u> and also in the shafts and the big-headed clubs. Calloway has got that fella from the space program – they had all the experts developing that golf club. They made those big-headed drivers and they all seem to be using them these days. They can't get any bigger. But the worst thing is those belly putters and those long handled putters, that's not golf. It's croquet. It just doesn't look the same. There are too many young people using them. Their nerves can't be that bad. The reason they developed the long putter was because the nervous system was bad – they used to have the yips. So they kept the two hands apart, then started sticking [anchoring] it to the body. But an 18-year-old? You can't tell me their nerves are that bad.

The equipment has changed over the years. In the early part of my career all the iron heads were drop forged; they would make them out of a round piece of steel – we had a lot of the old Scottish club makers come out. All the irons' heads were hand forged, whereas today most of them are manufactured in Thailand and different places; Korea. The art of club making sort of disappeared.

The golf ball is all different. We used the balata ball. I think the equipment is better today – they are more scientific about it. They go into swing weights and the technical side of dynamics and custom for each person with shafts with different 'kicks' – some people like the kick just under the grip, others like it down the bottom near the head. It is an art, assembling golf clubs. The major difference has been in the ball.

The problem is they haven't got enough land to build the golf courses that will contain those fellas, you know, and a lot of the lovely old golf courses are becoming obsolete. Players are driving over the traps (fairway bunkers) and what can they do? Try and make it more difficult and put big undulations in the greens? But the average person in the street ... they like to see the golf ball going that long way, don't they?

Peter Thomson: As far as golf is concerned, that is the biggest disappointment in my life: that the authorities didn't rein in the ball. It has changed the game so much. You have a ball that will penetrate the wind without any divergence. You have balls flying over fences in suburban areas where the members play – now, that wasn't possible in the '50s because you couldn't hit it over a fence because the ball wouldn't go that far. Technology is everywhere around us these days and there will always be technological advancements in golf.

Peter Toogood: I think it should be like cricket and table tennis … everyone uses the same ball. Then again, I guess all the big manufacturing companies wouldn't be able to claim their balls go further. It probably wouldn't help the other slogans they use in their marketing campaigns. In the '50s the Dunlop 65 was the best feeling ball. It is silly to try and compare the players from the '50s

and '60s to today's players because today's players have a tremendous advantage by hitting it 50 metres further using the same swing. The golf ball and the shaft have made a big difference to how far these young blokes are hitting it. They are hitting it enormous distances with not the most perfect swing. The thing is, there are a lot of very good golf courses and a lot of them will become obsolete. They can't keep pushing the tees back, extending the tees, buying another strip of land and rebuilding the holes forever.

Sir Bob Charles: Yes, it is sad. Technology is, more importantly, making great golf courses obsolete. The performance of a golf ball should be reduced to a maximum of 275 yards, which was the number one for distance statistics for Jack Nicklaus in 1967. By reducing it that far, it represents a 10% reduction in distance, which I believe the R & A have already tested. For the record, that same year [1967] Arnold Palmer was at 272 yards, Gary Player 256 yards and yours truly at 245 yards. At age 76 I still hit the ball 245 yards, but I am 60 yards behind my son David and thus not competitive with him. The 31 yards I was short of Nicklaus 45 years ago was still reasonably competitive. Reducing the ball performance by 10% and shortening golf courses to a max of 7000 yards will help restore the magic.

Norman Von Nida: Course construction today, I think, is doing a disservice to the game by creating what we call monsters: the courses are too long, the water hazards are too severe and the actual overall difficulty of competing and playing on the courses is such that its more of a chore now as against the pleasure of competing on a championship course. One can make a golf course a really great course by asking the competitors to display a great deal of skill in playing their shots, like fading it or drawing it, or

hitting it high or hitting it low, instead of this phobia for enormous great length. By making these monster golf courses, the course constructors are catering for brute strength and not skill.

Tom Watson: I agree they should bring it back about 10 percent. With the new golf ball I find it very hard to control downwind. The old golf ball you could spin more, you could loft the ball and get it up in the air, but with the new ball downwind it flattens out the trajectory as happened to Adam Scott on his second shot to the 16th at Royal Lytham and St Annes [Open Championship 2012] – it flattened out with the sand wedge and went fifty feet by. That's the new ball, right there. You can't get it in the air and spin it like the old ball.

In order to preserve the balance between power and the length of holes and in order to retain the special features of the game, the power of the ball should be limited.

The Royal & Ancient Rules of Golf Committee recommendation in 1919.

During the prime of his career, British Open champion Mark Calcavecchia was fourth in driving distance at 273 yards in the 1980s. Thirty years later in 2012, aged 52, he averaged 285 yards. John Daly averaged 302 yards in 1997, the first player to average over 300 yards.

Question: In your life, is there one round of golf that sticks out from the others as being your 'finest hour'? If so, what made it so special?

Jack Newton: Oh gee, that is a tough one. Probably the most satisfying – I didn't win it; I lost the playoff to **Tom Watson** – was playing with **Jack Nicklaus** in the third round of the British Open when I broke the course record at Carnoustie [Scotland] in 1975. I rate Carnoustie as an Open venue – it is a course that has stood the test of time. I shot 65 and it was lower than what **Ben Hogan** had shot there, but more importantly I was playing with Jack Nicklaus who I admired and he was very good to me. He shot 68 and he said to me, 'Jack, I felt like I was having 80 by the way you were going.'

A week prior, I had won a foursomes tournament with an Irish mate of mine called **John O'Leary**. **Tom Weiskopf** [USA] was a good friend of mine and I had taken money off him at Yarra Yarra [Melbourne] and he was always at me for a return match. I ran into him the Monday before the tournament and I agreed. I said, 'Get yourself a partner and I will get my man and we will play ya.' We get on the tee and we are all there, but I say to Tom, 'Where is your partner?' The next thing there are thousands of people running to the first tee – he's got **Jack [Nicklaus]**! My partner birdied the first and I birdied a couple and we were like 2 up after 6 and cruising. I jokingly said to Tom, 'You might have to go and get yourself another partner, because you are going to get your arse smacked.' Anyway, the story has it that Jack heard me say it and he apparently got Tom to one side and said, 'Come on, let's teach these young pups a lesson.' Anyway Weiskopf had a hole in one at the bloody 8th and I think he shot 65, Jack shot 66 and I had 66 or 67 myself and we got drowned, moneywise. Weiskopf was tugging at me to pay him and I said, 'No, I am not paying you. I am paying Jack.' Anyway Jack said, 'No, we will go upstairs and you can buy me a sandwich and a beer and we will call it quits.' I thought, 'that is a beautiful thing; it is going to cost me 300 quid otherwise'.

I noticed something, playing with them, about my putting, which helped me a lot that week in the British Open. The other one was that I played a practice round by myself with **Bobby Locke** that week and we were coming up the last and he said to me, 'You know, Jack, you can win this week as long as you keep that fifteenth club in your bag under control.'

Bob Shearer: I have had a lot of good deals, but I will have to say the Australian Open [1982]. I have been very fortunate in who I have been able to play with, but that day I was paired with **Jack Nicklaus** and **Jack Newton**. It was my home Open and I had a few chances to win it before that day, but I wanted to win it that bad that I think I was choking. I had won the Australian Amateur and the Australian PGA and I wanted to put the third one there. I had chances a few times and it actually came a little bit out of the blue at The Australian. Playing with Nicklaus and playing so well was as good as it gets. Years earlier, when I was the Australian Amateur champion [1969] I got drawn with **Jack Nicklaus** for the first time and I shit myself. I could barely tee it up and I hit it fair on the head, I mean absolutely topped it. I wouldn't have topped the ball in ten years. We were walking down the fairway and Jack put his arm around me and he said, 'Son, we both go to the bathroom in the same way; just settle down and we will have a nice day.' I had a couple of bogeys and a double, but then shot 2 under for the last 12 holes. Here we are 12 or 13 years later and I am teed up with him again. I had teed it up with him a lot in between, but here we are at the same golf course and I am leading the tournament and he is there. The difference was that I hit a driver and a 2-iron onto the front of the par 5 green. Jack Nicklaus was my hero all my young life and here we were, it all came back in the end. To do it in front of Jack, he is such a nice bloke and a nice bloke to play

with and again he put his arm around me coming down the 72nd hole.

Bill Dunk: No. Not especially. Not one round. There are a couple of golf tournaments that stick in my mind. The Victorian Open in 1981 around Metropolitan and the Chrysler classic at Royal Melbourne in 1975. In the Vic Open I had always run second, or down the mine somewhere there. One year I went in to the last round a shot behind **Nagle**. I shot 64 in the last round and ran second! Nagle shot 64 to win by a shot. That is why the '81 Open sticks in my mind; there was **Norman**, **Shearer** – and I had a wood into the last green for my second shot and I hit it into the middle of the green, two putts to win it.

The Chrysler tournament: **David Graham** nearly holed it on the last hole to tie me. I had played the Australian Open up in Sydney the week before and I played with **Nicklaus** in the last round and I bombed out nicely. I got down to Melbourne the next week for the Chrysler and I am sat in the clubhouse taking my shoes off after the first round and one of the 'scribes' [golf journalists] comes over and he says, 'How did you go today?' and I told him I was one under or whatever it was. He said, 'That's not bad' then he said, 'Now, after last week's bad performance how do you think you'll go this week?' In my nasty little way that I used to have I told him to POQ and go and annoy someone else. I went into the washroom to wash my hands and tidy myself up a bit and I was thinking 'bloody mongrels won't leave you alone' and the next thing I open the door to walk out of the washroom and here they all are waiting for me and I just said, 'You lot of mongrels.' A lot of the modern players are muzzled, but that was it, I let them have it. It was the first tournament that they roped off – the crowd had to walk behind the ropes. I hit my drive up the last hole needing to make a par to have a

chance to win. I had a 3-iron into the green, waiting for the green to clear and three of these 'scribes' came out and stood right behind me. If I had enough brains I would have said, get back behind the ropes will you. I couldn't get it out of my mind and I hit it into the right hand trap. I get to the bunker and there is a rough patch in the bunker (they call it 'Dunk's Island' these days) and I can only just see the back of the ball. I took the sand iron and I blew it up there about six feet past the hole. I have a slippery downhill putt from 6 feet. It comes my turn to putt. There are a few thousand people around the green and they went quiet and all I can hear is a magpie in the tree there squawking. As I get over the putt, there is the clubhouse over there and they are watching it on TV and I can hear it go quiet and all of a sudden I am there on my own. I was lucky enough to tickle it in. **David Graham** came up the last hole and he hit this 45-50 footer from the front of the green and it just lipped out. He gave it such a good run I couldn't believe it.

Jack Newton and Tom Watson 1975 British Open from Jack Newton's private collection

Question: In your life, is there one round of golf that sticks out from the others as being your 'finest hour'? If so, what made it so special?

Bruce Crampton: The last round of the Australian Open at Royal Sydney in 1956, and in particular the last two holes. The putt that I made on the 71st hole was a long putt from the front-right portion of the green. The hole was cut on a flat area at the back-left section of the green. I hit a nice 3-wood off the 18th tee and then hit a perfect 6-iron to about 4–5 feet below the hole and made the putt. That round and those two holes changed my life.

If it wasn't the last round of the 1956 Australian Open, then it had to be the last round of the Speedo Tournament a few weeks later at Victoria Golf Club. I had 9 birdies and broke the course record by four shots and ended up winning the tournament by 4 shots from **Peter Thomson**. It was five rounds and the Friday was my 21st birthday. We played 36 holes on Saturday. Standard scratch was 73. On the morning round Peter shot 70 and I shot 73. I could hear murmurs in the clubhouse during lunch as people expressed their belief that Peter would win the event. I went out in the final 18 holes and everything fell my way – it was a truly special round of golf.

The first tournament I won in the US was the Milwaukee Open in 1961. **Gene Littler** was one of my partners during the last round of that event. The last hole was a five par we couldn't reach in two. We left ourselves wedge shots to the green. I am sure people are aware what a great golf swing Gene Littler is known for. Gene was first to hit and he stood there with a wedge and 'shanked' his golf ball right into the crowd on the right side of the fairway. Now I am trying to win my first tournament in America and I have to get my ball on the green somehow. Talk about white-knuckling it.

I played the last two rounds with **Bobby Locke** in 1957 when he won at St Andrews in Scotland. I developed the 'shanks'. I 'shanked' it with a 7-iron, a 3-iron – you

name it. Talk about an embarrassing experience. That was also the tournament with the controversy on the 72nd green of the Championship where he failed to move his ball marker back to its original position. Bobby purposely hit his tee shot over on the first fairway from the 18th tee. The hole was cut in its customary last round position, just over the 'valley of sin'. Bobby hit a gorgeous second shot. It finished about 18 inches below the hole. I was beside him as he walked towards that final hole. He had tears in his eyes; the crowd was all around us. He gave the impression he was in another world because he knew he was about to win the British Open. I had to putt first. My first putt finished outside Bobby's coin which I had to ask him to move aside. I made my par putt, then turned and walked towards where the scoring table was located off the back-left section of the green without paying attention to whether or not Bobby moved his coin back to its original position. It wasn't until I was with a group of fellow pros the following day in Paris where the French Open was to be played, watching a replay of the British Open, that someone noticed Bobby failed to move his coin back. Nobody around the 18th green at St Andrews apparently noticed this mistake either. [Bobby Locke had effectively signed for an incorrect score and the penalty would be disqualification; however, the R&A tournament history states: 'The error was not spotted at the time, but reported to R&A officials later. The Championship Committee quickly decided that with his three-shot lead and no advantage having been gained, the equity and spirit of the game dictated that he should not be disqualified.' If Locke had been disqualified **Peter Thomson** would have won 5 times in a row from 1954–1958.]

Bruce Devlin: Can't say that it was an entire round, but getting the ball up and in at the last hole at the 1960 Australian Open changed my life. I was content to continue

being a plumber and in business with my Dad. That all changed 4 months later when my wife Gloria and **Norman Von Nida** talked me into turning professional.

Jack Nicklaus: I don't think so. I had a lot of good rounds – ones that I am proud of – but I can't see one of them standing out. I can go back and cite many, many rounds that I was proud of and very happy with, but to cite one over the other would be very difficult.

David Graham: Oh, well, that is pretty obvious – my final round when I won the US Open at Merion [1981]. By far. It was maybe not the best golf I have played – I think the best golf I have played over four rounds was when I won the American Golf Classic at Firestone [1976]. But the best single round of golf I ever played was the last round of the US Open. There are other great rounds of golf that I have played and others have played, but if you don't win it doesn't get recognised. There are a lot of great rounds played on Sunday by players who aren't in contention, they have shot a really great round and they don't even get to go to the press tent. Someone might have played the best round of golf of their life on a Sunday and finished tenth, but who cares?

Graham Marsh: When I shot 64 in the last round of the British Open [1983] at Royal Birkdale and was leader in the clubhouse for three hours. It was a howling gale when I went out in the morning and I was 8 shots behind. By the time I got to the 9th hole I was five under par and the leaders hadn't started. I was within three shots of the lead. I went on to shoot the back nine three under par and posted a 64. When I came back into the locker room **Arnold Palmer** was there and asked me what I had shot that day. When I told Arnold he said, 'You had better not go anywhere – that score might just about be good enough.' I sat in the locker room with my good friend and caddy Prof Don Watts (from Perth). For more than two hours we watched the flags at Royal Birkdale fully extended on the flagpole in front of the clubhouse. The leaders had gone out and dropped shots on the first few holes and by the time they reached the 9th hole I was still tied for the lead. Shortly after, as they started the back nine the flags on the clubhouse pole went half limp. As the wind continued to abate the leaders picked up a few birdies on the final nine and I finally finished 4th in the tournament. **Tom Watson** won beating me by two shots [for his 5th Open]. Hale Irwin and **Andy Bean** finished one back of Watson. That 64 was the best round of golf that I had ever played. [It was the last time Arnold Palmer made the cut in the British Open.]

David Graham shot a sensational final round 67 to win the 1981 US Open at Merion (Pennsylvania) to give Australia its first US Open champion, with rounds of 68,68, 70, 67. On June 21st 1967, in his final round 67, he hit every green in regulation and only missed one fairway. Some say it was the finest ball striking round of golf in the modern era. It earned David Graham a personal phone call with congratulations from none other than Ben Hogan. Painting of David Graham by Darren Love

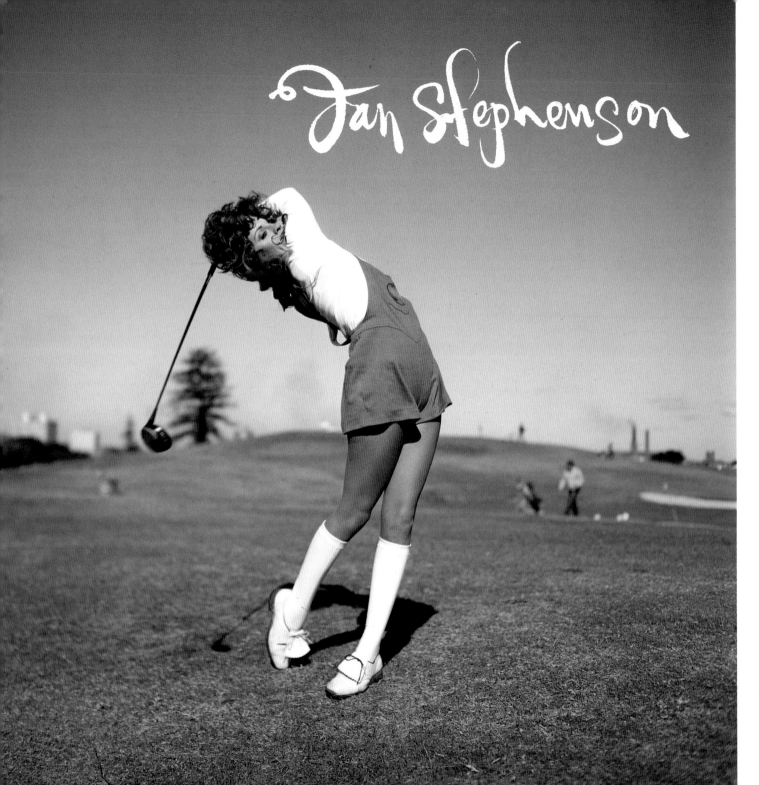

Jan Stephenson

Question: In your life, is there one round of golf that sticks out from the others as being your 'finest hour'? If so, what made it so special?

Jan Stephenson: There are a few rounds that are special. The last round of the Australian Open in 1977: my mother was caddying and I beat Pat Bradley in the play off. The last round of the Peter Jackson and LPGA Championship: they were 2 Majors that my father was caddying. Very special. When I won the US Open, my parents were there. That made it very special. I was nervous all day and it was in slow motion. I had led from the first round and I thought that it would never end!

Frank Phillips: I can remember a couple of the best shots I ever hit. The Australian Open in 1961 I was leading pretty easily and Kel Nagle made a burst at me and I double-bogeyed the 14th at Victoria Golf Club. I then hit a great iron shot into 16 but it went over the green. I stood on the 17th tee and I was level with Kel. I turned my driver over a little bit and I went over into a sandy lie down the left. I looked at the lie and thought I'd better punch a 5-iron down the middle of the fairway, but then I realised if I did that I would have a wood to get to the green for my third. So I took my courage in my hand, took my 4-wood and it's the best shot I ever hit. It went so far it just left me with a little wedge shot over the bunker and I knocked it stone dead.

The other one was coming down the final holes of the Hong Kong Open when I birdied 5 of the last 6 holes to win. I was a very good long-iron player and I used to carry a 1-iron which I would use in a heavy wind. I pulled the 1-iron out of the garage the other day to give to someone and I looked down at it and thought, 'How the bloody hell did I ever hit those?' It just made me realise how strong I was in those days – I used to belt that 1-iron 240 yards. Against the wind it used to fly for miles, but I couldn't even hit one these days – I couldn't even get it airborne.

Ian Stanley: It was in Fiji: the course is a par 62 and I shot 49. It was a lovely little course at the Fijian Resort; we used to play a little three-round event there. I had a hole in one and birdied the last to shoot 49. I played with the major sponsor, a guy from Fosters, and after the round we sat down and had a wonderful time with the Governor of Fiji. It was just one of those rounds where I couldn't miss a putt. I just wanted to get to the next hole and make another birdie.

Kel Nagle: Hard to say. I had a few moments. I remember when I won in Hong Kong in 1961. I had a putt for a 60 on the last green and I three putted. Thomson said 'serves you right'. [Laughs.] I was playing with him; he shot 65 and lost 3 more shots to me.

I had some good moments at Dublin in Ireland playing Woodbrook Golf Club. I shot 260 there as well. 260 for four rounds. I shot 260 in Hong Kong as well. In Hong Kong we played two different courses: two [rounds] on the old and two on the new. I suppose the scoring at St Andrews in 1960 in the first and second rounds – 69, 67 – sticks out in my mind too.

Peter Thomson: I can't answer that…

Peter Toogood: The first round of the British Open. In those days [1954] you had to play two rounds to qualify to enter the Open. I was nervous and a bit shaky; it was windy too down there by the coast near Birkdale. I played the first two holes OK and the third was a long par 5 that I hit two woods to the green to about 2 feet from the hole and I got an eagle. That calmed me down a bit. I would

say that those first two rounds to qualify to play in the British Open – I can remember them very vividly. To get into the Open itself I shot a 73 at Birkdale and a 71 at Hillside and that got me in the top 100 or whatever it was to play. And those rounds didn't count, of course, in the Open itself. Peter Thomson and I started out in the Australian Amateur at Metropolitan in 1948 and I was still at school. Here we were six years later accepting the prizes at the British Open. We were the only two players on the platform with the official presenting the British open trophy to Peter Thomson and the leading amateur medal to me. [Peter Toogood shot 72-75-73-71 to be leading amateur in the 1954 British Open.]

I did have one freakish day at Royal Hobart where I went out in 34 and for some reason every iron shot I hit on the back nine finished close and I had 28. I won the comp that day, playing Stableford off +2. It wasn't a course record because it wasn't a stroke event I was playing in.

Sir Bob Charles: I have no particular round that sticks out but a 64 in qualifying for the US Open in Memphis was memorable in that I never missed a putt under 30 feet.

Question: The future … some people are saying that golf needs to be shorter – perhaps 12 holes – to cater for the modern time-starved golfer. Can you see any changes on the horizon?

Jack Nicklaus: Well, I wouldn't have seen coming what has happened in the last 30 years, so I can't imagine what might happen in the next 30. I think you just have to wait and watch it unfold.

Bob Shearer: The 18 holes has got to stay, if it is tournament golf. Golf is a time-consuming thing and 9 holes is coming into play for the average bloke.

Bruce Devlin: I think the game is too traditional; I seriously doubt that it will change. The USGA came up with what I think is a good idea: what ever tees you normally play, go up one and play the hole a little shorter. Suits me just fine now that I am 75.

David Graham: I grew up in Australia in the '60s when young kids couldn't get on golf courses, particularly the nice courses. I learnt to play golf hitting balls in football fields and cricket fields and places like that. I think one thing that needs to happen is that private clubs, all over the world, need to have some type of a program so that for certain days of the year the younger generation or the less fortunate that can't afford the luxury of those kinds of memberships can at least be exposed to the great courses and exposed to the game.

Fostering better junior programs would be a really nice thing to see. Clearly we have to figure out a way to make it less expensive for a lot of people and better access for a lot of people. I think the governing bodies of the game know that and they are trying to rectify that in some small way. The 'first tee program' in this country [America] has been hugely successful.

Frank Phillips: You go out on the golf course; it is four, four and a half hours out on the course. People with young families, they don't want to spend that time away from their families so they go and take up something else. Then they don't come back to golf. When things get tough (financially) the first thing the wife says is, 'Well, you can't be a member of the golf club – we can't afford it.'

Gary Player: Golf takes so long. With the economy being bad, man and wife are spending more time at home and not spending money. When the husband goes to play golf it takes him 6 hours there and back, so the wife complains, so he is playing less. It may be more economically viable to make the game a bit shorter.

Ian Stanley: I have just done a concept plan of a golf course which is 3 lots of 6 holes, instead of two nines … a lot of the young guys with families don't really have time to play golf. They might play on Saturday, early in the morning, so they have the rest of the day with their families. We have to work out a way to quicken the game up and make it more affordable, particularly for younger people. Into the future, I think the cost of golf is going to be the big thing, and also the amount of time we are out there playing it.
Peter Toogood: They are just going to make the courses longer and that is going to affect the club members. Although, just recently I heard at Kingston Heath they are building tees in front of the ladies tees for the players who are 80 years and older. I think that is a good move. I'd like to see a sort of maximum length of golf course. I think they could tighten up courses a lot more without just adding length. This would help to retain 'club' membership.

Sir Bob Charles: Twelve holes – never! The eighteen holes need to be shorter with tees beside greens as was St Andrews when I first played there in 1958 at 6581 yards. As I said earlier, reduce the ball and shorten the courses.

'Walkin': watercolour art by Jamie Kasdaglis

Question: If when you reach the 'Pearly Gates' St Peter says that you can go back to Earth and play one more round of golf on your favourite course, which one would it be and who would you want to play with?

Bob Shearer: That is a hard question because there would be more than 3 people. First one would be my son, my older boy. I would have to bring **Jack (Nicklaus)** in. The other one ... I never met him but I wanted to meet him – Ben Hogan. I would like him to abuse me on the way around. I would have to have my younger son caddying for me and it would have to be at St Andrews.

Bill Dunk: Any one of the Melbourne sandbelt courses. I don't think they come any better than those.

Bruce Crampton: You got me between two minds there. Up until recently I would have always said Cypress Point up on the Monterey Peninsula because it is 4 or 5 different types of golf courses all in one. Starts out as a British Open type of course, goes into pine trees, comes out into the sand dunes and along the ocean. The 18th is different again amid all these eerie cypress trees with red moss on them. But ... the golf course I love the most is the NSW Golf Club layout at La Perouse in Sydney.

Jack Nicklaus: I would hope to do that before I get there. But if I had to pick, I would probably say Pebble Beach.

Jack Newton: Oh, God … I would say Carnoustie, but of the Melbourne sand belt courses I would say I am a very fond of Metropolitan. I guess Augusta, but if it has a fault ... the place is too perfect, the sand is so white you can't see the ball in the bunker if the sun is at the wrong angle; but I would have to say going down Magnolia Drive and the whole box and dice ... and the wine cellar they have got is pretty good. The people I would like to play with would be my father, and the others would be difficult to choose from ... probably **Jack [Nicklaus]** and **Trevino**, although that wouldn't be a good mix! Trevino threw that rubber snake down in the playoff for the US Open [1971] and no one had ever heard of Lee Trevino – what a character! [Trevino won the playoff.]

Graham Marsh: The course I would go back and play, not because it is the greatest course on the planet, would be St Andrews. I love the place. For me it is such a spiritual golfing experience playing at about 5 o'clock in the evening when the tide is down, the seagulls are flying and the light is soft. The trip out to the 9th, aptly named End, is then followed by one of the most remarkable walks in all of golf. As you head back to the town framed by steeples it is hard not to soak up the history – the whole ambience and magnificence embraces the true spirit of this great game. This is where it all started and this is where I would want to hang up my shoes.

Bruce Devlin: There is a golf course in South Carolina that I built – where my ashes will be spread off the 3rd tee – planning to swim with the dolphins – called 'Secession'. I would love to play with my Dad, **Norman Von Nida** and **Ben Hogan**. 'Secession' is certainly unlike any course I have designed. We have incorporated the traditional art of shot-making into every hole. You can run the ball onto virtually every green, and closely mowed chipping areas provide the chance to hit a variety of chip, bump and pitch shots around the green.

David Graham: It wouldn't even be on my wishlist. Nope. Where I play golf wouldn't be … I know what you are asking but if I get to the 'Pearly Gates' all I want to do is marry the same woman again. Beyond that, I can't answer your question because there are so many great experiences in golf. I wouldn't want to just play one round of golf – I would want to go and play Royal Melbourne, St Andrews, Preston Trail [Dallas], Augusta National, Cypress Point, Merion … I'd like to go play Riversdale. They would all be for completely different reasons. If I was to just pick one, I would most likely say that I would like to go fishing rather than play golf.

Frank Phillips: Either Kingston Heath, Royal Adelaide or Birkdale.

Gary Player: Probably Augusta because of the great beauty and it has been the best run tournament … or St Andrews because it is the home of golf and I admire what the R&A has done for golf. I played in 46 straight Opens, 52 Masters.

Ian Stanley: If I was hitting the ball well again, I would probably want to go and play St Andrews or Royal Melbourne.

Jan Stephenson: I would love to play with **Hogan** again, and talk to him about the new technology for teaching. I understand my swing so much better now, and I could talk to him more intelligently about my swing problems that he was always trying to fix. My father would be someone that I would love to play with again. He was the best father and supporter for me. He loved Pine Valley so that would be great to take him there.

Peter Toogood: Muirfield in Scotland. I thought that was a wonderful course. Has anybody else said that? No? Muirfield was such a well-designed course: no trees – just you, the ball, the hole, the greens, the fairways. The ideal four would be **Norman von Nida**, **Peter Thomson**, **Byron Nelson** and **Bobby Jones**.

Sir Bob Charles: St Andrews because it is unique and can be played clockwise or anti clockwise, all the tees are beside the greens, there are no trees, and with one water carry makes St Andrews the epitome of links golf. The ideal foursome would be **Ben Hogan**, **Bobby Jones** and **Old Tom Morris** playing St Andrews in reverse, which I have never had the privilege of playing.

If when you get to the pearly gates ...
Kel Nagle: Won't be long! *[Laughs.]*

If when you get to the pearly gates and you are told you can go back and play one course, which course would it be?
Kel Nagle: which golf course? Oh, St Andrews.

'Comrades': watercolour art by Jamie Kasdaglis

Art by Robert A. Wade

The Far East Circuit

The Australian Pros who played in the 1960 Far East Open in Manila, and then went to Hong Kong for the Hong Kong Open. Peter Thomson, Colin McGregor, Len Woodward, Darrel Welch (can only see his face), Bill See Hoe (front), Allan Murray (just see top of his head), Lenny Thomas (head tilted to the side), Frank Phillips (in rear, can only see half his face), Doug Canty, Bruce Crampton, Jim McInnes, Sid Cowling and Kel Nagle. Norman Von Nida and Eric Cremin also played. Frank Phillips was the winner in Manila. Peter Thomson won the Hong Kong Open. Photo from Bruce Crampton's archives.

THE FAR EAST CIRCUIT

The Asian Tour, as we know it today, was conceived and nurtured through its early teething problems by a small group of Australian professional golfers, who had a vision for the future. The vision would enable them to earn a living, while not having to travel so far and wide as America or Britain to apply their fledgling trade, in the late 1950s and early 1960s. Indeed, the 'Far East Circuit' cut its teeth on the back of prominent Australian golfers, most notably five times major champion Peter Thomson, who provided the Asian litmus test via his successful exhibition matches in Hong Kong, Singapore and Malaysia, with Norman Von Nida and, later, Kel Nagle. These exhibition matches provided a springboard to create national Opens for Hong Kong, Singapore, Malaysia, Taiwan and Thailand. The scent of the Asian currencies was wafting through the tropical air and into the Australians noses as far back as 1938, with Australian pioneer Norman Von Nida enticed to board a ship for his first International victory, at Wack Wack golf club in Manila, Philippines. He won.

'In 1938 I read that the Philippines Open was being played in Manila and that the first prize was roughly $5000; it was more money than I could play for in Australia, for the whole year. I was working for the sporting goods manufacturer, Slazenger, and they advanced me the money to go up there and play. It took about two and half weeks by boat from Sydney and fortunately for me I won, and I repeated the exercise again in 1939, and that was the beginning of my career, travelling around the world, playing golf for a living.'
Norman Von Nida (1914–2007)

The Philippines Open (formerly referred to as the 'Far East Open') is one of the world's longest-running men's golf tournaments. The tournament, which began in 1913, is also Asia's oldest golf tournament and national open. In its early years, the Philippines Open attracted some of the top players in the world, such as Norman Von Nida, Gary Player, Sam Snead, Doug Sanders, Lloyd Mangrum, Kel Nagle, Peter Thomson and Bruce Crampton. It was the pilgrimage to the Philippines that warranted further explorations into Asia, and naturally that led to Hong Kong and Singapore, countries that had healthy populations of British and Scottish expats, who loved their golf. Beyond the Philippines, the next country that attracted a professional tournament was Hong Kong.

'The first followers from Manila were the Hong Kongians. The Hong Kong golfers were expatriates and they were the ones who set the ball in motion, although the Royal Hong Kong Golf Club was an old, very old club that went back to the 1920s, that certainly started something in Hong Kong to popularise the game. Then, of course, the expatriates

in Bangkok and Hong Kong also wanted to have a golf course or two. There was also Indonesia and Singapore. Singapore golf went back to the 1930s. It was really the efforts of the British expatriates, mostly, that sparked the riot. Wherever the British went, they established golf.'

'I first went to Manila, to the Philippines Open, in 1950; that was my first introduction to golf in Asia, and that was with Norman Von Nida. I never played exhibition matches with Bobby Locke in Asia: it was mostly exhibitions matches with Von Nida and I think I played one with Kel Nagle in Kuala Lumpur (Malaysia). The first one with Norman Von Nida was in 1952, in Singapore.'
Peter Thomson

The exhibition matches of Norman Von Nida, Peter Thomson and Kel Nagle really provided the interest for the Asian population to get out and see world-class golfers in action. The public showed their interest by turning up in large numbers and appreciating the fine play. Hong Kong and Singapore had firm footings in golf, with the Hong Kong golf club having the 'Royal' prefix, dating back to 1889. After a sprinkling of exhibition matches providing the bait in the early to mid 1950s, the explosion of the late 50s was a victory away. Golf in Asia took a leap in the public eye of Asia when Japan had a historic victory in the 1957 Canada Cup (now known as the World Cup). The Japanese team putted their way to victory on the tricky Korai greens (in Japan) and won by 9 shots from the USA. Nakamura shot 68-68-67-71 to win the Individual honors by seven shots, from Sam Snead, Gary Player and a young David Thomas from Wales.

'In 1957 I was privileged to partner Peter Thomson in what was then called the 'Canada Cup' (now called the World Cup), where two players represent their country. Peter and I went to Japan to represent Australia, and the Japanese team won. It was Koichi Ono and Torakichi 'Pete' Nakamura, and their victory which really started the explosion, and the interest in golf in Japan. Torakichi Nakamura won the individual stroke play medal and beat players like myself, Peter Thomson and Sam Snead.'
Bruce Crampton

'1957 instigated the whole move in Japan; it really got it going. The Canada Cup was held in Tokyo and it was on television. The Japanese team won and Nakamura won the individual, beating guys like Jimmy Demaret, Sam Snead, Gary Player and Peter Thomson.'
Graham Marsh

'I feel enriched by it all. I have been charmed by the customs of Japan, intrigued by
the workings of the Chinese and stunned by the poverty in India.'

Peter Thomson

Crampton won the Far East Open in 1959.   Source: Bruce Crampton collection.

Professionals		1st 18	2nd 18	3rd 18	4th 18	Total 72 holes'	Prize
1st	Frank Phillips (Australia)	76	73	74	(68)	291	P6,000.00 & Trophy
2nd	Hsieh Yung-Yo (China)	75	(70)	73	74	292	4,000.00
3rd	Peter Thomson (Australia)	74	73	73	73	293	3,000.00
4th, 5th (tie)	Bruce Crampton (Australia)	78	72	74	(70)	294	2,250.00
	Norman Von Nida (Australia)	75	73	74	72	294	2,250.00
6th	Len Woodward (Australia)	79	(70)	76	72	297	1,750.00
7th, 8th	Ben Arda (Philippines)	75	(70)	76	77	298	1,375.00
	Larry Montes (Philippines)	79	74	73	74	298	1,375.00
9th, 10th	Pastor S. Domingo (Philippines)	75	72	77	76	300	875.00
	Yoshiro Hayashi (Japan)	75	73	75	77	300	875.00
11th, 12th	Sebastian Miguel (Spain)	81	72	76	72	301	675.00
	Chen Chien-Chung (China)	73	75	79	74	301	675.00
13th	Jim McInnes (Australia)	78	73	76	75	302	600.00
14th	Celestino Tugot (Philippines)	77	72	80	74	303	550.00
15th	Ken Nagle (Australia)	78	75	80	72	305	500.00
16th	Orville J. Moody (U.S.A.)	80	(71)	80	75	306	450.00
17th, 18th, 19th, 20th	Brian Huggett (Hong Kong)	78	77	77	75	307	325.00
	Justo de la Cruz (Philippines)	78	77	74	78	307	325.00
	Tomoo Ishii (Japan)	76	72	80	79	307	325.00
	Yusei Shimamura (Japan)	77	74	78	78	307	325.00
21st, 22nd	Angel Miguel (Spain)	80	76	77	75	308	200.00
	Euterio Nival (Philippines)	76	77	81	74	308	200.00
23rd	Uta Dabpavibul (Tailand)	78	74	79	78	309	200.00
24th, 25th, 26th	Eric Cremin (Australia)	77	76	79	78	310	166.67
	Diego Marmas, Jr. (Philippines)	76	76	76	82	310	166.67
	Vic Allin (Philippines)	80	(71)	84	75	310	166.66
27th, 28th	Pedro A. Garcia (Philippines)	73	78	80	81	311	100.00
	Dionisio Na... Jr. (Philippines)	80	72	77	82	311	100.00
9th	Emilio Biglel (Philippines)	77	75	78	82	312	100.00
th (tie)	Roberto S. Doi (Philippines)	78	77	77	82	314	50.00
	Carlos Martinez (Philippines)	79	78	75	82	314	50.00
Amateurs Low Amateur	M/Sgt. Lee Grimes (U.S.A.)	81	77	74	77	309	Trophy
2nd Low	M... (Philippines)	78	76	77	80	311	Trophy

JAPAN

Japan was officially dealt into the World golf picture in 1957, but they would never truly be part of the Far East Circuit and later the Asian tour, preferring to establish their own tour within the borders of Japan. Japan did host the Yomiuri Open for a short period of time, won in 1962 by Peter Thomson and in 1965 by Frank Phillips; the Yomiuri Open was the last leg of the Far East Circuit in the early days.

In 1958 Hong Kong golf club member Kim Hall, who many say was the entrepreneur behind establishing the Far East Circuit, wrote a letter to Australian professional Eric Cremin, asking if any of the Australian Pros who were headed for the 1959 Philippines Open would consider going to Hong Kong afterwards. The answer was 'yes', if there was a prize purse. Kim Hall approached the South China Morning Post newspaper and asked them to sponsor a professional event. 1000 pounds prize money was announced, and it was official: there would be a National Open in Hong Kong in 1959.

These early journeys to Asia would often involve staying at the homes of local golfers and officials, and being immersed in that country's way of life. An Australian wouldn't win the inaugural 1959 Hong Kong Open: that prestige would fall, fittingly, on the 'soon to be famous' Taiwanese player, 'Mister Lu' (Lu Liang Huan). The first Peter Thomson knew of Mister Lu's victory was reading a newspaper back home in Australia. Amazingly, the organisers of the inaugural Hong Kong Open had forgotten to invite him. Mister Lu would become an icon of the game, and global golf ambassador for Taiwan, after finishing second to Lee Trevino in the 1971 British Open and in 1972 winning the World Cup for Taiwan, with teammate Hsieh Min-Nan. This is the only time Taiwan has won the World Cup.

The Philippines pilgrimage had started with one lone Australian on a boat in 1938. Twenty years later, in 1958, there was 2 Australians arriving by airplane. In 1959 there were six Australians and by 1960 there were 13 Australians making the journey. During the Hong Kong Open of 1960, won by Peter Thomson, the first meeting of the Organising Committee commenced and Kim Hall, the top amateur in Hong Kong, was appointed the International Coordinator. Since the beginning, the Circuit has been managed by Alan Sutcliffe and Kim Hall as the Coordinating Committee based in Hong Kong. There was a representative from Singapore, and Leonardo 'Skip' Guinto represented the Philippines. The Committee had no powers to enforce rules or regulations, as each tournament was run by its respective country.

A year later, in 1961, more than twenty Australians boarded the plane bound for the Philippines Open – and onwards to the inaugural Singapore Open, won by Australian Frank Phillips. Again, an Australian, Kel Nagle, won the Hong Kong Open. These three events formed the backbone of what would become a genuine 'Far East Circuit.'

By 1961, the 'circuit' was in its third trimester of gestation. The midwives for the birth would be: golfing administrator Kim Hall in Hong Kong; Australian professional golfer Eric Cremin, then the President of the Australian PGA; five times British Open champion Peter Thomson; Japan's Atsushi Kida; and the President of the Philippines Golf Association Celso Tuason.

During the Far East Open in 1961 the meeting of these five gentlemen would have a ripple effect across the Asian golfing spectrum. Malaysia, Taiwan and Japan would be brought into the fray for the following year, 1962, and the Far East Circuit officially teed off on the 8th February 1962 with five tournaments. The 'circuit' began in the Philippines and went to Singapore, Malaysia, Hong Kong and Japan. In the first year of the Circuit, 1962, Peter Thomson won the Yomiuri Open in Japan, Len Woodward continued Australia's dominance of the Hong Kong Open and Frank Phillips won the inaugural Malayan Open … Peter Thomson was the official money leader at the end of the 1962 circuit.

Peter Thomson was pivotal to helping secure the sponsorship for the inaugural 1962 Malaysian Open.

'One of my Singapore and Malaysian friends, Loke Wan Tho, who chaired the Cathay Organisation, responded with a sponsorship, but he held out a warning. "I will sponsor, but not for the sole benefit of Australian and English golfers, but for our own young players. I want them to learn how to be champions." So it was. Dunlop became the most active sponsors and several others followed, as can be seen in the early files. It was not easy because there was no TV initially and sponsorship was not a big reward winner, but it grew.'
Peter Thomson

'Eric Cremin and myself were part of the birth of the Asian Tour. Celestino Tugot and Larry Montes (two outstanding Philippines golfers) had come to Australia to play in the McWilliams Wines tournament. Bill McWilliam was friendly with Larry Montes and Montes went on to win the Far East Open 12 times. So their trip to Australia highlighted the Far East Open for me, in Manila. I asked Slazenger to see if they could arrange a trip for me to play in the 1958 Far East Open.

I had played well in the tournaments in Australia in 1957 and thought playing in the Far East Open would provide further overseas experience, prior to getting ready to depart for the US. Eric Cremin came with me the first year I went, in 1958, so there were two of us from Australia. The next year we went over, there were six of us from Australia:

myself, Kel Nagle, Eric Cremin, Frank Phillips, Sid Cowling and Norman von Nida. I was fortunate enough to win the Far East Open in 1959, my first International victory. In 1959 we also played in some new territories in Hong Kong, which became the birth of the Hong Kong Open. I think the next year, 1960, there were thirteen Australians who went over, and Australia's Frank Phillips won. Then the Malaysian Open started and another one in India. That, to me, feels like the birth of the Asian tour, right there.'
Bruce Crampton

When talking to Peter Thomson about the birth of the Far East Circuit, it was suggested that he had single-handedly conceived and built up the circuit. In his usual graceful way, he said the following:

'It was not single handed at all. I reacted to their invitation. Of course, what they needed to promote their tournament was some sort of famed name, to come to play. I gave them the encouragement by saying "if you make the date and fix the prize money, then I will be there" So that is how we got started in Hong Kong. Although I didn't play in the first one (1959) they forgot to invite me to the first one and somebody else (Mr Lu from Taiwan) won. The second year I made it (and won). When we played the Hong Kong Open for the first time (1960) there was no golf at all in China because it was looked upon as a very elite activity and therefore not supportable. Particularly, as it swallowed up land to create the arena and that was against the ethics of the nation.'
Peter Thomson

THE P2,500 PUTT. Hsieh Yung-Yo, the steady Taipeh pro (on left edge of the green) studies his long putt for a par on the 18th hole. He missed the putt and lost the race for a P6,000 first prize in the Philippine Open yesterday afternoon on the Wack Wack course. Hsieh pocketed the P1,500 second prize. Standing at right is the big winner, Frank Phillips of Australia and the other golfer who is studying the Australian is Ben Arda.

Australia's Frank Phillips Wins Philippine Op[en]

Defeats Taipeh's Hsieh Yung-Yo In [St]irring Battle For Big Prize Money

(Continued from page 1)

[...]wrad. He hooked a long drive en route to No. 17 and his ball rolled out of the fairway and stopped on a bare lie near the tee of No. 18. He was behind a towering tamarind tree and it was impossible for him to pitch over. The trouble player elected to play-out and lose a stroke. He pitched on neatly and two-putted for a bogey but that left him the battle by the extra P3,000.

Sensing victory in the air and before a record gallery for a local golf show, the big Australian with a big golf [...]

But the big fight for top money in the rich Philippine Open was now really on with [...]

Thomson never got hot throughout the four-day meet. He got into trouble every once in a while and his putting was not up to par on the difficult Wack Wack greens.

After Thomson came veteran Norman Von Nida and Bruce Crampton, who tied for the fourth and fifth prizes, each carding a 294. Crampton also threatened to break the course record of 68 as he went four-under, but he was troubled on the closing holes and came home with a two-under 70.

Another Australian, Len Woodward, whose entry was sponsored by Al Sol Alcantara, finished in sixth place.

Then came the two leading Philippine pros, Larry Montes and Ben Arda, who tied for [...]

point, but Hsieh over-pitched and was left with a long 12-footer for a par.

Then the calm Australian blasted out of the sandtrap like a master and had only a four-foot putt for his par. Hsieh stroked his long putt straight but it didn't have the right allowance. The ball rolled to the left and stopped about three inches from the cup.

Pastor Domingo, another local pro and Yuchiro Hayashi of Japan tied for the ninth and tenth places, each shooting a 300 total.

Lee Grimes, U.S. Army player who was the best shooter in the recent PI American meet in Baguio also won the low amateurs in the Open. He posted a 308 total to beat the best local amateur, Mel Gana, by two strokes.

Frank Phillips was very happy and looked like a young Manila businessman as he put on a "barong" for the awarding ceremonies. He was very nice to the autograph seekers and answered questions to newsmen very frankly.

He said, "You have a very difficult course here. Over in [...]

route to No. 17. On the first hole, he sank a long one from almost the front edge of the green for his first bird. He hit a tremendous drive on No. 2 and had a short and easy pitch to bag another bird.

On the long No. 5, he missed an eagle which would have given him an additional P500. It was a long putt and the ball missed the cup by inches. He took his third birdie on this hole and bagged another neat bird on the sixth hole. He pitched a beauty which left him only a club-length putt. He sank the putt and was four-under, and from here he sailed right on until the 17th.

But Hsieh was very much in the show with Phillips. The 26-year old Taipeh hotshot came from a near stymie on [...]

stroke as they [...] 12.

But the [Si...] bogey on No. [...] out poorly tr[...] They were ti[...] the 15th Phi[...] birdie to be fi[...]

Ben Arda, w[...] man in the [...] was also in [...] one of the t[...] the 13th ho[...] cracked wide [...] to get out of [...] His third shot [...] and the hap[...] 6th on the [...]

It was the [...] in the lively [...] from here P[...] put on a...[...]

A crowd a[...] followed the [...]

CHAMPAGNE GOLF BY PHILLIPS

Birdie barrage climax of remarkable round

BY WILLIAM STONE AND ROBIN PARKE

GO . . . GO! THIS IS FRANK PHILLIPS WINNING YESTERDAY'S HONGKONG OPEN AT FANLING WITH A TREMENDOUS BIRDIE THREE ON THE LAST HOLE. THE PUTT WAS A DIFFICULT LEAP TO RIGHT TO FOOT[...]

$20,200 rekindles Phillips interest

Shrine title

TAIWAN AMATEUR'S FI[...] ROUND IN P.I. OPEN

Phillips Sinks 15-foot Putt To Share Lead

Manila, Feb. 24.

Frank Phillips of Australia sank a 15-foot putt on the 18th hole today for a three-under-par 69 to finish level with an unheralded amateur from Taiwan for the first round lead in the U.S.$35,000 Philippine Open Golf Championship.

[...]Phillips' putt gave him $8,000 in prize money [...] ($3,500) goes to the lowest scorer [...] carrying Chinese [...]here was Hsu Sheng-san [...]played a four-under round on [...] the 6,100-yard Wack [...]

Golf and Country Club, picking up four birdies, one bogey and 13 pars en route to his 69.

Eight players shot 5th and tied for third place. Among them were defending champion Lu Liang-huan of Taiwan, Ken Brown of the United States, Barry Coxon of Australia, Celestino Tugot and Ernesto Pizat of the Philippines, and Michio Ishii, Kenji Hosoishi and Marius Yamata, all of Japan.

The prominent favorite, Bruce Crampton, Billy Casper, faltered badly on the second nine to finish three successive bogeys and finished with a 38-36—73, four strokes [...]

H.K. OPEN FOR PHILLIPS — AT LAS[T]
Staves Off Late Challenge By Sugimoto

PHILLIPS BEATS RECORD WITH 64

THE STAGE IS SET FOR TREMENDOUS FINAL ROUND THIS MORNING

FRANK PHILLIPS, 28-year-old Australian professional golfer—the man who has gone on record as saying that the secret of the game is not to hit the ball too far—shattered the Selangor Golf Club old course record by three strokes with a third round of 64 in the Malayan Open yesterday morning.

It was a fantastic, brilliant round and the huge crowd that cheered him round got a sample of world class golf as he birdied hole after hole with some classic shots.

A remarkable point is that Phillips might well have had a round of 60. He missed several easy putts. His record-breaking round earned him a bonus of $1,000

this I did not have to fight for them and I had no worries."

His figures for the round:

MALAYSIA

The intricate, fiscal polarity between China and Hong Kong was quite evident in 1960, as the Hong Kong Open was the first professional sports event for the country. The notion of offering financial incentives to play a sport was a groundbreaking event for the Chinese settlement of Hong Kong and one that was encouraged by the political leaders of the era. For professional golf to succeed beyond Hong Kong and into countries like Singapore, Malaysia, Taiwan and India, it required the support of the political leaders.

'General Ne Win in Burma was a very keen golfer and he wanted to have plenty of golf in Burma. He had the military playing golf. They had nothing else to do. Also Lee Kuan Yew in Singapore: it was a habit of his to play nine holes in the morning when it was cool, before he went to his Prime Minister's office. The expatriates didn't need any encouraging to play golf, as they would in Britain or Australia. Malaysia too was in that category. In Kuala Lumpur there was Tunku Abdul Rahman (Prime Minister of Malaysia – the father of Independence 1957–1970); he was sympathetic to the golf, but he didn't play much – although Malaysia wasn't a free country until 1963. His successor, Abdul Razack Hussein, was a regular golfer and I think his son won the election this past weekend.'
Peter Thomson

'Ferdinand Marcos was President of the Philippines but he was also very high up in the golf club – Wack Wack golf club. He used to hand out the trophies. I never forget going to the cocktail party and Imelda Marcos is there and she wanted to dance with a few of us. So I danced with her, but I couldn't dance, I was bloody hopeless. Imelda used to think she had a magnificent singing voice. She used to get up and sing, and she wasn't … she wasn't that good.'
Lee Kuan Yew (Prime Minister of Singapore for three

decades) was a very interesting man to talk to, very brainy … a brilliant man. Without the support of the political leaders, the Far East circuit wouldn't have happened.

'Kim Hall used Peter Thomson as a big drawcard. Kim Hall was stationed in Hong Kong and he took over the running of the Far East circuit. Kim was a businessman in Hong Kong, who loved golf himself; he was a good golfer, who decided to take over the runnings and build up the Far East circuit. Eric Cremin was very important. He was good friends with Kim Hall and they helped kick-start it. It turned into a very good circuit.'

'My first trip to Asia, to play golf, was 1959 and we only played one tournament, the Philippines Open. That was the one that Bruce Crampton won. Then the Australian boys got together, with talk of trying to make the circuit larger. We all ganged up and there was the Von, Peter Thomson, Kel Nagle, myself, Sid Cowling and Bruce Crampton. Then there were the Japanese players and the other Asian players, who thought, 'what a good idea' – and they tried to get more tournaments. That's how it started.'

'The Singapore Open started in 1961 and I won that, and the year after we got the Malaysian Open that I also won, the first year it was played, in 1962. Then we went to Taiwan and then Japan. The tournament in Japan was the Yomiuri tournament. They were the five tournaments (Philippines, Hong Kong, Singapore, Malaysia, Taiwan, Japan) we started with, then later on India and Thailand came into it. I had a good run up there.'

'I played the East tournaments more than in America. I went to America and played twice but I didn't like the way it was run over there, so I stuck to the Far East. I could get home to my family pretty easily from up there too.

If you are over in Europe or America it would take a fair while to get back to Australia, but from Singapore and such place you were home in a few hours. I think that is one of the hard things to take when you are a professional golfer: being away from your family. I took the wife with me a couple of times, but when the kids came she didn't want to go anymore.'

'When I went to America in the late 50s and again in the early 60s it didn't take me long to realise that the American courses were watered, whereas the British courses were not. That is why Peter Thomson considers American golf to be target golf. In America you hit the ball on the green and it will stop, whereas in England you had to finesse the ball on the green.'
Frank Phillips

1963 was a another big year for the Australian golfers on the fledgling Far East Circuit, Bill Dunk won the Malayan Open in 1963, Peter Thomson won his first Indian Open and Kel Nagle finished the circuit as the official money leader. The Taiwanese golf force arrived in 1964 and it was not until 1972 that an Australian would again dominate the Far East Circuit, when Graham Marsh arrived.

Bill Dunk winning the Malaysian Open, 1963. Source: Bill Dunk's photo archives.

GRAHAM MARSH - THE 1970's

'There was a collaborative move by Peter Thomson, Kim Hall and Eric Cremin in the late 60s to create an Asian Tour. That was the generation that was really pushing to have a golf tour in Asia, probably because Asia was much closer to home than either Europe or America. When I first went to Asia in the 70s the tour was based on limited prize money. The total purses each week were around $15,000 with first prize between $1500 and $1800; it was lean pickings. The context of what that tour was all about – making it easier for Australians to play tournaments closer to home and developing the game in Asia – was particularly useful for me, because at the time there seemed to be a huge gap between the Australian golfers and the golfers in America. Around that time it was always thought that the Americans had a huge advantage because of the teachers, better equipment and superior conditioned golf courses.'

'Remember, also, that was in the days of persimmon heads and they were playing with a different sized golf ball (1.68 [inches], while we were playing with the 1.62). It was always perceived that they (the Americans) had an advantage over us. I think in the back of our minds we needed to prove we could win Internationally before we could actually challenge them over there on their home territory. In effect the Asian tour became more like a stepping-stone to go to the next level. If you couldn't win in Asia against the Asian players then you were probably not going to continue on with a successful career as a professional golfer. You can't learn the difficult maths, unless you learn the basic maths. As you go through in sport you don't want to be fighting Muhammad Ali if you are just a rookie boxer coming out of the gym. You have to earn your way towards a peak of excellence. This is what the Far East circuit gave us: the opportunity to compete against another level and then move from there to a higher level.'

'You have to remember that the professional tournament players in Australia at that time, whilst there were some world-class players, there wasn't the depth. So there really needed to be a progression from playing in Australia – in only a handful of tournaments – to go to playing 30 or 40 tournaments a year in the USA. This was a huge leap for most Australian golfers to deal with mentally and practically. Even going to Britain was a big change for Australian golfers as that tour was a rather spasmodic because they didn't have consecutive weeks of golf tournaments.'

'There would be a couple in Britain and then you would have a month off before playing a couple in Europe. It was very expensive for a young up-and-coming Australian golfer to go to that part of the world and then be taking weeks off. The consecutive weeks of playing in Asia was a huge plus for the development of many Australian players. It gave us a hint of what life on tour as a professional golfer was going to be all about.'

'When I first went to Japan in 1970 and played the Yomiuri Open, which was the last leg of the Far East tour, there were probably only five 4-round events in Japan: The Yomiuri Open, the Chunichi Crowns which was strictly invitational, The Japan Open, The Japan PGA and maybe one or two others events of 72 holes. It was very limited and pretty much a closed shop. In fact from 1970–1974 there were no Japan PGA tour records kept; they didn't start keeping their records until around 1974. It wasn't the Japanese PGA that initiated the record-keeping, it was done by a company called Dunlop Sports Enterprise and it was they primarily who grew the circuit, not the Japan Golf Association or the Japan PGA. It was Dunlop Sports Enterprise who gradually bumped the tour from four tournaments to ten, to fifteen and then finally about 38 tournaments over a 15-year period.'

'They were the company instrumental in bringing sponsors to the table and managing their events. Of course, during that time other promoters came in and did things as well. The big tournament to come along in Japan, after the Yomiuri and the Chunichi Crowns, was the Dunlop International.

Dunlop grew this event with the goal of making it the model golf tournament in Japan. They as visionaries wanted to continue to grow golf, to grow their own market for the golf ball along with their equipment and clothing lines.'

Do the Japanese hold Graham Marsh in that kind of god-like status with your success in Japan?

'In my era there was no doubt that was the case. They used to joke about the fact – that I had my own TV shows on Saturdays and Sundays! I was regularly in the final groups and the television coverage was a big deal. It had a big audience. There were only a few foreign players there competing regularly and finishing in the top handful; I think I won 25 times and I probably finished 2nd and 3rd forty or fifty times. When they saw there was a foreign player there to be beaten they would watch because they wanted to see their own win. If I won I was not all that popular, but if I lost it was always good for them. The name Marsh for better or worse was known.'

'One of Thomson's visions, to his credit, was that he felt there should be a Pacific tour that would stand beside the European and American Tours. He envisioned us in Australia combining resources in the region and hip-hopping between countries in relatively the same time zones. The future would then dictate that the stronger tournaments in America, Asia and Europe would then join forces to create a super F1 golf tour. Truthfully, that is where it is kind of headed now if you start looking at all the World Championship Events that US PGA Tour Commissioner Tim Finchem has set up and is starting to take to other countries in the World. In 1977 we tried to set up the Pacific Tour, but by then the Japanese tour had so far outpaced The Far East Tour and the Australian Tour they were not interested in joining because they felt that they could do things on their own. Japan suffered a downturn in its economy but before that happened they did end up bringing a number of tournaments to Australia – like the Daikyo, The Vines, Coca Cola at Royal Melbourne and an event at Sanctuary Cove.'

'There has been a lot of talk over the years about developing this relationship between Australia, South East Asia and Japan. Probably, by now the opportunity has been lost in terms of the big picture; however in time we may end up with a secondary tour. I think that it was a great shame and an opportunity lost for the region and World golf. In South-East Asia now there are all kinds of One Asia's 'this' tour and 'that' tour – America putting its nose in and Europe putting its nose in; not only with men's golf but also women's through the LPGA. It is fair to say it is really a fragmented mess throughout South-East Asia in terms of professional golf. Nobody knows who runs what and when it's going to happen. Had Japan co-operated at that time in the late 70s I think there would have been a much more positive and structured way forward for professional golf within the Pacific Basin.'
Graham Marsh

Australian dynamic duo Peter Thomson and Kel Nagle at Kai Tak airport, 1971. Source: South China Morning Post

AUSTRALIA & NEW ZEALAND VICTORIES IN THE FAR EAST

Philippines Open (established 1913)

Norman Von Nida 1938, 1939

Bruce Crampton 1959

Frank Phillips 1960

Peter Thomson 1964

Robert Whitlock 1996

Adam Le Vesconte 2005

Scott Strange 2006

Hong Kong Open (established 1959)

Peter Thomson 1960, 1965, 1967

Kel Nagle 1961

Frank Phillips 1966, 1973

Walter Godfrey 1972

Greg Norman 1979, 1983

Kurt Cox 1982

Frank Nobilo 1997

Singapore Open (established 1961)

Frank Phillips 1961, 1965

Ted Ball 1964

Ross Newdick 1966

Terry Gale 1978

Greg Turner 1986

Peter Fowler 1987

Paul Moloney 1993

Steven Conran 1995

Kenny Druce 1999

Adam Scott 2005, 2006, 2010

Malaysian Open (established 1962)

Frank Phillips 1962

Bill Dunk 1963

Graham Marsh 1974, 1975

Stewart Ginn 1977, 1986

Brian Jones 1978

Terry Gale 1983, 1985, 1987

Indian Open (established 1964)

Peter Thomson 1964, 1966, 1976

Graham Marsh 1971, 1973

Brian Jones 1972, 1977

Ted Ball 1975

Tony Grimes 1985

Stewart Ginn 1992

David Gleeson 2011

Yomiuri Open (Japan)

Peter Thomson 1962

Frank Phillips 1965

David Graham 1970

Thailand Open (established 1965)

Randall Vines 1968

David Graham 1970

Graham Marsh 1973

Jeff Senior 1988

Richard Lee 2005

Andre Stolz 2011

In 2012 the Singapore Open was a $6 million tournament, Asia's premier golf event, sponsored by a major bank, Barclays. The Hong Kong Open is a multimillion dollar event sponsored by a global financial services firm, UBS. The Malaysian Open is a multimillion dollar event sponsored by Maybank. The Thailand Open was a $1 million tournament in 2012. The Indian Open was a $1.25 million tournament in 2012. The Philippines Open has not yet reached the elusive million dollar prizemoney status, but did see an increase from $300,000 to $700,000 in 2013.

This chapter is dedicated to the late Eric Cremin, a former Australian professional golfer. Eric won the Australian Open (1949) and Australian PGA titles (1937 & 1938). He was runner up in the Australian PGA title seven times and won 25 times as a professional. Eric Cremin spent a large part of his life as a teaching pro in Singapore, aiding the development of professional golf in Asia. He died of a heart attack in Singapore and Australia's Alan Murray continues his work as the teaching professional.
Eric James Cremin 1914-1973

The Far East Circuit

'The first time I won the Singapore Open [1961] I think I got $2000 and the second time I got $5000. Adam Scott won it last year and he got a million.'
Frank Phillips

How do you feel looking at the Asian tour today? Some would say it is more successful than the Australian tour; you must be quite proud to have been part of it all in the beginning?

Peter Thomson: 'I was part of it and I still am. Last December (2011) I was non-playing Captain of the Asia-Pacific team that played in a kind of President's Cup tournament against China. We played at a course called the Tycoon Country Club in Shenzhen. There I am, at advanced age, still involved in the leadership of golf. We won, incidentally.'

Would you say that China needs a star golfer, like Japan had in 1957 in Nakamura?

Peter Thomson: 'They will certainly get one in due course. That is without a doubt. When we played the Hong Kong Open for the first time (1960) there was no golf at all in China because it was looked upon as a very elite activity and therefore not supportable. Particularly as it swallowed up land to create the arena and that was against the ethics of the nation. Golf in the next decade will probably see double the number of players, now that China is starting to show an interest.'

Photos World Sport Group: Robert Morrice, Chairman and Chief Executive of Barclays Asia with Australian Adam Scott.

ROBERT A. WADE OAM

AWI (LM), FVAS, FRSA (LON), PWS (LON), AWS (USA), KA (USA), ISMP (USA), MHSMA (MEXICO)

Robert A. Wade is one of the finest living watercolour artists in the world. He has won just about every major award an artist could hope to win and has travelled the world extensively following his passion. Three best-selling art books, most notably *Robert Wade's Watercolour Workshop Handbook*, leave a permanent bound record of the fine man's career in art and pass on his knowledge to the next generation of watercolour artists. His works adorn the walls of many of the premier art spaces and museums the world over and in the United States he has been dubbed the 'World Ambassador of Watercolour'. Music icon Tony Bennett is perhaps Robert A. Wade's biggest fan … their shared love of watercolour art has afforded them a wonderful friendship.

Beyond watercolour art, Robert A. Wade's other major passion is golf. A single figure golfer for 42 years and a member of the illustrious Metropolitan Club in Melbourne, Australian golf is lucky to have such a prolific watercolour talent. His golf art is visible on such esteemed walls as The R & A St Andrews Scotland, The Ryder Cup Room, World Golf Hall Of Fame USA, Royal Melbourne, Royal Sydney, Royal Adelaide, The National, Metropolitan, Huntingdale, Kingston Heath, Yarra Yarra, Commonwealth, Victoria and The Australian Golf Club.

Personally, as a gentleman you will not encounter a finer fellow. With his success he gives back, regularly donating his art and time to charity, hospitals and with a keen interest in helping disadvantaged children. What struck me about Robert A. Wade is that he is one of the happiest men I have ever met. Often with artists you find a tortured soul who feels under-appreciated and mis-understood. Mr Wade is the opposite of that: he is appreciated, he is understood and he is a testament to following your true inner passions leading to a healthy fruitful life. Indeed he is much like some of his cherished friends: Peter Thomson travelled the world with a golf club in his hands; Tony Bennett with a microphone and a silky voice that has swooned generations; Robert A. Wade has followed a very similar path, with a paintbrush in his hands visiting the far flung corners of the world.

'In art we have rare times when our vision extends beyond the normal and everyday. We seem to be on another plane, in another world of creativity and sensitivity that leads us on to seek understanding of the purpose for being what we are.'

Question: When did you start painting?

Aged 6. My father was an artist. When people used to say to me 'What are you going to be when you grow up, Bobby?' invariably my answer would be 'an artist like my dad'. That never ever changed.

I won a scholarship to Scotch College in Melbourne and I remember the Headmaster of Scotch looking at my report card and saying, 'This is a fine report, Wade. What professional course do you propose to follow after school?' When I replied 'An artist, sir', he sort of gave me a look that suggested 'A what?' then continued with a chuckle and 'We'll see about that!' I did French, Latin, Greek, English Expression, English Literature and at the start of my final year, the Headmaster said 'Now another good report, Wade. Have you ultimately decided what you are going to do with your career?' When I replied 'I am still going to be an artist, sir', he shook his head in dismay and said 'We didn't get that bee out of your bonnet after all'.

Ten years ago I was invited back to Scotch College to open their art show and as I stood up in the pulpit of the assembly hall where my old Headmaster used to stand every morning, I wondered that if he had still been with us maybe he would have acknowledged that I had made the right decision.

You left school early to run your family printing business because your father died of a brain haemorrhage when he was only 39. Was he a successful artist?
Yes. He was a commercial artist, now called a graphic artist. We used to do all the theatre advertising around Melbourne. Maybe if 'Beau Geste' was showing we would transform the foyer into a fort in the desert with the Arabs and the French Foreign Legion people and all that sort of stuff. This was really exciting for a little boy, as I was always allowed to have a bucket of paint and a big brush and maybe I could paint the yellow desert sand or the green fronds on a couple of the palm trees.

So how old were you when you had your first exhibition or sold your first piece of art?
I was never all that interested in selling paintings and I am still not. It is not the mark of how good you are. You could be the best artist of all time and people may not want to buy your paintings, but other artists and your peers perhaps would admire it and that would be to one's great satisfaction. The first exhibition I had would have been in 1958 and I was 28 years old. I always believed I never wanted to hold an exhibition until I was really right up there. So many people start painting, sell a picture to Aunt Mary or their grandmother and then they think they are professional artists, 'We'll have a show', and they are not ready for it and do their reputation irreparable harm. I waited until I was 52 years of age before I presented my first solo show: all the pieces were sold with rave reviews and I achieved what I had wanted to do.

Is it my understanding that you focused on golf art quite a while later in your career?
Quite a long while later. I had established an international career in watercolours based on landscapes, seascapes, genre paintings, people at work, people in native markets and things like that. However I had done a painting of Metropolitan and had it on the wall of my own office. It was the early 1980s when the late Tony Charlton (former ace television sports commentator) had come by, he saw it and said 'Oh, is that one of yours?' I said yes; he was rather surprised and said 'I didn't know you painted golf courses'. I told him that I usually didn't paint golf images – I just painted this one for myself. He said 'Good. Paint three of Metro for me: I want to put them in the brochure for the Victorian Open'. So I did, then Kingston Heath saw them; they contacted me and said 'We want three paintings for our Clubhouse'. Commonwealth Golf Club saw the paintings at Kingston Heath and from there it went on and on and on. That is how it happened. I never sought it; I never advertised.

Now your paintings are in most of the great golf clubhouses in Melbourne and you have travelled the world painting golf courses all over Britain and America. What are the highlights of the international courses for you, the artist?
To find out that my painting of St Andrews was used by the United States Golf Association for their Christmas card and then that same painting was acquired by St Andrews and hangs in their clubhouse in Scotland. There is also one of my paintings hanging in the Ryder Cup Room at Wentworth Golf Club.

Did you get more satisfaction out of being in Britain than being in America with your golf art?
Well, again, being a traditionalist, the UK took golf back to its very beginnings for me. [Laughs] The first time I played St Andrews I finished 4, 4, 4, 4 to break 80 at the Old Course and that was one of my big thrills. To go to all of those places where golf began is very special. America is very 'golfy' of course, but it is not as traditional as the courses in Britain. Just to go into those old British clubhouses (if you are allowed, that is) and sniff around, smell the old books, feel the tradition: everything is old. You could imagine the members coming into the same buildings years ago with their crooked sticks, taking off their periwigs and all that sort of stuff – it really gave me a big buzz.

Watercolour has opened up all those wonderful doors for me that my golf never would have done. I have paintings hung in many of these Clubhouses around the world ... but I always wanted to be remembered in those places for my golf, not for my painting. [Laughs]

'It is the requirement of mental discipline to hit the shots away from the flags that makes the old course unique, so special and so searchingly fascinating.'
Peter Thomson

St Andrews

"Morning on the Charles Bridge, Prague"

An incredible city with the most amazing examples of every sort of architectural style imaginable. I put it right alongside Venice as my two most mind boggling painting places.

"Girls' Talk, Fez Morocco"

One of my favourite watercolours, it hangs in my own home and is not for sale! I love the textures and the soft light in the alley way. I painted it in 1994, before the advent of mobile phones, but today I would have to wonder if the ladies were using an iPhone!

"Souk Sales, Marrakech" Morocco

Morocco was a real bonanza for me and exciting subjects like this just kept on popping up wherever I looked.

"The Hunt" Connecticut USA.

Great fun for me, trying to portray the swirling movement of the hound pack. The red jackets of the riders made attractive colour spots in the composition.

"Delivery in the Souk" Fez, Morocco

"Macau, an Old Resident"

"Venetian Reflections" Italy

Hardly a ripple on the canal's surface, so mirror-like reflections were created and became the focal point of the painting.

"The Atrium, Isabella Stewart Gardner Museum, Boston USA"

What a superb pattern those shadows made, and the Italianate architectural style gave it such a feeling of character. To me it was an irresistible invitation to paint it.

"The Sweeper, Singapore"

Ahmet, my brother-in-law's house man, seemed to sweep every minute of the day, except when a car entered the driveway and then he'd shoulder arms with his broom and salute the arrival. His shadow made a most interesting shape and an unusual composition.

"Chicken Vendors" Marrakech

Looks like a very quiet sales day for the poultry salesmen today! They were all pretty relaxed and co-operated with me to get themselves arranged to meet my requests!

Robert

A.

Wade

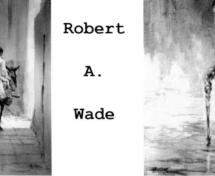

'The press has said, in the past, that my opinion of St Andrews is that it is unfair and that I couldn't play it. I played five tournaments there and I think I won twice at St Andrews and I was never out of the top ten in the others. It wasn't that I couldn't play the course; it was just that to me it could be unfair. In 1947 I won the Spalding tournament there. Dai Rees [Wales] and I, were friendly with a chap there called Jack Busson. Jack was a very good player, a Ryder Cup player before the War and he was leading this Spalding tournament by five shots going into the 14th at St Andrews; all he had to do was shoot par figures and he would beat me by five shots. His drive trickled down into the middle of the 'beardies' (bunker). He had about 15 swipes and never got out. He levered himself out of the 'beardies' several minutes later, tears rolling down his face and he never finished the tournament.'

Norman Von Nida

St Andrews, Fife, Scotland

Mansfield G.C.

WINNING
CLUB   Cancer Council Award

Sketch

Finished Painting

The National Golf Club old course 2nd

Kingston Heath 10th

The National Golf Club Ocean Course 6th hole

Moonah Links 8th

Opposite: National Golf Club old course 18th

Royal Sydney Golf Club 18th

Yarra Yarra Golf Club 12th

Royal Melbourne Golf Club 6th

Metropolitan Golf Club 'showers' 18th

Commonwealth Golf Club 16th

With your art career would you say you are better known internationally than you are in Australia?

I would think so, yes. My granddaughter set up a Facebook account for me and she is very proud to tell her friends that her grandfather has 3700 Facebook friends. She thinks that's COOL. I get emails from all over the world, from countries that I didn't even know painted in watercolour. They tell me how much they like my art and it is all very humbling. I am one of the luckiest blokes that you will ever get to talk to. To have spent my life doing what I love doing, it almost feels like cheating! I wouldn't do anything differently if I had my time all over again. The people, the terrific people that I have met, not just in art but in golf. It has been a wonderful life. Here, do you want a brush too? Should we get started? You will do the same with your writing and books, doing what you love.

If you wind the clock back to where you first started with golf, you are 21 years of age and a member at Metropolitan in Melbourne. Which golfers are in your consciousness as being great players?

Bobby Locke. He came out here at that time (1951); I went and watched him at Kingston Heath playing an exhibition match with Doug Bachli, Bill Edgar and Mick Ryan. [Bill Edgar beat Bobby Locke in a 1938 exhibition match at Commonwealth Golf Club.] I will always remember Bobby Locke, immaculate in his plus fours, his collar and tie and a white golf cap. A big man. He was hitting 2-irons from one end of the practice fairway to the other and his caddie is down the other end of the fairway with a towel catching the balls as they bounded up towards him. Bobby Locke was just knocking them dead and this was with the old clubs, not hickories, but old balls and things and Bobby Locke just had total control over what he was doing. So, Bobby Locke was the big name in those days and Norman Von Nida. Eric Cremin and Ossie Pickworth were also big names here in Australia. Peter Thomson was the big break through in Australian golf, and with the guidance of 'The Von', he went over and won some big tournaments in the UK . Peter brought a new respectability to the golf profession in this country and raised the bar forever.

Peter Thomson is a very different personality to Greg Norman, of course. Greg Norman's personality and his persona did more to promote the game of golf in this country than anyone, ever. You could feel it oozing from him, whereas Peter was a gentleman and a traditionalist, quite happy to sit in the background.

Is it true that you got offered a chance to paint Augusta National and you politely declined?

Absolutely. My London agent arranged the invitation which I knocked back ... and I still haven't changed my mind on that either.

And the reason for that?

The reason for that is that with the golf courses that I play, and the golf courses that I paint, I like to feel as if the course has just grown up out of the surrounding country, similar to the old courses in Scotland where they just mowed a bit of grass, put out some teemarkers, mowed some more grass, put a pin in a hole and that was it. It is totally natural stuff. In Scotland and Ireland, thinking about all of the rounds that have been played there just makes my spine tingle. To me Augusta is very artificial and I have no desire to play it or paint it.

Someone gave me some old hickory shafted clubs that were dated back to around the turn of the century. I used to hold them in my hands, and I know this will sound silly, but I would think 'Why can't you talk? Why can't you tell me how you got out here from Scotland? What events have you played in and what games have you been instrumental in winning or losing? Wouldn't that be interesting? Well, like those clubs, if only the courses could tell you their stories.

And you like trying to capture that in your art?

If I possibly can, yes. I hope that my works will always leave something for the viewer to imagine or remember. Don't forget, we are only the temporary custodians of the traditions of GOLF, the grandest game of all!"

I do not report the fact. The camera can do that! I have an intense dislike of any so-called painting rules that preclude my desire to rearrange my subject. My painting will not be an accurate facsimile of what appears before me, it will be a sincere representation of how I feel about what I see. I want complete freedom to dramatise, romanticise or fanaticise, or to do whatever allows me to make my personal statement.

Southern Golf Club, Victoria

GOLF COURSE DESIGN

For an artist, golf course design offers one of the largest 'canvases' to work with. As with any finished art piece it will draw acclaim from some and criticism from others in what is entirely a subjective opinion from golfers, judges and/or 'experts'. Many golf courses are built on wasteland, that is, land that is almost unusable for any other purposes. Conversely, some golf courses are built on quality land and generally speaking this is where the truly magnificent golf courses are located, having been built on a premium site and often with a large budget. Naturally there are exceptions to this rule, with the archetype, The Old Course in St Andrews, Scotland, being the obvious example. St Andrews still offers a template of timeless charm, simplicity personified by the ageing of time. Modernity and technological advancements in equipment and the way we view golf courses has changed the modern design brief to the extreme end where some courses are designed with television in mind. There are golf course projects with colossal budgets, supernova golf complexes that house several signature courses by the world's most famous players and or architects. Many famous and traditional courses are forced into being 'remodelled' – or, more accurately, lengthened – to keep up with the modern golf ball which now flies over 300 yards. Golf course design continues to be big business, particularly in the blossoming golf community of China. Big business and the monetary rewards that are afforded the leading horses in this golf course design race naturally lead to fierce competition within the industry.

Within the spectrum of personalities found amid golf course designers, some of them are like artists who create gargantuan art pieces for our perusal. Not only are they seeing natural lines and textures and working with them to enhance our visual delights as we wander over their creations, they are also immersing themselves with the local soils, plant life and more broadly the ancient culture of the land they are appointed to massage. Nature is at the core of their existence. They understand the symbiotic relationships around them with light and shade, drainage, seasonal airflows and animal migrations. The artist sees the big picture and wants to fit in with it. They finish their opus design and then put it on show in a sort of exhibition of their work. The public come and hack pieces of turf from its pristine presentation, washing the colours around and altering the brushstrokes of the finished piece before retreating to the abundantly stocked clubhouse to cast opinions on the new course. The artist behind the creation may well be hiding behind a tree peeking out to see if people are enjoying his work and, unlike Picasso, if the work is not appreciated the option to destroy the artpiece is not available. He must live with the retorts of disgruntled golfers and 'industry experts'.

On the other end of the spectrum from the artist, the entrepreneur golf course designer sees the whole process as a business. Art and Nature often play second fiddle to the prime motive, expansion and profit. Most golf course designers fit between these two polarities.

Australia has a firm heritage with golf course design dating back to the mid 1800s in Tasmania with Scottish immigrant Alexander Reid laying out a crude nine hole course. 'Ratho' (near Bothwell, Tasmania) is one of the oldest courses in the southern hemisphere and these days has a homely museum and attracts historians from all over the world to view its ancestry. Dr Alister Mackenzie (Britain) is the most glorified golf course architect to have weaved his magic on Australian golf courses in the early days. His work at Royal Melbourne is well known. He was paid handsomely. Mackenzie also affected the later design work of Royal Melbourne Club Captain, Alex Russell (1924 Australian Open Champion). Mackenzie also advised on the designs and remodels of several other prominent Australian courses in Melbourne and Sydney, providing a bona fide link back to the roots of design in Britain. Beyond Mackenzie we have a long line of successful Australian architects including five times British Open Champion Peter Thomson, Michael Wolveridge, Bruce Devlin, Graham Marsh and more recently names like Ross Perrett, Tony Cashmore and Bob Harrison. These architects have turned their hand to golf course design and designed top-class golf courses all over the world.

14th Hole, The Legends Course, Moonah Links. Designed by Ross Perrett. Photo by Kim Baker.

Photo: Tim Lobb, Peter Thomson and Ross Perrett

Ross Perrett is a nature warrior and an artist. He chose to study plants and architecture straight out of school and, luckily for him, one of Australia's most experienced golf course architects, Peter Thomson, welcomed him into his golf course architecture firm. Ross is an outgoing personality described by Peter Thomson as 'like a bee in a bottle', with energy to burn. Perrett is known and loved around the world, particularly in Asia where he has worked on nearly 100 projects. Perrett understands nature, plants and the sensitivities around him. He can paint, with watercolour and oils. He is an artist working in the big business of golf course design. For the last fifteen years he has spent considerable time in China.

'I well remember my first trip to China back in '96 to attend the first China Golf Show, held in Shanghai. My minder, Joseph Shi, who was the head barman at Metropolitan GC at the time, arranged for his taxi driver mate Mr Chen to collect us from the airport and take us out to dinner at a downtown Shanghai Bar. Two stunning Chinese models dressed in Fosters Brewing Formula 1 satin racing gear (promoting Australia's most famous beverage) greeted us at the entrance. They were university students and were happily recruited to help us at our humble booth the next day - dressed in their stunning satin attire. All the big name golf architects were there -Nicklaus, Palmer, RT Jones II - in big fancy booths but without interpreters. Despite our modest booth, with the help of the Chinese speaking Fosters girls, a stuffed kangaroo and Joseph's enthusiasm we managed to win the only job on offer - Yin Tao Golf Course, in Qingpu, near Shanghai. This was the first of over 130 trips to China and the start of a love/hate relationship that still has a long way to play out.'

There is talk of golf driving ranges in China, in the future, meshing their love of gambling with golf. Have you any desire to build a golf casino?

'Frankly I would much prefer to design a desert golf experience overlooking Uluru in outback Australia - one that makes a lasting contribution to the wellbeing of our indigenous people and excites all who play the course. It would be totally integrated with nature and not look like a golf course from the air and be full of wildlife, laughter and goodwill.'

'It would also be fun to 'mow in' a course on stunning natural 'links-like' land formed by glacial deposits in the mountains of Italy, India or Mongolia ... It might only be playable 4 months a year but would cost very little to build ... as it would simply be undressed from nature.'

'Developing ideas for golf courses that respect nature and culture interest me far more than building a Golf Casino. However, I can imagine a high-tech driving range where players are rewarded for skill and can potentially make millions - hitting at targets in a 3-dimensional giant 'dart board' - a fully integrated hedonistic experience with pretty women, music of all sorts (strictly headphones so as not to spoil anyone else's experience). It may help 'grow golf' as every greedy person on the planet may take up golf so they can have a crack at the jackpot.'

How many times have you been to China in the last ten years and can you describe how much it has changed (in relation to golf) in that time?

'China at the time was changing rapidly under the leadership of Deng Xiaoping (now regarded as the founder of Modern China). Shanghai was going nuts with a third of the world's cranes working 24/7. Our project was on low-lying land and was being filled at night with mud dug from the basements of the emerging skyline - the 'New York' of the East. Bicycles were the most common form of transport and the first freeways were under construction. It was an exciting place to be - a city that never slept and loads of fun to be had at venues like the famous 1930s art nouveau-style Peace Hotel. One fond memory is playing the saxophone with the Peace Hotel Band, with all players over 80 years old. Some 17 years later the place is nearly unrecognisable.'

Of all the modern golf course designers are there any that are inspiring your designs, or are you drawing your inspiration from other places ... if so, where?

'It my responsibility to be aware what is happening in golf course design around the world, such is the competitive nature of the business. Also magazines and the Internet are used to peddle the "latest and greatest" in the marketing of new projects. Where possible, I try to ignore fashion and "listen the land" which is fine for natural sites but the majority of our projects are on featureless marginal land. This is where our creative skills are truly tested. Upgrading an established course or building on a natural site are relatively easy projects compared to those reclaimed from the sea or built over a tip site.'

photo: Mt Merapi Golf Course Indonesia

China

Do you think Asia has its own 'style' of golf course design? Are they using Asian golf course designers or are they importing foreign designers to complete the projects?

'It probably did back in the 90s when the golf boom travelled quickly through South East Asia – Malaysia, Thailand, Philippines, Indonesia and Singapore. The climate and standard of player resulted in a playable resort-style of course. Since then, information explosion and the effects of globalisation have caused a homogenisation of tastes where the world now sings from the same hymn book. The increased mobility of Asian golfers to the mature golf markets of the USA, Australia and Europe has been a great education. The Asian developer is now very familiar with links golf and iconic courses like St Andrews Old Course, Augusta National and everything in between and therefore demands something that can truly compete on the international stage.'

'Golf was played in Shanghai in the very early 20th Century on a site near the Hongqiao Airport, now used as a zoo. I have also seen some fine golf clubs made in China at the time, which must have been in response to some level of demand. The post–Second World War Cultural Revolution regarded golf as a bourgeois pastime with no place in China. The first modern course was built in 1981 to a design by Arnold Palmer. Others followed slowly and by 1996 there may have been 30 or more. Today there are probably over 600. This pales in comparison to the USA who averaged 400 new courses a year between 1990 and 2005 (6000 in total). Currently golf development has almost stopped as the Chinese Government grapples with trying to develop new policies to regulate and balance the insatiable demand for golf with the perception of golf being an elitist sport for the rich. The emergence of home-grown young golfing stars like Shang Shang Feng and the even younger Guan Tianlang (played in The US Masters at 14 years old) and the decision to play golf in the Olympics should see common sense prevail. Hopefully in the future golf will be more accessible to the masses and China will be at the forefront of golf development globally.'

Where is the future with golf course architecture? Where do you see it going and are there any changes on the horizon for the time-starved modern golfer?

'The future is uncertain. The only certainty is change. In mature markets golf participation has been on the decline in recent years but this may be due to the Global Financial Crisis that has affected most industries.'

'In traditional golf clubs, the average age of members has been increasing in part due to the mobility of younger golfers who have embraced the flexibility of the multitude of daily fee courses on offer. Club life has little appeal to a hedonistic generation connected to each other and events by the Internet and social media.'
'Golf is a time-consuming pastime but I am not convinced we will see the proliferation of shorter courses with fewer holes that offer a more time-efficient golf experience. To date there has been a lot of talk but very few facilities built.'

Do you think in the future we will see golf courses rated by the public and the public only, or will there always be these 'lists' that pop up in the media created by a panel of opinionated experts?

'Course ratings are a joke and I believe that in most cases they are assembled by panels of so called "experts" who have a commercial conflict of interest in the result or at the very least friends or fans of the people assembling the panels.'

Design

'I think there will be a variety of golf courses in China, and there already is a great deal of variety within the golf that currently exists, certainly among the 20 or more courses we have designed. China is a large and diverse land, with the ability to dictate a variety of personalities within the golf. In China, you have mountains; you have high altitudes and you have low-altitude hills; you have seaside. And then you have places like Hainan Island – where we have several projects – that has a variety of different sands. So, to characterise China as having one particular type of golf course would be like saying Baskin-Robbins has only one flavour of ice cream. That would be like saying all the golf courses in Britain are seaside golf courses. Yes, there are seaside golf courses. Yes, there are some inland golf course. Yes, there are some open-field golf courses. It's the same as with the United States.'

Jack Nicklaus

photo: Spring City Golf resort, China. Designed by Jack Nicklaus.

You have designed dozens of golf courses in America. Would you say there is an 'American style' golf course? If so, what are the key differences between an American style course compared to say an old Scottish seaside layout?

Bruce Devlin: 'Not sure that there is such a thing as an American style golf course, but generally speaking I believe that most American architects have trended towards carrying the ball into most of the greens.'

photo: 14th hole at Secession Golf Club, USA. Designed by Bruce Devlin.

Hamilton Island designed by Thomson & Perrett photo by Gary Lisbon.

GOLF COURSE DESIGN WITH GRAHAM MARSH

Course design – when you started designing courses, what was the landing area with driver and how is technology influencing your designs?

'When I started in golf course design (1985) we were looking at a landing area around 220 metres and now we are out to 260 metres. In the next few years we will probably have to take that out to 270 or 280 metres to have any chance of producing a golf course that from the back tee is challenging for the tour players. To put it in context, back in the 1970s there was a handful of players who were hitting the ball over 300 yards, but a 300-yard drive was considered quite a feat. If you had a dry links course in the British Open the ball might bound on to 340 yards. Today the long hitters are averaging over 300 yards and the ball is just going ridiculous lengths. They are already playing tournaments on golf courses that are specially designed and prepared for championships and I find that somewhat of a shame because it is getting away from the grass roots and the historical value of the game. Most of the amateurs don't want to go and play those courses because they are simply too hard to play, but they have to make them that way to challenge the professionals. Not only is the ball travelling prodigious distances they have incredible accuracy, given the fact that the ball is so stable and the clubs are so forgiving. My question is this: "Is this where we want to continue to go?" In the last thirty years, the distance off the tee has gone up tremendously. If you want to project that out for the next thirty years ...where are we going to go with this?'

'We know beyond doubt the athletes will improve; look at what the athletes were doing thirty years ago and look at what they are doing today – there is a massive improvement. The shame in golf is that the improvements in technology have outperformed the athletic performance of the golfer. I am much more interested in seeing athletes improve without all the help from technology. Let technology run rampant, as it has done in the past, and couple this with athletic performance and we will be looking at courses the likes of what we have never seen before. Without a shadow of a doubt, most of the great championship golf courses of yesteryear have run out of land to accommodate the kind of length I am talking about. These courses are land locked and simply cannot be lengthened.'

'When are the governing bodies going to step up, recognise the problem and start to offer serious solutions? The intestinal fortitude they have shown in the past dealing with the technology issue tends to indicate it will be much later rather than sooner. A hole that was 340 yards back in the 70s was a driver and a 70-yard pitch for most of the field. Today there are some that would hit it on the green with a 3-metal from the same distance.'

Have you ever been asked to design a golf course with television in mind?

'No. We have never done that – never been asked. I am sure some clients have asked it of other designers but we have not had that request. Where this style of design becomes blatantly obvious is on the many TPC courses in the United States. It is mandatory that the finishing holes have water for the pretty television pictures on the weekends. Whilst I am not in principle against water on a golf course it has certainly been overused in some instances and a source of considerable frustration for many daily golfers.'

What are your thoughts and feeling towards the opinion polls on golf course design?

'I question their knowledge and only see it as an opinion poll. Most are simply not qualified to pass comment, but it is a business that they run – a self-fulfilling business. It is fulfilling for them to think they are re-inventing the wheel and that they are the self-endorsed experts. If you look at most of them, they have never designed a golf course – wouldn't know where to start if they were asked – yet they are leading the discussion and argument on ranking courses in the country. I find that rather interesting. In fact it is not very difficult for them to say whatever they want to say about anything because there are no checks and balances on them. They can run and they can hide because the average golfer doesn't question their authority. Statistical data is important if you are really trying to rate something. Any scientist that looks at something in a rational way would have to have considerable statistical data to back up his theory. Playing a course once and filling in a form hardly qualifies as statistical data. I have watched raters fly into town, jump on a golf buggy, charge around the course in under 4 hours then start to make profound statements about the design. On many occasions I have had to play a course multiple times under various conditions to truly appreciate the nuances and the subtleties of the design.'

'Any of the leading architects in the world who are serious about the business would tell you the more courses they design the more they realise how little they know. I find it laughable watching some golf writers setting themselves up as golf consultants offering their advice to clients and then rating that same course. It is obvious that we need dedicated journalists to write about golf and help promote the game honestly and fairly. When they cross the line and start to become self-professed golf-course design experts through the power of the pen then it is time for the industry to expose them for who they really are and what they represent.'

'It has been said of golf raters that most are more interested in being involved in the politics of golf rather than in the substance of golf course architecture. I can only concur.'

'Sadly we have had reporters in Australia who have taken handouts on the basis that they will promote certain golf developments and rate them highly in publications they write for on a weekly or annual basis. I guess you can categorise this as free enterprise — however, when your judgement is influenced by money it is difficult to gain credibility. Unfortunately the golfing public is the loser as they are the ones spending their hard-earned money based on guidance that is shady at best.'

'In Germany the courses are rated by the public. You can go and play any course in Germany and afterwards go onto a website and rate the golf course. We have a course in Germany that doesn't get great ratings by the "experts" but it comes in at number three in Germany on the public website. The clubhouse doesn't get very highly rated, but they love the golf course and it comes in the top three every year. This is how to rate golf courses — votes from people that play, not some self-proclaimed golf rater that has his own vision of what golf design is all about.'

'I cannot wait for the day when such a web site is implemented in Australia. Let golfers of all ability decide which courses are the best in the country. Golf course ratings will then at least become credible.'

In Japan ... course architecture ... you have plenty of experience. Do they have a style of golf course in Japan?

'By default many are penal, the reason being that most of the golf courses in Japan were built on the tops of mountains. Out of bounds on both sides of the fairway, carries across gorges, water hazards in front of greens and steep slopes up against edges of green complexes. All of these unplayable hazards fall into the penal category of design. The early courses that were built on the better parcels of land were much more orientated towards the strategic school of design. The huge boom that took place from the 1970s to the '90s forced golf into the mountains — there was no place else to build courses. Thus the penal school of design prospered.'

photo: Graham Marsh courtesy Australian Golf Digest Archives

photo: Sutton Bay Golf Course South Dakota USA by Graham Marsh designs courtesy of Gary W. Kellner at Dimpled Rock photography

BRUCE CRAMPTON

In 1956 Crampton held off Kel Nagle to win the Australian Open at Royal Sydney Golf Club and four weeks later he defeated the reigning British Open Champion Peter Thomson around his home course, Victoria Golf Club (Melbourne) to win the Speedo tournament. An invitation to the 1957 US Masters Tournament in Augusta, Georgia, soon arrived and the 21-year-old prodigy, Bruce Crampton, was bound for the United States.

During his time in America Crampton attained four second place finishes in the American majors, all to the great Jack Nicklaus; two Vardon Trophies, 14 PGA Tour wins, 20 Senior PGA Tour wins, 5 World Cup appearances and he was the first Australian (and first foreign) golfer to win more than a million dollars in prize money on the PGA Tour. When Bruce Crampton retired from the PGA Tour as a 41-year-old he was 5th on the US all time career prize money list behind four giants of the game — Jack Nicklaus, Arnold Palmer, Lee Trevino and Billy Casper.

*All photos from Bruce Cramptons private collection

'I had won 250 pounds for winning the Australian Open in 1956 and at that time it was the equivalent to about $500. In Houston, Texas, my first tournament over here, I shot even par and I tied for 13th. It was a $30,000 tournament and Arnold Palmer won it. My prize for tying for 13th place was more money than I won for winning the Australian Open. The decision was made there and then … I wanted to play my golf in America.'

Above (left to right) - Bruce with a set of miniature golf clubs. Holding and admiring the first wood he ever owned, a 4 wood bought with his own money from Slazengers. The presentation ceremony 1951 NSW Schoolboy Championship.

Below - Gary Player, Bruce and Frank Phillips. Signing scorecard 1951. 1956 at Sunningdale England. The follow-through. Final round winning card from the 1961 Milwaukee Open, his first Official Tournament victory in the U.S.

How important was your victory in the 1956 Australian Open at Royal Sydney where you finished strongly to beat the legend, that is, Kel Nagle?

Ever since I came to the United States whenever someone asks, 'What is the most important victory you have ever had', I always say, 'With all due respect to the 34 official victories I've had in the United States, it's the Australian Open.'

When I won the Australian Open in 1956, Peter Thomson wasn't in the field, so the press/ media started asking the question 'Would Crampton have won the Open if Thomson had played?' The next big tournament, after the Australian Open that year, was the Speedo tournament, which happened to be played at Peter Thomson's home course, Victoria Golf Club in Melbourne. As fate had it, I won the Speedo tournament. I don't know if it was just the Australian Open victory, the combination of both victories, or Norman Von Nida getting in touch with Clifford Roberts in Augusta, but I was invited to play in the 1957 Masters Tournament. That is what motivated me to come to the United States. So, all the good things which have followed in Bruce Crampton's career are a direct result of that Australian Open victory. Thus, I will always consider it my most important triumph.

You decided to head to the United States six weeks prior to the 1957 US Masters. What was it like arriving in America by yourself as a 21-year-old?

Australia didn't have television in 1957, nor were there jet aircraft. I had decided I would play six or seven tournaments leading up to Augusta to get acclimatised. The first one was in February in Houston, Texas. I didn't know anyone in the United States and was quite naïve. I carried a package of 15 dozen American size golf balls Slazengers made for me because I didn't know if I could get golf balls in America.

The only things I knew about Texas at the time were what I had seen at the 'pictures' (movie theatre); wild-west shoot-'em-up stories. In those movies, when a stranger arrived in town, nine times out of ten he was a trouble-maker and ended up getting shot or lynched.

I had been in the air some 40 hours by the time my plane landed at Houston's Hobby Airport. 32 hours flying time to San Francisco, with stops in Nandi, Fiji, and Honolulu, Hawaii, then another 8 hours non-stop to Houston. Driving from the airport to the Rice Hotel in downtown Houston, everybody I saw was dressed in Western gear. I saw a couple of covered wagons and people on horseback and just thought 'Hell, this really is Texas, and the way I imagined it would be'.

The next morning I went to the restaurant in the hotel to get breakfast. Every time I asked for something the waitress (dressed in Western gear) replied with 'well, I guess we don't have any of that', but as I looked around I could see people eating what I wanted! Now the wheels started to spin and I realised how far away from home I was. I started to think 'Bruce, if they find out you're a foreigner from Australia you're a gonner for sure.' Everyone in the restaurant was dressed in Western gear; it was like a scene from one of the movies I had seen. I tried to keep my mouth shut as much as possible and for three days I even leaned a chair up against the knob of my Hotel room door to stop people getting in; also just like it was done in those Wild West movies.

Eventually I met a very nice man named Spinney Gould in the lobby of the Hotel. Spinney was from St Louis. He was very good friends with several of the Northern golf pros and also Jack Fleck who won the 1955 US Open at The Olympic Club in San Francisco when he beat the great Ben Hogan. Spinney explained to me that it was 'fat stock show week' which meant all the 'western people' were in town. Boy, was I relieved. He introduced me to several of the pros he was friendly with after they arrived in town from the previous tournament in San Antonio (Texas Open). Later in the week I accompanied several of the pros to the Houston Colosseum where I saw Roy Rogers riding Trigger, in addition to outstanding rodeo performances.

That was my introduction to playing tournament golf in the United States.

photos: 1956 Australian Open Champion   source: Bruce Crampton's private collection

BRUCE CRAMPTON CONTINUED

You planned six months away from home. That must have been quite daunting for a 21-year-old.
Apprehensive, maybe, but I don't recall being frightened as far as travelling alone or my golf was concerned. Having observed quite a few visiting professional golfers from America while they were playing in Ampol Tournaments in Sydney, I was all pumped up about testing my skills against those I considered to be the best in the World at the time. You see, in my mind I had proved I could compete favourably with Australian players, so I wanted to find out if I could compete favourably against the best US Professionals on their home turf. There is no doubt that the experience I gained during my 1956 overseas trip with Norman Von Nida and Frank Phillips provided a certain sense of basic security. Besides, I had flown home to Australia by myself from Great Britain and Europe via the US because I wanted to complete that 1956 trip as a 'round the World' venture. On the way I spent a couple of days in New York as well as a couple of days in San Francisco. Norman and Frank flew home via the Middle East.

If anything was daunting it was the relatively small amount of US dollars I left Australia with. Back in those days Australian Exchange Control Regulations were very stringent. US dollars were very hard to come by. They were considered prized commodities. Under normal circumstances, an Australian going on a trip overseas could not take more than $US400 out of Australia. David Blacklock, Managing Director of Slazengers at the time, pulled some strings and managed to gain approval for me to get $US2500 for my contemplated six months stay in the United States. This equated to spending no more that thirty dollars per day. For the next several years, upon my return to Australia following each tour, I was required to provide the Australian Exchange Authorities with a detailed earning/expenses report, and guarantee to sell any surplus funds to the Australian Banking System. Prior to leaving the US for Great Britain following the

1957 Masters Tournament I opened a bank account in New York, and then kept asking the Australian Authorities for permission to leave my surplus US Dollars in that banking account for use the following year. For those interested, I about broke even that first year I competed in the United States.

You won the Vardon Trophy twice (1973 & 1975). How significant was having the lowest scoring average to you?
I thought each one of them was a very important accomplishment. To have the lowest scoring average on the Tour over eighty rounds had to be very special. At least it was in my mind anyway. The Vardon Trophy was more or less in name only when I won. There was no trophy or award. Later on I talked to the officials at the PGA of America and I said 'winning the Vardon Trophy is an important accomplishment; I think the winner should receive some sort of an award'. A decision was subsequently made by the PGA of America to start awarding a winning medal each year, and to make it retroactive so that all previous winners would receive a medal for each of their Vardon Trophy victories. The medals have the PGA of America logo on the front side and a pair of hands gripping a golf club illustrating the famous 'Vardon Grip' on the back side. It's my understanding the medal has now been replaced with an attractive bronze sculpture of what has become the most widely used method of gripping a golf club throughout the World.

While it has changed in recent years, back in those days (the early 1970s) without any question the best players in the World were in the United States. They were dominating the Ryder Cup Matches. There were very few tournaments in Europe.

Several European countries did hold open golf championships but because the sport was primarily an aristocratic game

on the Continent, such events did not have a very large following. On the occasions I played the French Open, the Belgian Open and German Open there was next to no gallery, and very few spectators on any of the courses. It's a different story today. The European Tour is huge. It has produced any number of world class players, which has resulted in recent Ryder Cup victories for the European Team.

Talking quality of opposition, Jack Nicklaus was at the top of his game when you were at the top of yours. I imagine 40 years on from that it must be quite a sobering or even a warm feeling to know you came second to perhaps the greatest ever golfer the world has seen.
Yes, a total of five times just in the 'Majors'. One US Open, one Masters Tournament, two PGA Championships on the Regular Tour and one Senior PGA Championship on the Senior Tour. I consoled myself on each of those occasions by telling myself, 'well, I'll be defending runner-up next year'.

I can tell you that whenever I see a replay of that 1-iron shot Jack Nicklaus hit on the 71st hole at Pebble Beach during the 1972 US Open Championship, I keep hoping his golf ball will go in the ocean. Of course it never does; instead it finishes really close to the cup. I was playing the 18th hole at the time. It was easy to tell from the huge roar that something dramatic had happened in the group behind me.

On the other end of the spectrum, Jack was often a tremendous help to me while we were both playing the Tour. Going into the 1965 Bing Crosby National Pro-Am Tournament I was playing very poorly. So much so, that I didn't want to go to the golf course on the Tuesday before the tournament. My wife talked me into going to hit some balls; she said 'maybe you will figure something

out'. In 1965 the pros used to practise to the right of
the 2nd fairway at Pebble Beach, and hit shots across the
fairway up into the pine trees. Not long after I started
hitting balls Jack Nicklaus came and started hitting balls
right behind me. We started talking. He offered some
suggestions, and ended up telling me I should try to 'cut'
(fade) every shot that week, in other words, try to move
my golf ball from left to right through the air. The more
I tried to hit 'cut' shots the straighter my golf ball
flew. Can you believe I ended up winning the tournament?

On another occasion Jack and I were paired together in
the Canadian Open. At one point during the round Jack
said to me, 'If you take the club any more to the inside
on your back swing, you are going to hit your right ankle
with it'.

*'Bruce Crampton was a very talented player who might have
been misunderstood by some, including the press, because
of his passion. Bruce was a very focused competitor, who
was very intense and intent on playing well. He was a
wonderful player. Bruce might not have won a Major but
the record books will show how well he played in a number
of Majors and how close he came to winning them. But
I imagine Bruce's competitiveness, the seriousness with
which he approached his game and his unwavering desire to
play well perhaps was mistaken for something else.'*
Jack Nicklaus

Jack Nicklaus congratulation after the 1969 Hawaiian Open
victory. Bruce shot closing rounds of 65-67 to beat Jack
Nicklaus by 4 strokes.

There have been some quite derogatory things written about you over the years. From what I can tell you were a fierce competitor who had a determined look on your face when you were focused, you were professional and treated golf like your job – the course was, as you say, 'your office'. In some ways I think you were ahead of your time with your professional nature.

I cannot argue with that point of view, but let me tell you what I think may well have been the 'birth' of all those negative articles.

As the Australian Open champion I signed a contract to write stories for Sydney's Daily Telegraph newspaper. My assignment was to prepare a preview for each tournament in which I played, and also a story following each tournament round giving my impression of that day's play. I didn't write the stories. They were ghost written. I would call Fleet Street in London when I was in Great Britain, or when I was in the United States I would call New York. In 1957 I had played in the US Masters. It is widely known how outstanding Augusta National Golf Club hospitality is, and how well the members take care of all the contestants in their world renowned tournament.

The next tournament I hoped to play in was one in Lancashire, England. By the time I got there the entry deadline had passed. Gary Player asked me if I would be willing to drive a little black Morris Minor car belonging to an amateur friend of his up to Glasgow (Scotland), where the next event was going to be played (The Swallow-Penfold Tournament). I said, 'yes, I would be glad to.' So, I drove up to Glasgow on the Saturday and I went to Glasgow Golf Club, or what the locals call 'Killermont' or just plain 'Killi'. After passing though large iron gates built into a tall stone fence which surrounded the club property, and negotiating the somewhat lengthy drive up to the clubhouse, I was met by the club porter,

who immediately informed me that 'professionals are not allowed on the premises at the weekend'. I said, 'Sir, I don't think you understand. I have travelled 13,000 miles to play in next week's golf tournament. May I leave my clubs?' He replied, 'No, you are not allowed on the premises.'

No 'welcome to Scotland, young man'? What did you do, where did you go?

Seeing I had met Eric Brown (Scottish Professional who topped the European Order of Merit in 1957) I telephoned him to see if it was all right for me to come out and practise at Buchanan Castle Golf Club where Eric was the Club Professional. It was, so that's where I went.

Then back to Royal Glasgow for the Swallow-Penfold Tournament?

In those days a tournament golf course was, more often than not, closed to play the day before the event. It was also customary for sponsors of golf tournaments in Great Britain to provide contestants playing in their respective tournaments with a lunch drink ticket, a lunch ticket and a tea ticket for afternoon tea. When tournament week arrived for the Swallow-Penfold, much to my dismay I found that Professionals were not being allowed to eat in the Clubhouse. A tent had been pitched outside in close proximity to the Clubhouse, in which food was being served to the Pros. Brian Wilkes, from South Africa, and I played our final morning practice round together, after which we headed to the tent to get something to eat. As I recall that day in Glasgow was a misty one with light rain falling. The entrance to the tent was pretty churned up and mushy because of all the foot traffic. Food was being served 'army style'. The Scottish women volunteers were spooning a helping of the food being offered onto one's paper plate as one passed by. When I got to the

last food station I noticed a rather hefty Scottish woman pouring cans of fruit salad into a metal bowl and mixing it up with her hands.

Now remember, I had just come from competing in the United States, where I played in the Masters at Augusta National, and this was what I encountered in Scotland, which I had been led to believe was the home of golf.

On Tuesday night, I called the Sydney Daily Telegraph correspondent in London to brief him about what type of preview I would like to have cabled to Sydney. As the current Australian Open champion I felt it was my duty to tell the Australian golfing community what my experiences had been like in the United States and what I had run into at Glasgow Golf Club in Scotland. The story was written, and published.

Brian Wilkes and I went to the pictures (movies) the next day. When we entered the lobby area of the hotel where we were staying flashbulbs on cameras started popping and members of the press who had assembled started calling out, 'there he is, there he is'. My immediate thought was 'my God, I've won the lottery.' What had actually happened was British correspondents in Australia had picked up my Sydney Daily Telegraph article and sent it back to Great Britain. The next day Bruce Crampton was front page news in every newspaper I saw. The rest of the week wherever I went at Glasgow Golf Club there were cameras pointed at me; from behind trees, around a corner of the Clubhouse; you name it. Commander Rowe, who was running the British PGA in those days, wrote a letter to the PGA of Australia. He wanted me expelled. Can you imagine that? All I did was request that the truth be told.

From that point on in my golfing career it seemed to me I was a marked man.

That is quite a story. Would you say this is at the roots of later problems you had with the media?

Experience has taught me that once an individual becomes involved in some sort of an incident and it's reported in the press, the story immediately becomes part of the individual's media record. Downstream the incident is quite often referred to, thus refocusing attention upon it.

Dave Hill is a good example. I happened to be in the locker room at Hazeltine National Golf Club during the 1970 US Open. Dave was sitting at a table visiting with several members of the press joking around with them. At some point, Dave, in jest, referred to Hazeltine being a 'cow pasture'. Some young upstart put it on the wire services. From that day forward when a reporter wanted a quote about the condition of a particular golf course the first person approached was Dave Hill.

Tommy Bolt is another good example. People will hear the name and instantly think 'the guy who threw his clubs'. But not so fast; Tommy Bolt (1958 US Open Champion) was a very likeable guy away from public scrutiny. He had a great sense of humour. Yes, he threw temper tantrums and broke clubs, but one could argue it was all for showmanship and publicity.

You only played the British Open half a dozen times. Was this due to that experience back in 1957?

The way the Pros were treated certainly left a bad taste in my mouth. I didn't appreciate the class distinction that was prevalent back in those days in Great Britain. In a lot of people's minds, being a Professional Golfer put me in a lower class. Also, because I was Australian I was a Colonial Outcast on top of that. Being so lucrative to play in America and being well established there it wasn't attractive to go over to Britain to play in bad weather. Besides, I really didn't enjoy playing over there. I am of the school that believes golf should be played through the air. I don't feel like I have any control over my golf ball once it hits the ground. I associate with hitting the ball through the air, landing it on the green and stopping it. I don't associate with hitting a wedge shot and seeing my golf ball run and bounce for forty yards before it stops.

While playing in America and being very successful, you repeatedly had problems with the media and you tried to change your image. Can you tell me the extent you went to change your image?

At one point in my career I talked to Jack Tuthill, who was in charge of the PGA Tour Rules Officials at the time, about my image and concerns. He suggested I start wearing a cap. I also paid a PR person for a while on the advice of my manager at the time, but concluded it was a waste of hard earned money. I never had any training as far as acting was concerned or public relations either. If my talents were in acting then I should gone to Hollywood, not play tournament golf. While I was living in Dallas, Texas, my dentist worked on my over-bite in an attempt to make my facial expression, when I was concentrating, look less severe.

To the best of my memory, I was only fined once, and certainly never suspended while playing either the regular PGA Tour or the Senior PGA Tour for anything I was accused of by members of the press, marshals, scorekeepers and volunteers. Apart from one particular incident, it turned out the accusations were either inaccurate, twisted because of a preconceived idea the accuser had about me or grossly misinterpreted in the first place.

Do you think the incident in Britain in 1957 changed the way you behaved on the golf course and around the media?
No, I don't believe so, because I didn't believe I had done anything wrong. All I did was tell the truth. It did, however, make me more fully aware of how vindictive members of the press can be, what a large role sensationalism plays in media stories and, depending what headline a story is given, the degree to which it has a major bearing on how the story itself is interpreted. Take what happened in 1957 at Glasgow Golf Club as an example. The professionals were not 'BANNED' from the clubhouse, we were just not allowed to eat in there, yet the headline on the story under my name in the Sydney Daily Telegraph contained this word.

Later on I became aware that reporters are basically required by their editors to write stories about what the readers want to read about, regardless of whether the details in a particular story are right, wrong or indifferent, as well as how certain facts are twisted to achieve that objective. Pieces written for magazines and periodicals tend to be more accurate than newspaper pieces simply because of less urgent filing and timeline constraints. To this day I only believe a fairly small percentage of what I read in print. First of all it's only one person's interpretation of what took place. Secondly, one only has to pay attention to a given story that reaches the courts to find out what the true facts are once they come out 'under oath', and how much those facts can differ from what one was originally led to believe.

REMOVALS, STORAGE by DAWSONS LTD.
3 DOUGLAS ST. GLASGOW Phone CEN 0995

Evening Citizen
No. 29,007 WEDNESDAY MAY 15 1957 PRICE 3d

LATE CITY

MODERN LIGHTING
PETER FISHER

'Insulted golfers

→ FROM PAGE ONE

Professionals must walk or take 6d bus from gate to the clubhouse

GOLF ROW FLARES AGAIN

Officials angry as two competitors arrive in a car

THE row over facilities for professionals at the Glasgow Golf Club, Killermont, flared up again today at the start of the Swallow Professional £4,000 Tournament.

Only the cars of officials were allowed past the gates of the course, half-a-mile from the clubhouse. Professionals had either to walk there or pay 6d for a special bus which is running from the gates to the clubhouse.

And at the clubhouse they were being allowed only the use of locker rooms.

Alex. Fox, the young professional at the Dalmahoy Club, near Edinburgh, was stopped at the gates in his taxi.

After arguing with officials, Fox's taxi was allowed to go through. But when he reached the clubhouse angry officials waved the taxi back.

Fox jumped from the car and waved it away.

HIS CAR
Sent back

Angelo Angelini, the Italian, also got past the gates in a car driven by brother professional Antonio Silva.

At the clubhouse Angelini jumped from the car but officials refused to permit Silva to park the car.

Silva had to turn the car around, drive back to the gates, park the car there and get on the bus for the clubhouse.

Meanwhile, the man who sparked off the row—Australian Bruce Crampton—practised on ground adjoining the first fairway. He, too, had to travel by bus to the clubhouse.

Crampton has a contract with the Melbourne Sun to report his overseas golfing tour for them.

When he arrived in Glasgow on Saturday he found that on Sunday the course was restricted to members only.

GUSTY WINDS

Star golfers storm at 'insults'

Express Staff Reporter

GLASGOW GOLF CLUB at Killermont—venue of today's Swallow-Penfold international tournament—was denounced as "insulting" by British and overseas professionals last

---

Crampton under fire

From Don Kelleher

GLASGOW, Wed. — Australian Open Champion Bruce Crampton is the centre of the bitterest golf controversy in Britain for some time.

His straight-from-the-shoulder criticism of the £A.5000 Swallow Penfold tournament in Glasgow started the trouble.

The tournament started today.

Other competitors will agree that they feel the same about the event as Crampton.

But they refuse to have their name put to any quote.

Some, however, like close champion Peter Allis, have publicly agreed with Crampton.

Tournament organisers and club officials are unrepentent.

Mr. Dick Penfold, director of the firm backing the event, told me:

"Crampton is only a boy yet.

"I think he's been spoiled by luxury American courses and club houses."

Some British pressmen say that if Crampton shoots a high score in this tournament they will "roast him alive."

No one appears to want to upset the organisers.

Yet the criticisms are perfectly justified.

Mr. Penfold himself shrugged when I suggested this course was far too small for a tournament of this calibre.

"It's the best in the area," he said.

Crampton yesterday claimed that he and other professionals competing in the Penfold tournament had been barred from the clubhouse of the Glasgow Golf Club.

15th May 1957

GOLFERS STORM AT THE 'SNOBS' OF KILLERMONT

Express Staff Reporter

GLASGOW GOLF CLUB at Killermont—venue of today's £4,000 Swallow-Penfold tournament was denounced as "snobbish and insulting" by British and overseas professionals last night.

AUSTRALIAN GOLFER'S COMPLAINT

"Rudeness" at Glasgow Club

Australian Open golf champion, Bruce Crampton, yesterday made an attack on the "rudeness and snobbery" of the Glasgow Golf Club where

---

Scots ban pros. from clubhouse

From Bruce Crampton

GLASGOW, Tues. — I never expected to be barred from a golf clubhouse, especially in Scotland.

Yet this is just what happened to me here at Glasgow Golf Club.

This exclusive club has banned all professionals competing in the £A.5000 Swallow Penfold tournament from eating in the clubhouse.

The tournament starts tomorrow.

Already internationally known stars such as Welshman Dai Rees have been ejected from the club restaurant, merely because they are pros.

Club members have made us feel most unwelcome, making it obvious we are only here on sufferance.

Cars barred

From today the committee also banned all pros' cars from the spacious club parking area on the grounds of lack of space.

This means a half mile walk to the course in the morning and again in the evening, after a tough day's golf.

To add to our difficulties, the committee, without telling us why, has restricted our practice to two rounds, and we had to use forward tees.

As a result, about a dozen of us boycotted the course yesterday, and

The Glasgow Club is getting world-wide publicity, and thousands of pounds, from spectators and television interests, yet seems to want to give the pros nothing.

How the committee expects to control the huge crowds which will flock to the tiny course, I fail to see.

The course is only 6058 yards long, and is very narrow in places.

Worst section is at the centre of the course, where it narrows to a mere 200 to 250 yards.

Here flanked by thick clumps of trees and a river are three greens and three tees.

The spectators, by sheer weight of numbers, will stampede over the greens and bunkers at this point as they won't have anywhere else to go.

I am staggered that a course of such poor quality has been chosen for a tournament which is the biggest in Britain's golfing calendar outside the Open.

15th May 195

---

people are not like this, but hasn't helped their reputation.

"Now, of course, we are doing our best to give them the shoulder.

"Instead of asking for large Scotches and giving the steward a two-bob tip we are ignoring the place.

"I'm very annoyed, too, at the way our caddies are treated. They have to walk 300 yards to their lunch."

Commander Roe, secretary of the Professional Golfers' Association, said:

"Bruce Crampton's remarks are a lot of nonsense. The club has gone to a great deal of trouble to accommodate us, and our welcome has been far from hostile.

"A luxury coach has been laid on for the competitors to the course, and club members have given up their lockers to professionals.

"The dining-room at the clubhouse isn't big enough, and has been converted into a refreshment bar. Members and competitors will have their meals in the catering tent alike.

"The car park isn't available because it is crowded with B.B.C. television vans and Press cars."

'A SACRIFICE

Mr. J. C. Monachan, secretary of the Glasgow Golf Club, said: "The Glasgow Club does not make a penny out of this tournament. The promoters get the money and the Professional Golfers' Association benevolent fund get the programme money.

"Members are doing everything to make the tournament a success in helping to steward and sell programmes. They are sacrificing a week's golf to accommodate the competitors.

"They, too, cannot use the park."

Mr. Monachan added that the competitors were all written to about the times they would be allowed to practice.

He said: "In fairness to the competitors, there were some at Stockport at another tournament and others were travelling. They may not be

GOLF 'SNOBBERY' SAYS CHAMP

BRUCE CRAMPTON

TOP golf pros. joined in a chorus of accusations and complaints against the Glasgow Golf Club yesterday.

Their protests came on the eve of the £4000 Swallow-Penfold tournament at the Killermont course.

The row flared up after allegations of "snobbery" and "lack of hospitality" appeared in an Australian newspaper.

They were signed by Australian "Open" champion Bruce Crampton, one of the favourites for the tournament.

Crampton said some competitors had been barred from the club house, from using the club car park, and had been made to feel "unwelcome."

Poor course

"Dai Rees has been ejected from the club restaurant," Crampton wrote.

And he added: "I am staggered that a course of such poor quality has been chosen for a tournament which is the biggest in Britain outside the Open."

Crampton's attack aroused widespread comment in Australia. where columnists bitterly attacked "ARROGANT BRITISH SPORTING CLUBS LIKE GLASGOW."

The Crampton article said too: "The Glasgow Club is getting world-wide publicity and thousands of pounds from spectators and television, but is unwilling to give anything in return."

'A bad show . . .'

Other pros. complained yesterday when the course was closed at 3 p.m.

Said Peter Alliss: "It's a bad show and most unfortunate for Britain's golfing reputation.

"Two or three of the boys were ordered out of the clubhouse. I don't know why. But there seems to be a rule that we can't stand at the bar for a drink.

"The steward looks to see if we are wearing spiked shoes."

He complained about the lunching arrangements. "We pay 8s for lunch which we have to carry to a soggy wet tent set up for professionals."

And former "Open" champion, Max Faulkner, talked of having to "change in my car in front of the public."

both club officials and the tournament organisers.

Said Mr. John Monachan, secretary of the club: *"We have had many tournaments at Killermont before.. But we have never had complaints or allegations like these. I can answer every point.*

"The club doesn't get a ha'penny from the tournament. That goes to the promoters and the sale of programmes is for the Pros' benevolent fund.

"Everything about the tournament was agreed to by the promoters and the P.G.A. six months ago.

Rees 'incident'

"And the Dai Rees incident?

"The club restaurant was closed to everyone on Sunday at 2 p.m. Shortly afterwards Dai Rees arrived and asked for tea and sandwiches.

"He spoke to the clubmaster, then the secretary of the P.G.A. Commander Rowe, spoke to him then Rees left."

And Fred Thirlaway, Scottish representative of Swallow-Penfold, said: "Neither Crampton nor any of the other pros have complained to me.

"Crampton is talking through a hole in his hat. Killermont is one of the finest courses in the country."

Crampton said in his Glasgow hotel last night: "We Australians say what we think.

Crampton's views

"But what I meant to convey was the feeling of irritation among my fellow pros."

But he claimed that certain phrases credited to him in his reports had been misquotes.

"I HAVE NOT SUFFERED ACTUAL RUDENESS OR SNOBBERY PERSONALLY . . .

"But there WAS a lack of warmth in the welcome we got. It would never happen in Australia.

"There visiting pros. are made members of clubs during tournaments. This wasn't done at Killermont."

PHILIP TO FLY IN A GLIDER

PRINCE PHILIP will make his first trip in a glider today. At the controls will be either Peter Scott, the bird expert and TV celebrity, or a gliding instructor.

They will take off in a two-seater "Eagle" from the Bristol Gliding Club's site in the Cotswolds.

Asked his advice

The Prince is already a qualified pilot for powered planes, and when he heard of Peter Scott's enthusiasm for gliding he asked his advice about it.

Salisbury speech may spread Tory revolt on Suez

LORD SALISBURY, speaking for the first time in the Lords since he resigned from the Government in March, said yesterday:

"The statement by the Prime Minister yesterday was received by many of us with a feeling of very great regret. It goes far too near to complete capitulation to Colonel Nasser to be palatable or endurable."

Lord Salisbury resigned in protest against the Government's decision to free the exiled Greek Cypriot leader, Archbishop Makarios.

Yesterday, he was protesting against the Government's decision to use the Suez canal again, largely on Colonel Nasser's terms.

There was applause in the House when Lord Salisbury rose. Later he tabled a motion demanding a debate.

A new threat

Last night, despite efforts by the whips, about 20 Conservative M.P.s were still threatening not to vote for the Government when the Commons debate on Suez ends tomorrow.

They will not, however, vote for the Labour motion of censure, for that might bring down the Government.

Another Tory M.P. threatened also to resign from the Parliamentary Conservative Party. He said he would decide finally

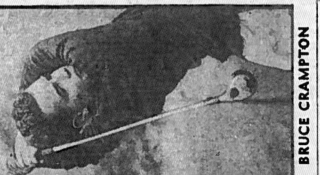

---

before the court are James Zarb, 37; Charles Pettuck, 45; and John Thornton Stanley, 40.

Another three Britons, in addition to Reynolds, are being tried in their absence.

Bruce tees off at Sunningdale Golf Club in England [1956]. The Von, Frank Phillips and Arthur the Club Professional watch.

You talk of how many of the best friends you made were during Pro-Ams. Can you describe how important the Pro-Ams were to the whole week and also, how difficult it was for you to go from being a jokey pro-am guy to mister serious the next day?

I've always believed I have a great sense of humour. I never tried to be a comedian myself during tournament play, but I sure did enjoy something amusing when it occurred.

I considered Pro-Ams very important. We, the professionals, or our organisation, came in, took over the golf course for a week, tore up the practice tee, as well as caused major damage to the playing area on the course itself, and then left as soon as our final round was completed.

Playing in a Pro-Am provided an opportunity to give something back to members, sponsors or guests with whom I was paired. The day was dedicated to them. If when we got through my playing partners could honestly say 'Gee whizz, that sure beat the hell out of working', then our day was a good one. If our group scored well enough to win, or come close to winning, then all the better. I was well aware of what a big occasion the day was for most of my partners, and how scary it could be. After all, few of them were used to playing in front of a large gallery, or actually being inside the ropes at a golf tournament, and having to hit golf shots.

While I could win prize money, which certainly would help pay the week's expenses, it was not considered 'Official', so a Pro-Am round didn't carry the same importance from my perspective as one of the 'Official' rounds in the tournament.

Photo: Tony Lema, Bing Crosby, and Bruce beside the 18th green at Pebble Beach after Bruce had won the 1965 Bing Crosby National Pro-Am tournament.

Over the years I accumulated a large number of stories and jokes. I also had a name for most of the shots. This material was used to help keep my playing partners relaxed. Many lasting friendships resulted.

Once the 'official' rounds of the tournament began, it was not difficult for me to put my game face on, and address the business at hand.

When you were going through personal problems off the course, how difficult was it to get focused and try and win a tournament? Can you give an example of how things happening off the course affected your performance on the course?

It can be extremely difficult. First of all, I would not get enough peaceful rest. When one is tired, things tend to look worse, and one becomes less patient, as well as less able to fully concentrate and keep one's mind totally focused on the task at hand. On many occasions I was just trying to get off the golf course, so I could focus on finding a solution to whatever was bothering me.

I recall something that happened on Saturday night during a four-ball tournament at Laurel Valley Golf Club in Ligonier, Pennsylvania, the heart of Arnold Palmer Country. My partner was Orville Moody. After three rounds we were either in the lead, tied for the lead or close to the lead. We were paired with Arnold Palmer and Jack Nicklaus for the final round on Sunday. My younger son, Jay, became really ill during the night. My wife and I had to take him to a hospital around 2 or 2.30 am. It was a night without sleep, so you can imagine how difficult Sunday's round was. Members of the huge gallery had no idea what was going on with me.

Photos: Far left is the presentation ceremony 1959 Far East Open (Philippines) and Bruce putting on the 18th green (72nd hole) at Wack Wack golf club when he won the 1959 Far East Open.

Top left – Norman Von Nida, Frank Phillips and Bruce Crampton on their International travels adjacent to Frank Phillips and Bruce Crampton 1956 England.

Below – visiting International players who competed in the 1956 Egyptian Open in Cairo. The Von became ill and went on to London.

Right – 1956 practice putt during Australian Open preparations.

Bruce Crampton

photos: 1956 Sunningdale, England. Bruce Crampton, Gary Player, Norman Von Nida, Trevor Wilkes from South Africa and Frank Phillips.   Right, Peter Thomson and Bruce with their Japanese caddies during the 1957 Canada Cup matches outside of Tokyo.

You retired from the US tour as a 41-year-old and didn't really play again until you turned 50. After 8 years away from the game how long did it take you to get your short game back?

I am forever grateful to the 6 Professionals – namely Don January, Bob Goalby, Julius Boros, Dan Sikes, Gardner Dickinson and Sam Snead – who initially met with Commissioner Dean Beaman to discuss the concept of starting a Senior Golf Tour. By the time I turned 50 there was a full schedule. The Senior PGA Tour gave me a mulligan at age 50. It gave me a second chance.

Once I made up my mind, it didn't take me long at all. There were those who didn't think I would ever get back to the level of winning again. I felt differently about it. I started a fitness regimen and practised every afternoon. The first Senior PGA Tour event I was eligible for and played in was the Hilton Head Seniors International, which took place 10–13 October 1985 on Hilton Head, South Carolina. My first official Senior PGA Tour victory came four months later at the Benson & Hedges Invitational in San Antonio, Texas. (Bruce went on to be the year's leading money winner in 1986, winning 7 times in his rookie year on the Senior PGA Tour. He was voted Senior Player of The Year, and awarded The Arnold Palmer Trophy.)

You had two runner-ups in Major Senior tournaments. How do you compare the Senior Majors to the regular tour, was it a similar pressure when it came down to the final nine holes on Sunday?

You bet. There is always pressure when one is trying to win any golf tournament. For one thing, one never wins often enough to ever get used to it. As for the so called 'Majors', there are only four of those on each of the Tours each calendar year, so one's odds of winning one is reduced. To people not closely associated with the Senior Majors there may not be the same prestige, but to the Senior PGA Tour players and members of their inner circle a win in one or more of them was, and still is, something highly desirable, and earnestly worked towards.

You still travel on an Australian passport and maintain your citizenship, but you have not lived in Australia for over 50 years. I guess there is part of you that still calls Australia home?

I'm still an Aussie at heart, and I'm guilty of still doing many things the 'Australian Way'. People over here still detect my Australian accent. During visits to my homeland, I'm told that I talk like 'A Bloody Yank'. My mother always had in her mind that I would never permanently live in Australia again. While she was alive I maintained my citizenship so I could tell her it hadn't changed. She passed away in 1984.

RANDOM QUOTES

I am very grateful to Arnold Palmer. He had the charisma and the style of playing golf that attracted the fans. Television was the real medium that caused a surge for tournament golf in the United States and Arnold Palmer was the catalyst that made the interest of the public at large really explode.

In those days the only way to make any large amount of money from a sporting goods company contract was to have your own autographed model golf clubs.

The 16-mm film I used to record movies of my swing had to be sent away to be developed. It was ten days or more before I got to it back and could run the film through a projector in order to see what my action looked like. By then I was more than likely doing something differently. While this was better than having nothing at all to aid me, it was nowhere near as efficient as having a video recorder right on the practice tee with me, so I could get instant feed-back.

Bruce Crampton, whom I caddied for on the senior tour, was misunderstood. The course was his office. He was at work, and there was no conversation, just the business at hand. He played to win for himself and his caddie. He'd apologise when he handed you a smaller cheque than others. At Pro-Ams he always had jokes for his amateur partners. He really enjoyed those rounds.
Quinn T. Jerriey

I don't know if the story about Scotland and the players starting out with a bottle of whisky is factual. They would take a nip after each hole. When the bottle of whisky was empty they had played 18 holes. I don't know if that's how a standard golf course having 18 holes got started, but that is what I have read. I also understand the bunkers on the famous links style golf courses were formed from where the cattle used to sleep for protection from the wind.

If the blue bloods in Britain had known in 1957 that my forebears were all convicts, it surely would have provided additional nails for my coffin.

I do not identify with blind shots or blind golf. I think the player should be able to see what the architect has designed and then the player should be required to craft and fit the shot into what the architect has created.

You can't get any more excitement than the last round, and particularly during the last nine holes of the Masters Tournament in Augusta, Georgia each year; the course just lends itself to all sorts of unexpected things happening.

I used to allow myself to get pretty upset at the USGA about the US Open: the way the course was set up; the rough, the severity of the greens; and how quick they were. Finally I came to the conclusion that the USGA really doesn't care all that much about score. It is trying to find a champion who is worthy of wearing the US Open crown for the next 12 months. To me, the United Sates Golf Association Open Championship is the premier championship in golf.

You can widen your stance, shorten your backswing, hit the ball lower, take an extra club or two and knock it down to keep it on line. You can also learn to turn it into the wind. Hold it both ways. Norman Von Nida schooled me well about each of these finer points of playing in the wind.

I would go out to NSW Golf Club with Norman, on occasions spending an hour or more in one bunker while he explained how go about hitting all types of shots from all sorts of lies out of the sand. He was renowned for his bunker play. Ask Gary Player what a great bunker player Norman Von Nida was.

If a top surfer is on a surfboard on a wave and he is thinking through every manoeuvre, what he has got to do and how he is going to do it mechanically, I don't think it would work. I think the good surfers must surely rely on their reflexes; they just automatically react, without thinking through every move. It is the same with golf.

If you had to tee it up tomorrow with Gary Player, Greg Norman and Adam Scott, for instance, hell, you probably wouldn't sleep a wink. But if you played with them every day for a month, it would become second nature to you, and end up not bothering you at all.

photo: 1956 at Sunningdale. Bruce, Gary Player, The Von, Trevor Wilkes from South Africa and Frank Phillips.

NORMAN VON NIDA - TRAILBLAZER 1914-2007

Norman Von Nida will forever be a name synonymous with Australian golf and a name recognised internationally for his contributions to the game and its top players. 'The Von' as he was known began his golfing life, as many in the 1920s did, as a caddie. By the age of 11, the pint-sized Von Nida won 'the caddies championship'

at Royal Queensland, then won the Courier Mail Caddies Championships the following two years. His life may have changed forever when, in 1929, he was chosen to caddy for the flamboyant American Walter Hagen at Royal Queensland. Hagen, the international superstar and flamboyant showman, became Norman Von Nida's idol. His reverence for Walter Hagen helped to set the trajectory that Von Nida's life would take, a life spreading the love of the game to an international audience and a life of taking young fledgling golfers and helping them spread their wings beyond the shores of Australia. Norman von Nida won over 100 tournaments.

'**Walter Hagen** was the man who travelled the world and projected the image of the professional golfer, much like Arnold Palmer did later on. Hagen was one of the most entertaining of all people and one of the most elegant of personalities. His demeanour, his attitude and his body language communicating with the people watching … it was really great to watch. It was illuminating to a young boy like myself; I thought he was something special. As a golfer he was something special, but as a personality he was even more special. I played a challenge match against him six years later at Gailes. I was fortunate enough to beat Sarazen and Hagen and both men influenced my direction in life enormously. They were both marvellous people.'

'The charisma of **Walter Hagen** was such that he was the original man who altered the attitude of amateurs towards professionals, because he felt that a professional was the equal socially to any amateur. When he competed at the British Open at St Andrews he was informed when he got to the club that he couldn't change his dress in the club house, so he hired a Rolls Royce and changed in the Rolls Royce right outside of the club house. From then on, professional golfers have been accepted throughout the world as equal.'

In 1936 **Gene Sarazen** came to Australia for the second time. Sarazen, then the greatest player in the world having won all the major golf tournaments, boldly stated in the media that he would play anyone in Australia for any amount of money. Von Nida resourcefully managed to raise the 50 pounds, even though at that time his only major golf victory was the 1935 Queensland Open, an event he went on to win eight times. 3000 people followed the 'challenge match' between Gene Sarazen and Norman Von Nida with 'The Von' winning 2 up in the biggest match in Queensland's history at that time.

'The words that Gene Sarazen spoke to me when I beat him … I asked him, 'Mr Sarazen, would it be possible for me to become a player such as you, travelling the world?' He answered, "Little man, who did you beat today?" He said, "You displayed skills today, you played the shots in such a way that demonstrates to me that you were not over-awed by playing the number one player in the world. But I will give you one piece of advice: instead of practising on the practice tee, like people do today, you have already developed the skill and the skilled shots. You must develop those skills by going out onto the golf course and experimenting with clubs to play certain types of shots so that when you have to play that difficult type of shot in a tournament you don't have any self-doubt about your ability."'

'Champions of today I don't believe have the charisma of the champions of yesteryear.'

Norman Von Nida

photo: Walter Hagen from John W Fischer III archives

photo: Walter Hagen and Archie Compston in Britain from John W Fischer III archives.

NORMAN VON NIDA CONTINUED

Von Nida won most of the events he could possibly win in Australia before taking a boat to Manila to win the then lucrative Philippines Open at Wack Wack golf club in 1938 and 1939. Von Nida was in America when the Second World War was declared and he had to hurry back to Australia. Five years later, after the war, Von Nida hopped on a boat headed for Britain where he really made a name for himself and put Australian golf on the world map.

'In those days, after the war, a man had to have permission from his wife if he wanted to leave the country, because in those days the husband was responsible for the wife and the family/children of that marriage. So, before I went to Britain in 1946 I had to deposit enough money for 12 months sustenance for my wife and my two children. I set off for Great Britain in a Navy ship, which was taking back the soldiers and sailors who were out here in a sort of administrative capacity during the Second World War. I was the only passenger on the boat. It took five weeks.'

'After I had paid the money for my family in Australia and paid [for] my ticket to Britain, I arrived in Britain with about 17 pounds. It was pretty daunting. I knew I had to do well in the first tournament at Wentworth Golf Club to pay my hotel account. I was fortunate in that I played a practice round at Wentworth with the local pro, **Archie Compston**, *on the short course at Wentworth and I shot a 62. Mr Compston asked me if I could play for money and I explained to him that I had raised the funds to come to Great Britain by betting with the bookies back in Australia and that I was very used to playing for money. I added that I didn't have any money to bet and he said, "Don't worry about that, I will put up the money, there are these two amateurs who have been robbing me for quite some time and we will play them." Fortunately for me, Mr Compston won 1500 pounds and he gave me 750 pounds, so I had enough money to continue playing in Great Britain.'*

photo: Norman Von Nida Far East Open presentation 1939, Philippines. From Von Nida family.

'After I was there for two or three weeks I realised that there was no player in Great Britain that I felt had any possible chance of beating me. The only player that had any possible chance of sort of competing with me on an equal basis was the international South African Bobby Locke … it was from this that one sort of gets the necessary confidence that allows one to be an international champion.'

Aside from his very lucrative betting matches, Von Nida succeeded in 1946, winning tournaments and coming second on the British Order of Merit, including tied 4th at the Open at St Andrews the year Sam Snead won. For his first season in Britain he won 1034 pounds in prize money. The following year he won seven tournaments and topped the order of merit and again competed well in the Open Championship with a tie for 6th. He became a well known figure in Britain, so much so that he once had King George VI follow him around 18 holes during a golf tournament. It wasn't just his golf that won Von Nida fans; his generous personality was to shine through in later years when he ushered the next crop of Australian professionals towards the vintage golf lands of Britain and the lucrative career option of America. **Von Nida's travels as a professional golfer took him to America, Britain, South Africa, the Philippines, Singapore, Egypt, Germany, France, Belgium, New Zealand, Canada, Hawaii and Switzerland. His fine play saw him in the company of luminaries of the game including Walter Hagen, Gene Sarazen, Bobby Jones, Henry Cotton, Sam Snead, Bobby Locke, Ben Hogan, Peter Thomson and later Jack Nicklaus.** The Von rose from a very poor family in Australia to become close friends of one of the richest families in Australia, the Packer family. Norman Von Nida was close friends with Sir Frank Packer and later he taught Kerry Packer how to play; he was so loved by the Packer family that Norman Von Nida continued to receive a weekly sum of money from the Packer family until his death, aged 93.

'I won the Queensland Open at Royal Queensland and for seven rounds averaged 69 during my stay in Brisbane, but all the press was interested in was the contents of my wardrobe, which they said was worth 700 pounds. They even reported that it contained 20 pairs of shoes. They were wrong. It contained 25.'

Von Nida's legacy in Australian golf as the 'trailblazer' is etched into history. He went further than blazing trails; he dragged other younger players with him, taking his role of mentor to the next generation. He aided the careers of some of Australia's finest golfers: Peter Thomson, Bruce Crampton, Bruce Devlin, Frank Phillips and David Graham. An outstanding bunker player, he aided and passed on these skills to the great Gary Player.

Norman von Nida *'I believe that a very important facet of the game – when a champion becomes a champion – that he should help some other young person to come along and be a champion after him.'*

Gary Player *'I first met Norman in 1956 at Sunningdale golf club, after I had just won the tournament with a world record score. He came up to me and he said, "Son, you have really got it; you are going to be a world champ." Gee, at that stage of my career it was such an encouraging thing. He then asked me if I would like to visit Australia and I said I would love to. That was the start of my wonderful trek to Australia where I won seven Australia Opens, thanks to Norman Von Nida. He not only invited me there but he got me the return air ticket to South Africa, he got me some appearance money and I played some exhibition matches at 25 pounds a game, travelling throughout the country for Slazenger at that time. But Norman was a wonderful golfer and teacher. He was always helping people and giving. People talk about leaving the world a better place; the only way you can do that is by giving something to the world and this is indicative of what Norman Von Nida did: he was always giving and helping people, giving them bits of money, arranging this, arranging that, letting you stay at his house – he was just unbelievable. He was a bit of a feisty golfer, but that is quite an advantage. He was cocky and had confidence in himself and played very well wherever he went. The big thing was, he was a giver. He helped Frank Phillips, Bruce Crampton … he just helped everyone I can think of. I know when I went over there every day he would come along and ask, "Is there anything I can do for you?" We used to hit bunker shots together at one pound per shot because we both thought we were the best bunker player around. Norman just helped to make everyone happy and if you can do something like that and be proud of your country, what a proud Australian he was. I just love Norman Von Nida and he had a great wife in Elva; that is a very big thing for a pro to have a good wife. I cannot speak highly enough of this man.'*

Kel Nagle *'Norman was the flag bearer for Aussie golfers when he went to England just after the war. Norman established himself over there. He was a great player. Lovely bunker player. Jim Ferrier as well; he went across to America just before the war. Ferrier was a great player, won the American PGA and all that sort of stuff. Von Nida was really the start, after the war, to get all our young fellas going across to practise. Von Nida, Eric Cremin and myself went across in 1951 and we played about 6 tournaments over there. I didn't play very well because I was in the boonies all the time. Hitting it long, but in the bush. Then I came back to Australia and took the job at Pymble Golf Club and worked on keeping it in play.'*

Peter Thomson *'Friends of mine introduced me to him when I was about 19. He was the big figure in the game in Australia and he came to Melbourne frequently to play golf, socially apart from a tournament once a year, perhaps. Soon enough he really encouraged me to follow his own lead and try it in the professional game, which seemed to me a pretty romantic kind of a life if one could roam the world and dress in all those beautiful clothes that he used to wear. So an impressionable youth like me fell for it. He was really a pathfinder for all of we Australians who eventually went to play golf overseas. He had gone to the Philippines twice before the Second World War and then after the war finished he continued that kind of roaming; he went to England in the first Hastings bombers (aeroplanes) that were used to transport us to Britain. As I say, that seemed like a very romantic thing for a young man like me to see Buckingham Palace and all the sights of London, so I was right in it without any second thoughts. Norman was an extraordinarily generous man who seemed to go out of his way to be kind to people like me, not of his own generation – I was a lot younger than him. I was really bowled over by his generosity.'*

Jack Nicklaus *'The Von! Well you know, I was very fond of Norman. Norman and I played a lot of golf together. When I played my first time in Australia, I played with Norman. I got to know Norman – saw him around the world as we played. He was a great competitor; he was a great friend and became an even better friend later as he came and taught in the United States. He taught at Muirfield Village Golf Club – my home club in Ohio – every year for many years. Norman was, in many ways, the face of Australian golf in the 1950s, '60s, '70s and even '80s. Norman passed away about 10 years ago, I suppose, but up until the time he died, he came every year.'*

photo of Von Nida: National Archives of Australia A1805, CU29/13.

Norman Von Nida

NORMAN VON NIDA CONTINUED

Bruce Crampton 'One day (in 1951) I was hitting 5-iron shots in the park across the street from Beverley Park golf course and a black Jaguar automobile, with red upholstery, pulled up on the wrong side of the street close to where I was practising. Out got Norman Von Nida. He watched me hit a number of shots. To this day I don't know why he came and showed such an interest in me, although I suspect Bill McWilliam may have spoken with him about me.'

'When I started working, one of the first jobs I had was at Slazengers, then a giant in the sporting goods business in Australia. I began in the packing department, graduated to hosting factory tours, but had the luxury of being able to go out with Norman Von Nida to work on my golf game at least three times per week. So, Von Nida literally took me under his wing and I was led to believe that his objective was to train me to take his place as Slazengers Australia Pty. Ltd.'s top golf ambassador.'

'The time I spent learning from Norman undoubtedly helped me build the foundation for so many of the things I was to so heavily rely upon throughout the rest of my golfing career. We were playing with the small ball then (1.62 in. as opposed to the larger 1.68 in. diameter ball). Without hesitation or any exaggeration I, to this day, consider Norman Von Nida to be best manoeuvrer of a golf ball I have ever seen.'

'I also had the privilege of accompanying "The Von" on an exhibition tour throughout Australia. This was not only lots of fun, and great experience, but it also gave me an on-site example, at each location we played a match, about how a golf "clinic" should be properly conducted. I can remember watching Norman as a member of his gallery when I went to the Australian Golf Club in Sydney. I was in short pants. He always wore colourful outfits. Watching him when he won the McWilliams Wines Tournament wearing such striking clothes, before such a huge gallery, left a lasting impression on me. I was both envious and inspired.'

'Once I turned pro Norman promised he would take me overseas as soon as I finished my apprenticeship. Thanks to Norman's efforts, and with aid from the PGA of Australia, and many of Norman's wealthier business acquaintances, enough money was raised for Frank Phillips and me to accompany him when he left for overseas in March of 1956. Our first stop was Singapore where we played an exhibition match. I also did some shopping while there. I purchased a 16 mm movie camera so I could record as much as possible about our overseas travels. Then it was on to Cairo, Egypt, for the Egyptian Open, and Alexandria, Egypt, for the Egyptian Match-Play Championship before flying on to Great Britain. Norman became violently ill in Egypt, and did not play in either of the golf tournaments. Frank and I put him on a middle of the night flight to London. He was so ill we literally did not know if we would ever see him again. Thankfully he was well and full of pep again by the time Frank and I reached England.'

'I have nothing but loving and fond memories of Norman Von Nida. Thanks to Norman and Bill McWilliam I received the foundation and incentive to accomplish what I did during my career as a tournament-playing Professional Golfer.'

Frank Phillips 'I did my first trip with The Von in 1956. He took Bruce Crampton and myself to England and it was a great experience. Norman wasn't a great teacher but he was a great motivator. He taught me how to play out of the bunkers and he was brilliant at that, but he was a great motivator. He would pick you up.'

'Norman took a lot of young Australians to England and taught them the ropes. Norman knew Ben Hogan very well. I had the pleasure of playing with Hogan a few times, but only because Norman knew him. I played with Kel Nagle in the Canada Cup many years ago (1958) in Mexico City and we played the first two rounds with Sam Snead and Ben Hogan [won by Ireland's Harry Bradshaw & Christy O'Connor].

'Norman was the one who started the Australian players playing overseas. He was the one who went to England first and he was quite successful over there himself. He took the young Australian golfers away, he was the founder of that, so all these players playing today have a great debt of gratitude to Norman, because he was the one who kicked it off. We always consider Norman as a trailblazer. Von Nida said to me before he died, "You know, Chops, you could never tell how you were playing, you were always the same." He said "you were not controlled by your golf" and I took that as a great compliment actually.'

Bob Shearer 'He was probably the first one who had a bit of grit in him and he went over there and took on the Poms. He was a feisty little fella. I remember one day at a tournament at Commonwealth he told me to bring a bag of practice balls up to the practice fairway. I was just a kid, probably 17 years old. He took me out in front of the bloody beer tent and tipped all the practice balls out about 15-20 yards away from all these blokes drinking, then gave me a 3-iron and said 'Hit it'. I shit myself. I turned around and The Von had walked away into the crowd. I couldn't see him; I just had to keep hitting the balls. I hit some awful ones to start with, but then I started to rip them! When I got to the stage where I was confident and I was ripping them to the end of the practice range at Commonwealth, The Von walked out and sort of said 'That's not bad. You have learned how to play in front of a gallery now.'

photo: Frank Phillips scrapbook

Norman Von Nida

Sir Bob Charles 'On my 18th birthday my parents presented me with a set of Slazenger Norman Von Nida irons (2 – SW) and including a putter. I won the NZ open less than 8 months later with these clubs, finishing ahead of Bruce Crampton and Peter Thomson. Norman had little influence on my career, living in NZ, unlike the Australians of my era: Thomson, Crampton and Phillips. However I do remember him as a generous man who loaned Bobby Verwey (South Africa) and myself a Slazenger-owned car for us to drive from Sunningdale to Sandwich for the St Georges Gold Vase, a 36-hole amateur event in 1958. Unfortunately I only had the privilege of playing a couple of rounds with Norman, early in my career.'

Jan Stephenson 'I remember watching The Von play when I was a junior in the late '60s. It was encouraging to see a man of small stature be such a great golfer. I was pretty small and they said I was too small to ever make it, so he was an inspiration. Towards the end, his eyesight was pretty bad, but he loved to come to our events and be part of the action.'

Jack Newton 'First of all I see him as the godfather of Australian golf. He established some of the platforms, particularly in Europe and here in Australia. He was a good coach, but he was an even better motivator. If you had ten minutes on the practice fairway with Norman Von Nida, by the time he had finished with you, you would think you could give Nicklaus a two-up start and beat the shit out of him. He certainly helped me a lot. He introduced me to Britain when I went over to play the British Amateur in 1969. Sunningdale was his base and he had two spinsters looking after him when he was there; they cleaned his shoes and gave him breakfast, lunch and dinner. Off he would go to Sunningdale, which was a pretty famous betting club – you could get a bet on just about anything you wanted. "The Von" was the best bunker player I have ever seen and he taught Gary Player. It is often overlooked what a cracking player he was, but unfortunately the war years precluded him from doing what he was quite capable of doing.'

Peter Toogood 'He was a great influence on me because he was a great friend of my father. My father had played against him during the '30s in pro events and dad had beaten him a couple of times. We hit it off and he used to give me a lot of real information without sort of teaching me or getting too technical. When he gave advice it was usually succinct and spot on and the way he advised players spilled over to all of us and that was the way we went onwards and treated other young players – just one little thing at a time: you don't go and try and change their swing completely.'

'I used to draw him in the Australian Open every year there for about five years. He was very kind to me, guided me and looked after me. He was there when I went to England in 1954 and I played with him at the Dax tournament and practice rounds with him at Royal Birkdale too. I wouldn't say he coached me, but he sort of looked after me a lot and cared for me.'

'There is a story about when I came third in the Australian Open at Lake Karringyup and at the presentation the first five or six pros all gave speeches, then away they all went, the governor left after the presentation, the crowd had gone and we were back in the locker rooms and 'The Von' suddenly realised they hadn't presented me with the leading amateur of the Australian open. He charged over and blew hell out of them. When you consider he was a pro and he had just won the Australian Open and there he was carrying on and caring about this young amateur. There he was sat out the front of the clubhouse in a chair and made them present the trophy to me while he clapped and applauded me. He couldn't stand people who thought they were bigger than the game. He was very genuine. His contribution to Australian golf was enormous, particularly with how much he helped the players.'

David Graham 'My memories of him are pretty strong and pretty deep and they are all extremely good. I always thought Norman was the sort of man that if he knew someone who needed $40 and Norman only had $50, he would give him that $40. He was extremely generous. His ability to help young players in Australia, for his generation, that was very unique. He led a great life, I mean he loved his life and what he did. He was very helpful with Peter Thomson and Bruce Devlin and also Bruce Crampton. He came into my life at a time where I wanted to win major championships, so I flew him to America and he spent a great deal of time with me and he was very helpful in teaching me to swing the club in a manner that was more conducive to playing the high ball flight. Norman was a unique individual and Australian golf needs to remember Norman – he played a huge part in the early success of the young players in those days. He was rough around the edges, like a lot of us were of that generation, but once you got to know him he was a remarkable man.'

photo: courtesy of the Australian PGA

WORLD FAMOUS GOLFERS

Norman Von Nida,
Aust. Open Champion.

Max Faulkner,
British Ryder Cup Player.

Eric Cremin,
N.S.W. Pro. Champion.

Kel Nagle,
Ex-Aust. Pro. Champion.

Dai Rees,
British Match Play

"G

People have asked me why have I done the things I have done, relative to helping other players who were taking my place in the game. Well, through golf, I have probably had the best life of anybody in the world. From being a caddie with no expectation of doing anything other than labouring through my career, I consider it has been a privilege for me to help all of the people I have been fortunate enough to assist with regard to their game. The fact that I have been able to do the things that I have done and have the life that I have had and being able to contribute to the lives of some people in golf and outside of the game – I am 88 years old now and I doubt that anyone in the world has had a better life than me, so I consider myself a very lucky person.

Norman Von Nida

Bruce Devlin *'When I was in the early stages of my golf career my father took me to Sydney to have Norman Von Nida take a look at me and evaluate my golf game. He told my Dad that he should take me back to Goulburn and teach me all he could about plumbing!! In the later years after I won the Australian Amateur and the Australian Open he was instrumental in me turning professional. He has helped many other players including Crampton, Player, Graham and in my opinion the most significant teacher that Australia has ever had.'*

Alan Murray *'He always kept things very simple with every part of the game. His main emphasis was on tempo, timing and co-ordination, three things he was very good at. Just watching him play was always helpful. I will always remember how he would give me confidence by praising my swing, especially when I was doubting myself. At the 1966 Wills Masters at Victoria Golf Club (Melbourne) after two rounds I was leading after hitting the ball great. I had even had a hole-in-one. Before the final two rounds on the Saturday, I was on the practice tee and hooking and pushing the ball, thinking that I was suddenly swinging like a 'hack'. As I was about to play with two of the world's greatest golfers, Kel Nagle and Roberto de Vincenzo, I was as nervous as a kitten. Right about then I hit another shot a bit left and I looked back and there was 'The Von' watching me and he said, 'Geez, Al, you are swinging it great!' It was incredible and probably the greatest wake-up call I ever had in golf. The lesson was – don't exaggerate your errors in the mind, as your confidence dips and you start to too many mechanical thoughts in your head. I walked to the first tee using visual swing imagery and feel, thinking of the day before, which really relaxed*

me, and I almost holed in one the par 4 1st hole. I did not win the tourney, even though I hit the ball well, as I putted a bit rough, probably because I was a bit too wrapped up in my long game. What a great lesson 'The Von' gave me there and it stayed for the rest of my life. So simple, just four little words: 'You are swinging great.'

'When Gary Player came to Australia in the 1950s as a young guy already doing well on the tour, he was a bit weak from bunkers. As 'The Von' was known then as one of the great bunker players in the world, Gary Player sought his advice. As I recall, 'The Von' invited him to stay at his house in Sydney for a few months and almost every day they were playing bunker shots at various venues. Gary Player, before long, became one of the great bunker players in the world, helping him win many tourneys. I heard that years later Gary Player built a huge bunker around his house in South Africa so he could get up early every morning and practise in the sand.'

'Norman Von Nida is without doubt a legend, one of Australia's greatest golfers and also a great ambassador who was likely our first international golfer to play in the USA, Europe, Asia etc. He was a kind generous person who was always there to help all of us young pros develop our confidence. Alongside 'The Von' I would also like to mention many other Australian PGA pros who taught me and most of the younger guys. They taught us everything they knew about golf, but also about life itself. Eric Cremin, Kel Nagle, Peter Thomson, Sam Richardson, Jim McGuinness, Dave Mercer, Alex Mercer, Ian Alexander, Dan Cullen, Colin deGroot, Graham Watson, Jim Moran, Doug Canty, Colin Johnstone and Tom Moore.'

This chapter made possible by the following resources;

'Norman Von Nida with Geoff Gough', a video recorded interview supplied by Tom Moore @ Australian Golf Heritage Society.

Neil Bennett's interview with Norman Von Nida in 1980, part of the Oral Histories and Folklore collection of the National Library of Australia.

'Bruce Young media interview and tribute' conducted by Bruce Young.

Book: *The Von – Stories and suggestions from Australian Golf's Little Master* by Ben Robertson, University of Queensland Press, 1999.

'To play brilliant golf for four testing rounds and then lose it all on the last two holes is the price that this merciless game sometimes demands.'

Norman Von Nida

HICKORY STICKS

In the modern era of golf where the game seems to be more sterilised and the equipment is morphing into digital gizmos from the future, there is a whole gamut of golfers around the world who have not been hornswoggled by technology; in fact, they have gone the other way ... back to hickory sticks.

Hickory Golf is a subculture within golf that has a firm link to the traditions and roots of the game. The modern renaissance in playing with hickory golf clubs started back in the 1970s with small gatherings of golfing enthusiasts, avid historians and collectors who would meet to talk golf, show off pieces from their collections and perhaps play a few holes to really get a feel for how it once was. It is all about the feeling of playing golf how it was intended to be played, with a nice smooth swing, where tempo beats macho and where playing the game is more appealing than studying the science.

'Playing with hickories requires a certain mindset. You have to see golf as a game, rather than an exact science. If you can't hit your wedge to the green before knowing to the nearest centimetre how far it is to the flag, the game may not be for you. The hickory joy is learning – relearning, if you like – to be creative with a limited amount of clubs. It means having to hit half and three-quarter shots, along with a variety of punch and cut-up shots. And it's that sense of challenge that, for me, has brought the enjoyment back to the game. A 7-iron will always remain just that. A 7-iron. But a mashie can become a friend. Treat your friends well and you'll be rewarded. Hit the sweet spot and there's magic in the air. Miss it by half an inch and you're fifty yards in the wrong direction. By way of a contrast, the modern club will let you get away with murder. But then, what kind of friend can that be?'

Iain Forrester, PGA professional

What were once humble gatherings are now National championships in countries like America, Australia, England, Austria, Czech Republic, Denmark, Finland, France, Germany, Poland, Sweden, Wales and of course Scotland. Each country has its own 'society' with dedicated members in some countries hosting dozens of events. Finland and Sweden have a Ryder Cup-style hickory matchplay contest against each other and in America there are a dozen events annually, which attract a strong field of like-minded competitors. Unique 'hickory handicap' systems have been devised and the hickory aficionados seek out old-school links golf courses under 6500 yards in length. Hickory Golf seems to attract the finest gentlemen of the game and also some superb golfers ... 17-year-old **Zack Saltman** shot 67 with 5 clubs in the 2006 World Hickory championships at Craigielaw in the UK.

'There is a way to deal with the curse of distance and return much golf to its original challenge. Play the courses with hickory. I have in mind not the courses now greatly stretched, but instead others, particularly the Scottish village courses under 6000 yards.'

David Hamilton (World Hickory Open)

The love of hickory all comes back to the equipment and the devoted collectors who ensured that history wasn't lost in a wave of modernism. In the modern era you can source a hand-made golf club made from local timbers, constructed by a master craftsman such as Ross Baker in Tasmania. Lovingly crafted from wood, lead weight and ram's horn, these golf clubs are exquisite works of art and use construction techniques which date back to the 1500s.

*'Having always had an interest in golf's fascinating history, playing Hickory Golf has enhanced my huge respect for the skills of **Harry Vardon**, **Bobby Jones**, **James Braid** and co. When you think about how the courses back then were presented, in comparison to modern day standards of green keeping, the game hardly bears any resemblance.'*

Perry Somers, Australia
(a winner of several hickory events worldwide)

'The Championship Series of the Society of Hickory Golfers is comprised of six major hickory tournaments and they also have the "Gutty Slam" which winds the clock back even further to pre-1900 and using replica gutta-percha golf balls and equipment ... while playing by the rules as they were in that era.'

Roger Andrew of Jenks, Oklahoma. Photo: Jan Tellstrom
photo opposite Zack Saltman by Robert Brown courtesy
of Lionel Freedman at the World Hickory Open, Britain.

Hickory Sticks

Johnny Fischer was the last person to win a Major championship, the 1936 American Amateur, using hickory-shafted clubs. By the early 1930s most tournament players had changed over to steel, but Fischer stayed with the girl he brought to the dance and who had been so faithful to him. Among the players he defeated with his hickories were **Chick Evans** (twice in the Amateur), **Eugene Homans**, **Tommy Armour**, **Gene Sarazen**, **Walter Hagen**, **Johnny Goodman**, **Lawson Little** and the Argentinian **José Jurado**.

'The Art of Grumpy & Beth' by Hannah Snider-Muldoon

photo: Jan Tellstrom

Roger Andrew of Jenks, Oklahoma. Photo: Jan Tellstrom

Bob Platt of Lynchburg, Virginia. Photo: Jan Tellstrom

'Golf is the closest game to the game we call life. You get bad breaks from good shots; you get good breaks from bad shots – but you have to play the ball where it lies.'

Bobby Jones

Mr Alan Grieve, you have now won a US Open and an Australian Open with your hickory sticks and you rarely pick up your modern clubs any more. How does a young man from Brisbane, Australia get interested in Hickory Golf in the first place?

I always had a Calamity Jane putter. I have had it for twenty years. One night I was looking around on the internet about hickory golf and found 'an introduction to hickory golf' and I thought, 'Why not? I will shout myself a Christmas present.' I bought an introductory set and away I went.

Where did you buy that introductory set from?

From Louisville Golf in Kentucky, America. Once I bought them and played with them I just thought, 'How good does this feel?' When you hit one of them out of the middle it just feels so pure and the sound is amazing. Where I bought the clubs from was linked to the 'Society of Hickory Golfers'. I had a look at their tournament schedule in America and lined up a trip to the US in 2011. I practised with the hickory clubs for a year here in Australia, then went over to the US and played their hickory events and was lucky enough to win their US open.

The course I won the US Open on (French Lick Springs Resort) was the same course they played the 1924 US PGA, won by Walter Hagen. They set the tees up in the same spots and put the pins in the same positions. You are dressed in 1920s clothes and using the same equipment, walking the same turf as Walter Hagen – it was fantastic. (foto of French lick old photo b/w)

Did you shoot similar numbers?

Oh, no. I averaged around 75, they were shooting in the 60s.

You ended up going to the Louisville factory that makes the hickory clubs and that was quite an eye opener …

The factory was quite close to where the tournament was held, so I went down there and I couldn't believe how well these hickory clubs were made. You can pick up an original old hickory club and pick up a modern reproduction and you simply cannot tell the difference. The people there at Louisville Golf are brilliant technicians – really passionate about what they are doing. It is an art form and they love their art. It was just amazing seeing how they manufacture a wood, a shaft, an iron, a putter and everything else they do. You can basically give them any old club that you like and they can recreate it.

With the hickory shafts is there just one stiffness?

No. Believe it or not the hickory shafts come in four different stiffnesses. The first question I asked them when I went to the factory in Louisville was, 'How do you determine what is a stiff and what is a regular shaft?' They put the shaft in a vice and they flick the other end and count the number of repetitions or vibrations and they have a band: between x and y number is a stiff shaft and between y and z is regular and so on.

Can you tell me a bit more about the hickory scene in America? Did they welcome you into their scene as an Australian?

Yes, definitely. I arrived for a practice round at the French Lick course where the tournament was played and the first thing I noticed was the Australian flag hanging off the balcony of the clubhouse, right next to the Canadian and US flag. They welcomed me in with open arms, bought me a beer and I didn't buy a beer for the whole tournament.

When you won the US open and took the trophy, were they still as friendly?

Yes, they were. Just an amazing bunch of guys. Sure, they were having a few friendly digs at me and when I went back as the defending champion I think I had to buy my own beer.

As much as playing with hickory seems to put the fun back into golf, I imagine the camaraderie with the like-minded people is a big part of the enjoyment.

Oh, it's huge. You have little subgroups from around America all getting together in one place having a really good time, plenty of good food, beer and wine and golf is an add-on. Having said that, there are quite a few really good golfers who are there to win the event. One of the guys, John Bloggs, plays off a one handicap with his hickory clubs. I play off 5.

If someone wants to get into hickory golf, how much does a set of remodelled clubs actually cost?

About the same as a normal set of clubs. It is a bit more personal though, if you go through Louisville Golf you can get your name inscribed on each of the shafts and get them fully custom made to your requirements. It is a lot easier and more reliable to get an introductory set of remodelled clubs from Louisville (Kentucky) or Tad Moore (Alabama) golf; they work. You can still get some good old original clubs but they are hard to find and not replaceable when you inevitably break a shaft.

And what is in a set of modern reproduction hickory clubs?

I have ten in my set: driver, spoon or cleek, bulldog, mid iron, mashie, betty or a spade, a mashie niblick, you'll carry two niblicks (which are your wedges) and your putter. No one really carries more than 11 clubs. We don't use the older golf balls; we use a soft modern ball because the hard balls seem to ruin your woods. The modern soft ball almost matches the feel you used to get with an old featherie golf ball.

How far do you average off the tee with a hickory-shafted persimmon-headed driver?
I average about 200-220 metres. Generally if you are going to play hickory golf you have
to set up the course to suit it, keep it short and don't tuck the pins away. You cannot
play off the modern back tees – it is just too hard. Most of the hickory golfers draw
the line at a course that is 6000 metres long. You don't want to be hitting a cleek into
every green – it is just not as much fun. You change your expectations, playing with
hickories. My target is 78 or 79 every time I play.

Do you think hickory golf works best on a links style course rather than parkland?
Links golf tends to feel right with hickories and hickory golf is all about feel.

The clothing seems to be a big part of the whole hickory movement.
You are playing with 1920s golf clubs and you are dressed like a 1920s' golfer. The first
tournament I went to I just thought 'yes, this is where I belong'. Up to that point,
wherever I played I just felt people looked at me and thought, 'Why are you wearing plus
fours?' or 'What are you hitting that old club for?' I wear plus fours even when I use
my modern clubs; this year I played Pennants in my plus fours and quite often it got in
my opponent's head and I won the first hole.

**How long does it take you to go from your hickory clubs and back to the modern ones and
feel comfortable again?**
About two or three rounds. It is mostly to do with your irons and wedges and realising
you can fire at the pin and stop it. With the hickories you play conservative golf and
leave your ego at home when you strike the ball; with the modern clubs you play more
attacking golf. You tend to think one or even two shots ahead with the hickories, whereas
you just bomb away with the moderns.

**When you play in America you can use modern reproductions or the authentic old clubs, but
in Australia you can only use the old authentic clubs – is that correct?**
All the tournaments I played over in America were run really well. The Australian scene
is slowly getting there. There are not as many tournaments to play in Australia, but I do
play the Australian Open at the end of November every year in Sydney and I have to use
my set of old authentic hickories – they won't let you use a set of modern reproductions.

**As the US Open champion for 2011 and the Australian Open Hickory champion for 2012, what
were the endorsement deals like? Did you end up with heavy sponsorship logos on your
plus fours … a new car?**
No. It is all for the love of the game.

photo Jan Tellstrom

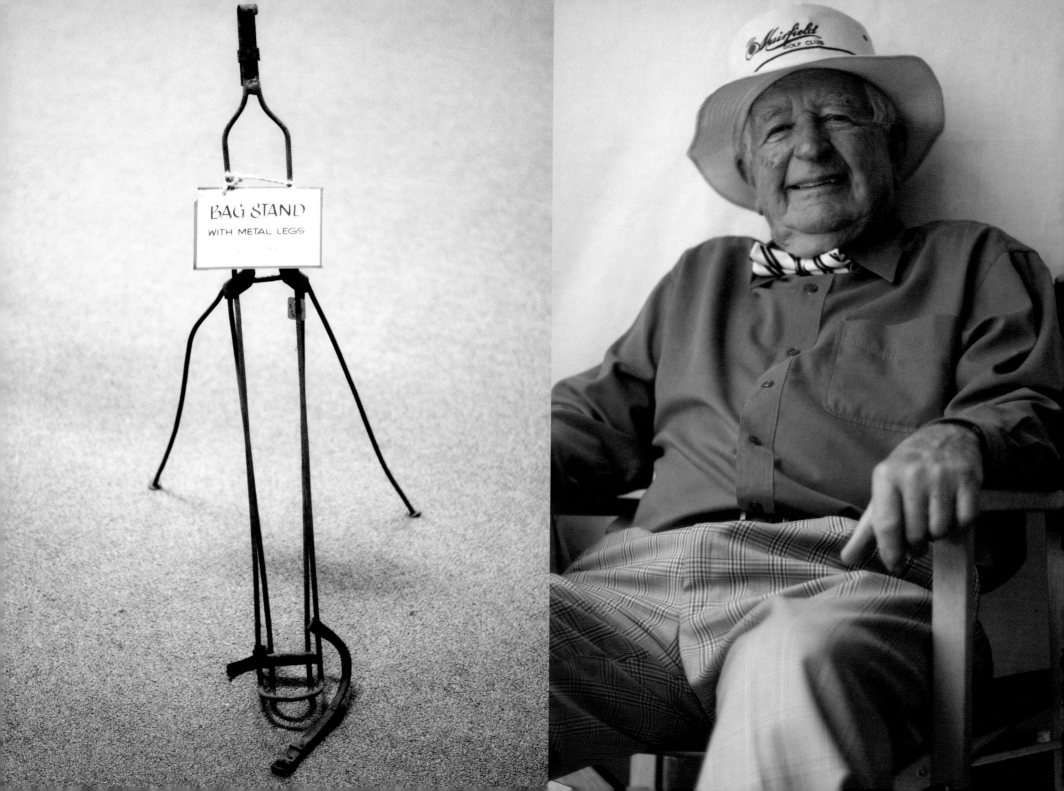

BAG STAND

WITH METAL LEGS

TOM MOORE

Mr Tom Moore is one of Australia's keenest golfing historians. He lives in Sydney and has established the Australian Golf Heritage Society Museum, a fine museum, in the western suburbs. Tom Moore is a vital part of the traditions of golf in Australia. This interview was conducted during the Australian Open in 2012 at The Lakes Golf Club in Sydney.

'Fellas like **Al Howard**, who is 100, his mind is as clear as a bell – he can go back to 1930 or before. **Kel Nagle** is another, **Dan Cullen** is another. There would be 100 people like this that we have to talk to and capture the aural histories. We are embarking now on a program of interviews.'

When did your passion for the history of Australian golf really kick in?
1973. My wife and I did a trip for Britain, I entered for the British Open. Up to that time, we were cutting up hickory-shafted clubs by the hundreds to make little wooden plugs for the top of the steel shafted clubs, which were hollow. On a journey around Britain you go to castles and cathedrals and eventually the penny drops that they never threw anything out over there. So I thought, 'Wait a minute – in another fifty years someone is going to say "Tom, where is all our golf history?" and I will reply, "Oh, it all got chopped up!"'

So I came back from Britain and I started putting things aside. As it got known that I was doing that, other people started to bring stuff in and I put it in the corner of the pro shop. I always had it in the back of my mind that I would one day display it. Time went on and I formed the Australian Golf Collectors Society. We started playing hickory events. In 2000 Dennis Brosnan gave us the entire upstairs of his warehouse (Parramatta, Sydney), free of charge, for a museum. I moved everything in there and that is where it is today and it keeps extending out of all

proportion. 80% of it would be stuff I collected myself. People find stuff in cupboards, in lofts – all over the place. One bloke was selling his car and he thought he'd better clean it out and he put his hand up under the front seat and there was a pristine set of a dozen golf balls still in their packet.

When did you first put the hickory golf days together?
1990. I was working at the Auburn municipal golf course and they were celebrating 100 years of local government and they wanted to put on events to celebrate that and

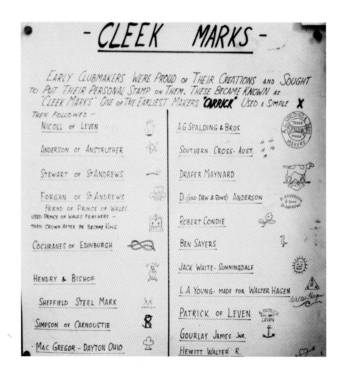

I thought, 'What better way than to put on a hickory championship?' So we gathered a few sets of clubs and nine people played in the first one. It has gone on from there and it is getting bigger and bigger. The Hickory Australian Open has been played every year since.

What is it about playing with hickory clubs that you love?
You have to swing the club – you can't bash at it. It is more of a pure swing. When you really hit it in the middle it is a lovely feel. It gives you an idea of what golf was all about. Mind you, golf was played, you might say, along the ground and nearly all the greens were shaped so that you could run the ball on from 30–40 yards out. Whereas today ... there would be a big pond or a deep bunker and you have to fly the ball onto the green. These hickory clubs weren't made to do that. It is a different ball skill altogether. Some courses are more fun to play with hickories than other courses.

That style of modern golf and flighting it in – do you think that is coming from America?
Oh, yes. The resort courses. It is a natural progression with the improvements in golf balls. We couldn't make the older balls stop as quickly as they can today. These days you can fly it in and get it to stop after the first bounce in what we call 'aerial golf'.

How does someone get into playing hickory golf?
Join the Australian Golf Heritage Society and we email and post out all the news of the hickory events. We have fifty little sets of hickory clubs we bring along. I have heard they let the players use replica hickories in the US, but to this point we have stated the clubs used in Australia must be pre-1940.

Tom Moore

FACTS from the Moore mind

- Our champions very quickly fall off the peg. You can ask young people about **Peter Thomson** and they will say, 'Who is he?' Kel Nagle? They know the current crop but they are not interested in the ones from the past.

- Australia was largely amateur golf up until the 1930s and then the Americans came. Walter Hagen came out with Australia's Joe Kirkwood and Gene Sarazen came out and that really kicked the game on.

- Around 1930 they changed from the hickory to the steel shaft and that made the whole thing so much cheaper.

- Television was another thing that boosted golf. It was the first time golf came into people's living rooms and they thought, 'Gee, I would like to try that.' It was around 1956 ... that was an explosion in golf right there.

- **Norman Von Nida**'s legacy is enormous in Australian history. He was virtually our first full-time player. He won most of his money on racehorses and he mixed with jockeys that gave him a lot of information. That financed him into playing his golf. He was a showman. He dressed to attract attention and he would get up to any trick at all to get his name in the paper, on the radio or wherever. He was our first full-time player and the war years cruelled him in a way took away five years in his prime. Gurus tell me that before the war he was unbeatable and the five years of the war didn't do him any good. He showed the way – took the young blokes overseas (**Thomson**, **Crampton**, **Phillips**) and showed them there was money overseas for their efforts.

- I speak to schoolkids a bit and when I ask them 'Where did golf originate?' they have no idea. China? They have no idea. I would say none of the kids know it started in Scotland and when I ask them how old it is they say 'Oh, 100 years'. It's 600 years old.

- The course in Ratho was done by a grazier who took up land down there in Bothwell, Tasmania. He laid out Ratho for his friends and they played golf there in the early 1800s, but they didn't form a club. Had he formed a club it would have possibly been the first golf club outside of Scotland and England. That honour is now claimed by Royal Calcutta (India), I think.

- One thing we are trying to do with our society is to get every golf club to appoint a historian. His job is simply to protect the club's history. Far too often a 'secretary manager' will move in and there are cupboards full of records and they get burnt. The club gets to 100 years old and wants to write a history and one of the older members goes to find all the old records and they are not there. Clubhouses want to extend and get bigger and they take the honour boards down and put them in the old greenkeeping shed where they get covered in oil and dust and eventually someone just puts them on a fire.

- The Robertson Collection at Royal Sydney Golf Club lay around in some room for fifty years until someone realised what they were. It is one of the most valuable collections in Australia.

- The first pros came to Royal Sydney about 1890. **Taylor**, **Carnegie Clark** and **Dan Soutar**. Soutar was an amateur when he came, a carpenter – he came out to marry Carnegie's sister … but it all fell through, I believe, and caused a great furore in the family. Dan Soutar went on to lay out lots of golf courses all over the countryside.

- When we went to Shanghai the communists had turned the golf course into a zoo. There were no golf courses in China when we were there in 1990.

1928	FRED POPPLEWELL	ROYAL SYDNEY	295
1929	IVO WHITTON (a)	ROYAL ADELAIDE	309
1930	FRANK EYRE	METROPOLITAN	306
1931	IVO WHITTON (a)	KENSINGTON	301
1932	MICK RYAN (a)	ROYAL ADELAIDE	296
1933	LOU KELLY	ROYAL MELBOURNE	302
1934	BILL BOLGER	ROYAL SYDNEY	283
1935	FERGUS McMAHON	ROYAL ADELAIDE	293
1936	GENE SARAZEN (U.S.A.)	METROPOLITAN	282
1937	GEORGE NAISMITH	KENSINGTON	299
1938	JIM FERRIER (a)	ROYAL ADELAIDE	283
1939	JIM FERRIER (a)	ROYAL MELBOURNE	285
1940 – 1945	NOT PLAYED		
1946	OSSIE PICKWORTH	ROYAL SYDNEY	289
1947	OSSIE PICKWORTH	ROYAL QUEENSLAND	285
1948	OSSIE PICKWORTH	KINGSTON HEATH	289
1949	ERIC CREMIN	KENSINGTON	287
1950	NORM VON NIDA	KOOYONGA	286
1951	PETER THOMSON	METROPOLITAN	288
1952	NORM VON NIDA	LAKE KARRINYUP	278
1953	NORM VON NIDA	ROYAL MELBOURNE	278
1954	OSSIE PICKWORTH	KOOYONGA	280
1955	BOBBY LOCKE (S.A.)	GAILES	290
1956	BRUCE CRAMPTON	ROYAL SYDNEY	289
1957	FRANK PHILLIPS	KINGSTON HEATH	287
1958	GARY PLAYER (S.A.)	KOOYONGA	271
1959	KEL NAGLE	KENSINGTON	284
1960	BRUCE DEVLIN (a)	LAKE KARRINYUP	282
1961	FRANK PHILLIPS	VICTORIA	275
1962	GARY PLAYER (S.A.)	ROYAL ADELAIDE	281
1963	GARY PLAYER (S.A.)	ROYAL MELBOURNE	278
1964	JACK NICKLAUS (U.S.A.)	THE LAKES	287
1965	GARY PLAYER (S.A.)	KOOYONGA	264
1966	ARNOLD PALMER (U.S.A.)	ROYAL QUEENSLAND	276
1967	PETER THOMSON	COMMONWEALTH	281

YEAR	WINNER	VENUE	SCORE
1968	JACK NICKLAUS (U.S.A.)	LAKE KARRINYUP	270
1969	GARY PLAYER (S.A.)	ROYAL SYDNEY	288
1970	GARY PLAYER (S.A.)	KINGSTON HEATH	280
1971	JACK NICKLAUS (U.S.A.)	ROYAL HOBART	269
1972	PETER THOMSON	KOOYONGA	281
1973	JESSE SNEAD (U.S.A.)	ROYAL QUEENSLAND	280
1974	GARY PLAYER (S.A.)	LAKE KARRINYUP	277
1975	JACK NICKLAUS (U.S.A.)	KENSINGTON	279
1976	JACK NICKLAUS (U.S.A.)	KENSINGTON	286
1977	DAVID GRAHAM	KENSINGTON	284
1978	JACK NICKLAUS (U.S.A.)	KENSINGTON	284
1979	JACK NEWTON	METROPOLITAN	288
1980	GREG NORMAN	THE LAKES	284
1981	BILL ROGERS (U.S.A.)	VICTORIA	282
1982	BOB SHEARER	KENSINGTON	287
1983	PETER FOWLER	KINGSTON HEATH	285
1984	TOM WATSON (U.S.A.)	ROYAL MELBOURNE	281
1985	GREG NORMAN	ROYAL MELBOURNE	272
1986	ROGER DAVIS	METROPOLITAN	278
1987	GREG NORMAN	ROYAL MELBOURNE	273
1988	MARK CALCAVECCHIA (U.S.A.)	ROYAL SYDNEY	269
1989	PETER SENIOR	KINGSTON HEATH	271

Australian Open 1904

Gary Player: 'We all used to go to the Slazenger factory and have lunch, work on our golf clubs. They had an old Scot there called 'Sandy' and he used to work on our clubs. Noel Morris, the head of Slazenger's, would be inviting all the best players from around the world to come out and play. I mean, golf was humming in Australia. It was a special time. Nicklaus and I were battling to have the record and it was a battle right down to the end, but I'm just so proud to have the most Australian Opens ever. Everyone wanted to come to Australia and play the Australian Open and I don't know what the hell has happened; I guess that is just the way life goes, but in my mind it is still a great tournament.' photo: courtesy of Black Knight International Archives.

Grand Slam Golf champion, Gary Player, is the most prolific winner of the Australian Open tournament with seven victories. The great Jack Nicklaus won the tournament six times, Australians Greg Norman and Ivo Whitton (Amateur) won the tournament five times.

The illustrious list of champions also includes major golf champions Gene Sarazen, Jim Ferrier, Bobby Locke, Peter Thomson, Kel Nagle, Arnold Palmer, Tom Watson, Bill Rogers, David Graham, Mark Calcavecchia, Steve Elkington, Geoff Ogilvy and Adam Scott.

The 1960s and 1970s were the 'golden era' of professional golf in Australia, attracting the biggest names from around the world to come and win the Australian Open. In 1971 Jack Nicklaus shot 19 under par at Royal Hobart to beat a stellar field by eight shots and during his victory speech he referred to the Australian Open as 'the fifth Major'.

Stonehaven Cup

THE AUSTRALIAN OPEN - THE GOLDEN ERA

Beginning in Sydney as the 'AustralAsian Open' in 1904, the tournament is one of the oldest National Opens in the world of golf. The tournament is 30 years older than one of golf's Majors, the US Masters, which was established by Bobby Jones in 1934, then called the 'Augusta National Invitational'; it later adopted the moniker of 'US Masters' in 1939 and continues its 'invitational' format. In 1916 the Professional Golfers Association of America was established and the US PGA championship was first played at Siwanoy Country Club (New York) as a matchplay event, also won by an Englishman Jim Barnes (1916). The US PGA championship continued as a matchplay event until 1957. The Australian Open is older than the French Open (1906), the German Open (1911), the Spanish Open (1912), the Philippines Open (1913), the Italian Open (1925), the Irish Open (1927) and the Japan Open (1927).

The 'AustralAsian' Open started in Sydney at the Australian Golf Club, then went to Royal Melbourne in 1905, then to Royal Sydney Golf Club in 1906 then back to Royal Melbourne in 1907. The tussle between Sydney and Melbourne hosting the championship has continued ever since. Royal Adelaide Golf Club joined the roster in 1910 and the three major cities hosted the championship until after World War II when **Ossie Pickworth** won at Royal Queensland (Brisbane) in 1947, the second of his three successive wins. Western Australia joined the roster in 1952 with **Norman Von Nida** winning at Lake Karrinyup and by 1971 the championship was played in Tasmania at Royal Hobart Golf Club, won by the great **Jack Nicklaus**. Sydney and Melbourne no longer had a stranglehold over the championship.

The pre-World War I champions **Michael Scott**, **Dan Soutar**, **Carnegie Clark**, **Clyde Pearce** and **Ivo Whitton** were shooting 300+ for the four rounds. In 1920 the soon-to-be-legendary golfer **Joe Kirkwood** shot 290 around the Australian Golf Club and it would take an International superstar, **Gene Sarazen**, to beat that mark albeit 16 years later at Metropolitan Golf Club in Melbourne (1936) with a score of 282. Two years earlier and in the company of Australian ambassador **Joe Kirkwood**, **Gene Sarazen** was brought to Australia via ship from America; the journey took 3 weeks. Gene Sarazen, having already won golf's 'Grand Slam', had a large impact on Australian golfers, particularly **Norman Von Nida**. Sarazen and Kirkwood were given half the gate's takings just to play the tournament, thus beginning the Australian Open's tumultuous relationship with appearance money. It wasn't Sarazen or Kirkwood who won the tournament that honour fell to Australian **Bill Bolger** who shot a tournament record score of 283 to win.

photo left: 1934 Australian Mick Ryan and Grand Slam golf champion Gene Sarazen (USA) at the 18th at Rose Bay Royal Sydney Golf Club. [Gene Sarazen won the Australian open in 1936 at Metropolitan Golf Club] NSW State Library hood_02612. Artwork by Jamie Kasdaglis

Ivo Harrington Whitton (1893–1967) was an outstanding amateur golfer who won 5 Australian Opens (1912, 1913, 1926, 1929, 1931). Ivo was at his peak in the 1920s and got his handicap down to +8. His first great sporting love was cricket, but when he missed out on being selected for Melbourne Grammar's first XI as a fourteen-year-old he chose to focus his sporting ability on golf. His father was honorary secretary at Metropolitan Golf Club. He won his first Australian Open as an 18-year-old at Royal Melbourne (1912) and defended the title the following year before World War I interrupted this fine sportsman's career. In 1914 when the war broke out, he was rejected from the AIF on medical grounds due to a weak ankle, but chose to return to England and enlist in the British Army and saw active service in Greece and Bulgaria.

Ivo Whitton won 5 Australian Open Championships; 2 Australian Amateur Championships (1922 and 1923) and 5 Victorian Amateur Championships (1919, 1920, 1922, 1923 and 1924). The VGA introduced the Ivo Whitton Trophy in 1960 for the lowest average stroke score in designated tournaments held each year. The inaugural winner was **Kevin Hartley** with an average of 72.72 from 32 rounds. Hartley went on to take the trophy 12 times out of the first 18 years of the competition. Other winners include **Michael Clayton** (1978 and 1980), **Brad Hughes** (1987), **Robert Allenby** (1990 and 1991), **Stephen Allan** (1994) and **Geoff Ogilvy** (1995 and 1997).

In 1931 Ivo was in 8th place when he teed off for the final round of the Australian Open at the Australian Golf Club. Playing in strong winds he managed to pass the legendary **Harry Williams** and **Jim Ferrier** for his 5th Australian Open victory. The victory was marred by losing his famous floppy hat, which he claimed was like a lucky charm … Ivo said he would never win another championship without his lucky hat. He never did.

photo: Victorian state team in Sydney, 1931. Charlie Smith, Alec Russell, Harry Williams (aged 16), Ivo Whitton, Henry Schlapp, Mick Ryan (captain) and L.M. McPherson. Photo courtesy Ryan Publishing.

Ossie Pickworth

Short-game maestro big **Jim Ferrier** won the Australian Open in 1938 and 1939 as an amateur, a precursor to his fine professional career in America. After serving four-and-a-half years as a cook in the army during World War II, **Ossie Pickworth** returned to Sydney as assistant club professional at Manly Golf Club and he won the Australian Open for the next three years (1946, 1947 and 1948). 1948 was a pivotal year for Ossie Pickworth as he held off his Manly Golf club colleague **Jim Ferrier**. Ferrier was the club secretary's privileged son; Pickworth was the battler from the proshop who often had to take orders from Ferrier off the golf course. In 1948 at Kingston Heath Golf Club they finished the four rounds tied on 289, seven shots ahead of the field. Golf was not played on Sundays in that era, but the Monday play-off was enthralling with Ossie Pickworth's straight hitting being too good for the wild Ferrier, Pickworth winning 71 to 74 and becoming the first player to win the Australian Open three years in succession. Ossie Pickworth relocated to Victoria in January 1949 to become the professional at Royal Melbourne Golf Club, rubbing shoulders with the prolific Australian open winner **Ivo Whitton**.

Ossie Pickworth was a chain-smoking wise-cracking happy man that was loved by the Australian public. In the 1950s exhibition matches were a lucrative pursuit for the world's finest golfers and Pickworth was privy to play one against the great South African **Bobby Locke** on the West course at Royal Melbourne. Pickworth had a 12 under par 63 to Locke's 65 in a stunning display of golf. He played the British circuit in 1950 and finished third on the order or merit, winning the Irish Open. Pickworth won the Australian PGA three times. During the Dunlop tournament at Commonwealth Golf Club in the 1950s Pickworth, playing the final 36 holes on a Saturday drove the 335 yard par 4 17th and holed a 20-footer for eagle and repeated the feat in the afternoon, holing a pitch shot from pin high. Pickworth won the Tattersalls Lottery in the late 1950s, bought a hotel and retired from competitive golf. He died aged 52. A true legend of Australian golf.

Horace Henry Alfred Pickworth (1917–1969)

Norman Von Nida: **Ossie Pickworth** was the best fairway wood player I ever played with. Very, very quick player and a chain smoker. It is one of the tragedies of golf that he died too soon, a bit like **Bobby Locke**.

photos: Ossie Pickworth putting in the 1953 Ampol
Tournament at The Lakes Sydney National Archives of
Australia A1805, CU29/ photographer J Fitzpatrick
National Archives of Australia A1805, CU29/19.

Peter Thomson's outstanding success in Britain in the 1950s brought with it a renewed interest in Australian golf and the Australian Open championship had another golf superstar **Bobby Locke** win the Stonehaven Cup in 1955 played at Gailes Golf Club in Brisbane. Following in the footsteps of Australian **Joe Kirkwood** who had encouraged **Walter Hagen** and **Gene Sarazen** to visit Australia in the 1930s, **Norman Von Nida** personally encouraged many of the international players of his era to come to Australia and try and win the national Open. After all to win it they would have to beat **Von Nida** himself and the prodigious **Peter Thomson** not to mention the resident rising stars of **Bruce Crampton**, **Frank Phillips** and **Kel Nagle**. Von Nida's foresight to see the potential champion in South African **Gary Player** would start a love affair with Australia and golf's superstars that would lead the Australian Open tournament into its 'golden era' where prizemoney grew and the competition was fierce. The Stonehaven Cup became a championship that golf's finest players wanted to win.

Gary Player: *'Norman Von Nida was a real beauty. I mean, he was travelling around the world inviting players to come and play in Australia. What a marvellous ambassador he was for Australia! The reason I went to Australia was that when I won the tournament in England, Von Nida came up to me and said, "Son, you are going to be a great player one day – we would love you to come to Australia and play." He was always travelling around and getting people to come and play in Australia.'*

In the 1960s and 1970s the Australian Open was one of the most sought-after trophies in world golf and Australia was a world leader in manufacturing golf equipment with sporting goods companies Slazengers, East Brothers and Spalding providing the financial backbone. Elite players like **Jack Nicklaus**, **Arnold Palmer** and **Gary Player** would be paid by their sponsors to come to Australia and promote the brand that was manufacturing their equipment. For years Dunlop had a clause in their contract that ensured these great players came to Australia each year. The Australian Open became an annual pilgrimage that would involve ample domestic travel and promotional exercises to raise the awareness of the brands that had paid the players to come to Australia.

Gary Player: *'They would probably give you about $10,000 for the whole trip. I remember going to play matches in Wagga Wagga, Alice Springs, Darwin and all these far-off places for 25 pounds per game, travelling in a car with no air conditioning, just travelling in your underpants it was so damn hot! We would get to these remote courses and we would play, there would be cracks in the fairways, these little old clubhouses, any shot – even one out of bounds – got clapped, anything that went forward got applause, we had luncheons there, stayed overnight, danced to the band ... it was just a different time. Nothing like that happens anymore.'*

'Australia has a lot of great golf courses, particularly in the sandbelt in Melbourne. You know, it used to take me forty hours to get to Australia from South Africa, we would stop in Mauritius and Cocos Island before Perth. You would land in the Cocos Islands and get off the plane and have a swim in the bloody ocean. You would have a beer and put a bit of 'Sea & Ski' on and lie in the sun for a while then you would hear a loud whistle and everybody would get dressed and get on the plane. It was a different world; it was a great time and I tell you what, there was great excitement in Australia at that time. Peter Thomson was winning the British Open regularly, all the top players were going to Australia: **Arnold Palmer**, **Jack Nicklaus**, **Lee Trevino**, **Greg Norman**. Everybody was going to Australia and playing in the Australian Open and the other tournaments there.'

Jack Nicklaus: 'Well, back in the 1960s and '70s, I came to Australia almost every year, and I not only enjoyed the trip because I loved the country, but I enjoyed my ability to play well down there. I had a great relationship with Slazenger. I think Slazenger was very important to bringing Gary Player and me to Australia. I think they were very important to the growth of the game in Australia, particularly Noel Morris who ran Slazenger at the time. He was a very forward-thinking, aggressive gentleman who I happened to like very much. He also did a good job in those years with the company. We looked at the Australian Open as being the fifth Major at that time. Unfortunately, with what's happened with the global landscape in golf, countries with the population of Australia have a hard time competing on the world tournament stage. Australia, however, still produces a number of wonderfully talented golfers, including this year's Masters Tournament winner Adam Scott, and a tremendous number of good athletes continue to represent their country well.'

From 1962 to 1972 the Australian Open was won exclusively by the four big names in golf: **Jack Nicklaus** (3 times), **Gary Player** (5 times), **Peter Thomson** (twice) and **Arnold Palmer** (once – 1966). Other tournaments like the Ampol and the Wills Masters were also attracting big prizemoney and Australia was in the spotlight on the world stage with other leading players, like **Lee Trevino**, venturing to Australia to pursue the rewards.

Photos: Left – South Africans Gary Player and Bobby Locke in 1956. Far right Gary Player in Melbourne. Courtesy Black Knight International Archives.

Col McGregor (former President of the NSW PGA): 'Being able to entice these champions to our shores was a huge boost for the Australian Open, and a wonderful opportunity for the golfing public to see the world's best players in action on our golf courses.'

'At this time, Dunlop Slazenger was the prominent golf club manufacturing company in Australia, and they put all three of these great players under contract, whereby they designed and manufactured golf clubs bearing their names. This in turn encouraged **Nicklaus**, **Palmer** and **Player** to come to Australia regularly to promote sales of their personalised models.'

'The manufacturing process of golf irons at this time was called drop forging, whereby the rough forging had to be hand finished. The loft and lie and the final shape was adjusted by hand and required great expertise. Slazenger fortunately had such a specialist in a Scottish gentleman named Sandy Faichney. It was incredible how he could hand-make these irons so that even these discerning champion golfers were entirely happy with the golf clubs made to their specifications, and were able to play in Australia to their normal high standard. Being assured of such quality equipment played a big part in making them happy to return here time after time. The Mexican superstar, **Lee Trevino**, took a set of clubs made by Sandy Faichney back to the United States and used them to win the 1971 U.S. Open.'

'Karsten Solheim, an engineer with General Electric, revolutionised golf club design and manufacturing. In 1969 he applied the concept of perimeter weighting to irons, increasing the sweet spot by removing the weight from the centre of the head and redistributing it to the toe and heel of the club. The manufacturing method was called Investment Casting. When the iron head comes from the cast, it requires no adjustment – each set of irons is identical.'

'We have no golf manufacturing companies in Australia now, only assemblers. To entice the world's best to our Australian Open now is far more difficult and much more expensive.'

Photo: NSW State Library hood_32449u & hood_32446u golf club making at East Bros.

Australian Open

Gary Player: 'Every year I went to Australia I won. The Ampol tournament in Melbourne enabled me to get married! That was during the Olympic Games in 1956. There was a first prize of 5000 pounds, which was the biggest prize in the world, outside of America. It was 5 times the money that first prize in the British Open had. I went to Australia with all the Americans and the **Peter Thomsons** and the man called **Ossie Pickworth** – he could play like hell! There was **Bruce Crampton** and **Frank Phillips** … there were a lot of wonderful golfers in Australia and I went and I said to my wife, "Well, I don't know if I am that good, but if I win it will get married." I won the tournament and there was this old pressman called MacDougal and he went and sent a telegram to my wife for me, it read, "Will you marry me?" It was through the Ampol tournament at the Yarra Yarra golf course that enabled me to get married.'

'Even today with all the modern day equipment … in 1965 I shot 264 for 72 holes and it is still a record today and nobody has come close. You just don't see those records lasting any more. Every year when I see the Australian Open being played I like to see if anybody is going to break that record. When we played at Kooyonga (Adelaide), **Nicklaus** and I were playing together and the first day I shoot 62 and he shoots 66. So we are going back to the hotel in Adelaide and he says, "How the hell can I shoot 66 and be four shots back? Tomorrow I am going to kick your little South African butt!" The next day I shoot 70 and Nicklaus shoots 63. Now he has a total of 129 and I've got a total of 132. Now 132 is an average of 66. So I said to him, on the second day, going back to the hotel, "How the hell can I have an average of 66 for the first two days and be three behind you?" I said, "I am going to get your big Yankie ass tomorrow!" The next day I am out and we didn't have all these electrical scoreboards and Nicklaus sends his caddie up to me on the tenth hole and asks, "Mister Nicklaus wants to know how you are doing after ten holes." I said, "I am ten under." He says, "No, not for the tournament – for the ten holes." I said, "Can't you hear me, mate? I'm ten under." So he runs back and he tells Nicklaus and Nicklaus shouts across, "You are lying! You are trying to put me off." I shot another 62 and I went on to win the tournament. I had a friend from South Africa who used to love to travel and watch golf. I can see him sitting on a seat stick there just shaking his head. I can see him just shaking his head. It was hard to believe. Two 62s I shot in the same tournament. But now the bad news. I am in the airport and I am dressed in a pair of white pants and a yellow shirt with all these multicolours on. This little old lady comes up to me and she says, "Excuse me, sir, I see you're the bus driver. Where

do I get my ticket to go downtown?" I gave her my medal and said, "Listen, lady, I just won your National Open, your National Championship which was a great honour. Here is the medal." We searched for her for years to get the medal back for my museum.'

Scorecard courtesy of Golf Australia: Gary Players first round in 1965. In his third round he did not have a 5 on the card. Newspaper clipping from Black Knight International archives. Right: News Ltd NP113278 October 30th 1965 spectators watch Gary Player competing in the Australian Open Golf Tournament at Kooyonga Golf Club in Adelaide South Australia.

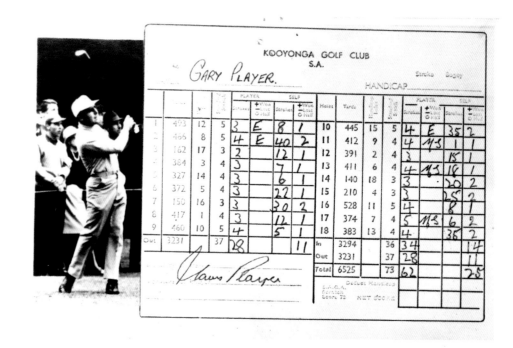

The Black Knight

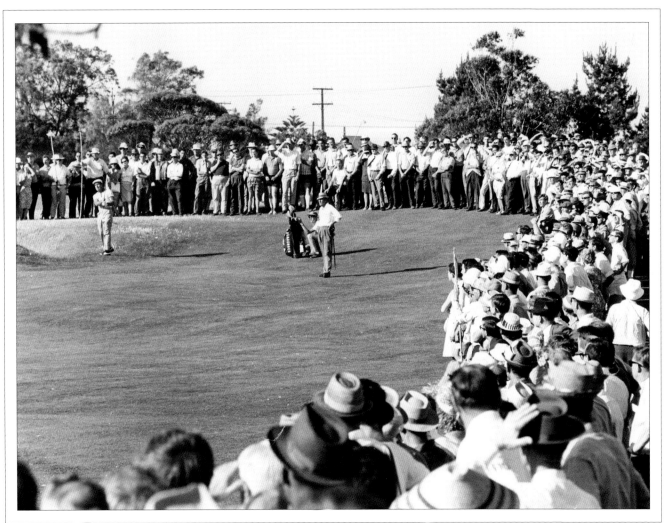

WORDS WITH MR PLAYER

'After the major championships, I always thought the Australian Open was the most important tournament that I won. For me. Maybe I was influenced by my great love for Australia – the people were unbelievable to me. They used to call me "Gazza". I was there with the plumbers, the gardeners and the businessmen. They treated me like a king in Oz.'

'When we played at the Australian in Sydney, Mr Kerry Packer was very helpful to me. These people were demonstrating (apartheid) against me, charging me on the greens, writing slogans on the greens and they had a police van driving down the middle of every fairway with me. These protestors would jump out of the galleries and start screaming at me and the cops would grab them and put them in the van.'

'One of the sad things in my life is that I spent years travelling throughout Australia and I have designed nearly 300 golf courses around the world and never built a course in Australia. I would love to come back to Australia and build a golf course, to be able to get the juniors in that town to come along with me and be part of building that golf course and, you know, visit their schools and teach them how to play golf because I could really help them a lot.'

'You might have two drivers, one that draws it and one that fades it and you can change those according to the golf course you are playing. When I think of the crappy equipment we played with and the condition of the golf courses, it is a miracle the scores we shot. That was one of the treats about going to the Melbourne sandbelt in that era – the golf courses were always in great shape.'

'I played Peter Thomson in the final of the Australian PGA at Huntingdale; it was one of the greatest matches of my career. We were even, one up, even, one down, even, one up, even, the whole way for the whole 36 holes. The toughest Australians I played against were Kel Nagle, Ossie Pickworth, Bruce Crampton, Peter Thomson, Greg Norman and a host of others. But the greatest of all time has got to be Thomson. You've got to go by the record books, and he won five Majors.'

'The harder you work the luckier you get.'

'What god takes away he gives back in another way.'

'As a teenager I thought "If I can become a champion of the world it will be a university degree".'

'To become a champion is how you accept adversity.'

'Instinct is a special gift – you have to learn to trust that instinct.'

'I would have loved to have seen the Americans come to South Africa and play the big tournaments against me on my home turf, let me tell you that.'

'Only your wife and your dog know about second.'

'Exercise for the body is like reading for the mind.'

'Arnold Palmer fell out of bed with charisma.'

'Standing over a three foot putt … sometimes, under pressure, the hole looks the size of a Bayer aspirin.'

photo courtesy of Golf Australia archives Gary Player with Stonehaven Cup in 1963 at Royal Melbourne.

Stonehaven Cup

Jack Nicklaus

By the mid 1970s the sporting contracts of superstars Jack Nicklaus, Arnold Palmer and Gary Player had changed and no longer included annual trips to Australia. **Appearance money** began a new and ugly chapter that continues to this day. One school of thought is that the only way a world-class golfer will come and play in Australia is if they are paid to play; the other school of thought is that if you have a premier tournament with sufficient prizemoney and status the players will come, like they do the British Open.

In 1976 Australian media mogul/billionaire **Kerry Packer**, a keen golfer, stepped in and raised the prizemoney for the Australian Open from $35,000 to $165, 000. He also spent $800,000 on the layout of the **Australian Golf Club** and employed none other than Jack Nicklaus to make the changes. Part of the deal was that the Australian Golf Club (Packer's home course) would become the home of the tournament. For the first time in the championship's 70-year history it was to be played at the same course in successive years 1975–1979. Jack Nicklaus was the headline act and won the title three of the four years that Kerry Packer was funding a pipedream at the Australian Golf Club.

Jack Nicklaus and his design team turned the Australian Golf Club into one of the toughest tests of golf in Australia. With Kerry Packer providing the finances he invited and paid for many of the international stars to play the tournament. Packer had the television coverage beaming into living rooms all over the world and was soon to revolutionise World Series Cricket. The list of players and champions of that era is testament to Packer's vision. It worked. Money talks. The vision to host the championship exclusively at the Australian Golf Club in Sydney was Kerry Packer's only fundamental error – Australian golf is known for the sandbelt in Melbourne. Packer's vision was soon clouded by the officials of the Australian Golf Union who traditionally ran the tournament, as they demanded the Australian Open return to Melbourne in 1979. Rumour has it that the AGU was in charge of the car parking at the Australian and they put the price up by a dollar and tried to keep the money – when Kerry Packer found out about 'the dollar' he said something like, 'No-one tries to make a dollar out of Kerry Packer'. That was the end of Kerry Packer's association with the Australian Open and the championship has never recovered to be a truly international event.

Jack Newton: *'Ah look, that whole Packer affair … I played a practice round with Jack Nicklaus and I talked to him about appearance money and all the rest of it. At that time the Australian Open was probably the equivalent of the third or fourth biggest tournament in America. Kerry Packer was putting up the dough. Jack said he thought the Australian Open should be able to stand up on its own two feet as one of the biggest tournaments in the world, one that the best players in the world want to win. Jack*

actually went back after that practice round and gave his appearance money back saying he wanted it added to the prize money. Tournament director Tony Charlton said, "You can't do that." Jack said, "I'm doing it and I want it to go into the prizemoney pool." And so it was …'

'It was the only other time in my life when the Australian Dollar was beyond parity. Packer had the right idea – he paid them all the same money, I think it was $8000 or $10,000 if they brought their wives and the players paid their own expenses. I remember one year he had 19 of the top 20 Yanks here, with Jack's help. Packer would look after the players, take them up to North Queensland fishing on his boat. He had the right idea.'

'Everything was going well, but there was this sniping behind the scenes where the AGU wanted to flex their muscles, as they liked to do in those days. So, they had a "bit of a blue" about gate money (the money taken for entry) and Packer just told them to stick it and that was the end of it. The standard answer is "oh, it's only $2500 we were talking about", but they just don't play the game the right way. Rich cats like that you have to sort of smoodge to them a bit and go their way and it was just a little thing like the gate money that was the straw that broke the camel's back. We are probably still paying the price for that. You can't afford to lose people like that out of the game. Packer started to revolutionise the television coverage and to this day Seven is still at the forefront of television golf and has been, through Graham Rowlands who is without peer as far as producing golf tournaments is concerned.'

'Quite frankly you cannot have an amateur body trying to run a major event. Sure, they might be good at organising an Australian amateur or a NSW amateur, but why not let people who run major events week in, week out take care of our big golf events?'

Norman Von Nida: *'The worst thing to ever happen to Australian golf … I think the AGU did themselves a dis-service when they got offside with Kerry Packer in regards to the Australian Open. The way Kerry had the tournament run, by bringing out players like Jack Nicklaus, Lee Trevino and the best players in the world and also put up the money for the tournament and televise every hole … with a camera on every hole it was the best televised tournament in the world. It also had the best television commentary in the world. For the AGU to get offside with somebody who was so involved and interested in promoting Australia, through the game of golf and the way he did it … was just absolutely unreal.'*

Above: The Australian Open 1908 won by Tasmanian Clyde Pearce.

Left & bottom: courtesy of Golf Australia's archives.

Below: The Australian Golf Club watercolour by Robert A Wade.

CAIRNS GAME FISHING CLUB

ANGLER	J NICKLAUS
FISH	BLACK MARLIN
WEIGHT	616 KG 1358 lb
TACKLE	130 lb
LAUNCH	OSPREY
DATE	11-11-78

(BNE1) BRISBANE, Australia, Nov.13--BIGGEST CATCH OF THE SEASON--Pro gol[f]
Jack Nicklaus shows off a black marlin weighing 1,358 lbs. that he cau[ght]
recently after a six-hour battle that ran into the night off Cairns, N[orth]
Queensland. The fish is the biggest caught this season and the fourth
biggest on record in the area.(AP Laserphoto)(gs21325mbr) 1978

CAIRNS GAME FISHING CLUB

P.O. BOX 674, CAIRNS, Q. 4870   743

CAPTURE AND WEIGHT RECORDING CERTIFICATE

Angler J NICKLAUS   Species BLACK MARLIN   Nett Weight 616 KG p
Address 11387 Cold Harbour Rd N'Palm Beach Florida   Weighed at CAIRNS
Where Caught AGIN COURTS I   Date Caught 11-11-78   Time 16.05 hrs.
Length overall 15' 6"   Length to crotch 12' 6"   Girth 7'
Line class 130 lb   Type of Line MONO K   Name of Craft OSPREY
Length of double   Length of trace   Number of hooks
Length of rod tip   ft.   ins.   Butt length   ft.
Witness of capture Bernard Tyler   Address
Witness of weighting   Address
Weightmaster's signature Joe Ball   Address
DECLARATION : I, the undersigned, hereby declare that the above named fish was brought to gaff by [me]
in accordance with the rules of the G.F.A.A., and my club, and that the above infor-
mation and statements are true.

Signature of angler

Witnessed by me this   day of   19

Question: Australian Open and the 'golden era' of golf in Australia. Australia used to attract the best golfers in the world – today the tournament schedule really struggles to compete. Does it make you sad to see the Australian Open fading from the International radar and what can the golfing bodies do about it?

Jack Nicklaus: I think they might have a difficult time trying to bring the event back to the status as the fifth Major, simply because of the amount of money that's being offered elsewhere, the strength of the European Tour and, to a smaller degree, because of the location of the country and the distances needed to travel. The Australian Open is still a very strong tournament, and considered one of the prized tournaments to win in the world, as far as I'm concerned. I think Kerry Packer had a great deal to do with helping elevate that event, too.

Bob Shearer: 'I think it is a little sad that they don't cop the players, but that is what has happened now – they play the whole year and make millions of bloody dollars. When they were coming to the Australian Open they were paid to come here and they got first class airfares and accommodation. These days it is hard to get our blokes, the Australians, to come and play.'

Frank Phillips: 'It does make me sad actually. It used to be known as the fifth Major. Paying players to come out and play, to me ... our home grown players should come home and play in it for nothing, but they don't. I think that's wrong. They learn their golf out here – they should put something back into the game that they have made their livelihood out of. I don't think they can recover it. They paid **Tiger Woods** something like 2 million dollars to turn up and unless they pay those top players they are not going to come out to Australia to play. In the old days, **Player**, **Palmer** and **Nicklaus** would come out here and promote Slazengers golf clubs and it would all make sense.'

'It was great, we used to have **Palmer**, **Player**, **Nicklaus** and all those players that used to come out and play every year, just about. It was unbelievable. They were the three best players in the world and we had them out here in Australia. We learnt a lot from playing with them, but more importantly I feel like I became firm friends with Arnold and Jack.'

Bruce Crampton: 'No, to the contrary, it is usually televised over here in the United States on the Golf Channel. Because the major portion of the US golf season is over by November/December it gets good coverage. The "Aussie Open" is well thought of in this country. Last year when it was played just before the President Cup Matches in Melbourne, it received even more attention.'

'The thing to remember is that there is so much money to play for over here, it has got to be made attractive for the top name players to go overseas to play. For instance **Rory McIlroy** and **Tiger Woods** recently played that exhibition match in China – I read they both received $3 million to play that round of golf. I remember **Jack Nicklaus** was guaranteed $400,000 one year to play the Australian Open at the Australian Golf Club plus he was reimbursed for the fuel costs of his own private jet. I can tell you that when I came back to play the Wills Masters in Australia it didn't make economic sense for me to pay my own expenses to do so.'

Bruce Devlin: 'It is sad to see the Australian Open off the radar screen but the fact that the European and Asian tours have grown so lucrative and the Australian Tour hasn't really grown much, I doubt that it will ever be what it was. Heavy financial sponsorship would help but that is going on everywhere else in the world.'

David Graham: 'Not much. Unfortunately it is an economic issue. Golf, in Australia, ever since I started playing has had a terrible issue with appearance fees, cost of operation and needing international star power. The cost of sponsoring now is in the tens of millions of dollars and it is very difficult to find Australian corporations that can justify that kind of budget. It is not just the prizemoney, it is the television, the tents, the spectator amenities … across the board it is just a very expensive thing to pull together.'

'Australia now competes with every other country in the world: Korea, Dubai, the Asian Tour, the strength of the European Tour, the Japanese tour – it is just very difficult and at that time of the year (December) it is hard to get people to play. It is tough to even re-schedule any more because there are so many tournaments all over the world that it is tough to find the perfect date ... and then you have the dreaded appearance fee issue, which has just been ongoing for fifty years. Today these top players want millions to show up and I don't think the sponsors want to spend that kind of money. When you have players that want half-a-million and million-dollar appearance fees and you want dozens of players, that is just not going to work. Even if they are playing for ten million in prizemoney it is not going to make a top player pay his own expenses to come and play the Australian Open. It doesn't matter what the prizemoney is.'

'The PGA in Australia doesn't have a lot of strength mainly because it doesn't have a lot of the top players. It can't be too dogmatic because it doesn't have the players. The sponsors can't justify being involved unless he has players, you know, like myself, who occasionally shoot four bad rounds but still get to go to the press tent and produce a lot of ink. I can get more ink for a sponsor by playing badly than some young player can by playing the best golf of his career. That's why we are going to have to continue importing players.'

'I can remember when people were furious that **Gary Player** was getting $20,000 to come and play in the Australian Open or **Jack Nicklaus** getting $20,000 when the purse was $20,000. I mean, people were ugly, people were rude and so spiteful about those players coming. You know, **Greg Norman** went through the same thing. I went through the same thing. Even today when they pay appearance fees, there is a segment that are just complainers. These players today are pretty independent these days and you have to make a pretty lucrative offer for them to even think about putting it on their schedule. I don't know how the Australian Open can compete. Players are becoming so affluent so quickly that I don't know how the Australian Open will be able to retain its status as it once was … I think it would be virtually impossible.'

Kel Nagle: 'It was always nice to win your own national tournament. But our prizemoney hasn't increased like it has in America or Britain. We find it hard to get the sponsors because the players are all away. The top players have been playing so much during the year that they don't really want to play at the end of the year, they want to have a bit of a holiday. Unfortunately, where Australia is situated in world, down under, it is a long way to travel and half the time they can't get the best players to come unless they pay them. It makes it difficult for the sponsors.'

Peter Thomson: 'I used to play in the Japan Open each year and they had a policy that they would never pay anybody to simply turn up. It was not dignified. It was against all the principles of fair go. So I thought, if Japan can do this, so can Australia. We didn't get our way …'

Peter Toogood: 'Yes, it is sad. In the '50s and '60s Australian amateurs and pros had the opportunity to play in competition with or at least to observe many of the world's best touring pros, e.g. **Bobby Locke**, **Gary Player**, **Roberto de Vincenzo**, **Jimmy Adams**, **Max Faulkner**, **Dai Rees**. Perhaps with promotional support from a group of business "houses" a mini tour with the Australian Open as the final event could be established with the other events leading up to the grand finale.'

'It was great to witness the 1971 Australian Open at Royal Hobart Golf Club with so many overseas touring pros present, including **Jack Nicklaus** who won.'

Jan Stephenson: 'It has become a reality that the world is smaller, with a world tour, and the electronic era. The money is so lucrative elsewhere. We have always expected our Aussie stars to return for free, yet pay other big names to come Down Under. It is difficult without big business to pay for the superstars. We can watch the best golfers on TV almost every week now in Australia, so it is not such a big deal to see them at the Australian tournaments. It should help that **Adam Scott** won the US Masters. It was a very popular win, and he is a perfect role model for our Juniors.'

Norman Von Nida: 'It's absolutely essential, for the progression of golf in Australia, that players like **Nicklaus** do compete here, so that people in Australia can make a comparative basis on how good we are or how good they are and this is the reason why one must always accept the fact of appearance money and large sums being paid to these really great international stars. I believe it should only be paid to the really great international ones – like **Nicklaus**, **Tom Watson** and **Lee Trevino**.'

Sir Bob Charles: 'By Golden Era I presume you mean the big three – **Nicklaus**, **Palmer** and **Player** – who were paid large sums by equipment companies to play in Australia together with appearance fees and exhibition match fees. We have a similar problem in NZ … the only way to get major players to compete Down Under is to pay huge appearance fees.'

Tom Watson: 'The reason is that there are other tournaments that take the place of the Australian Open: the World Golf Championships, the Presidents Cup and others. The best players in the World are basically required to play a lot more so-called 'major-type' tournaments. If you add the four major tournaments we have, the three or four World Golf Championships, add a Ryder Cup and/or a Presidents Cup and the Players Championship in America – that is nine tournaments right there. A lot of the players only want to play eighteen tournaments a year, so it puts a hamper on the playing schedule of the players. I was always looking forward to playing Royal Melbourne. I had heard some great stories about Royal Melbourne and fortunately for me, I won there.'

Question: Australian Open and the 'golden era' of golf in Australia. Australia used to attract the best golfers in the world – today the tournament schedule really struggles to compete. Does it make you sad to see the Australian Open fading from the International radar and what can the golfing bodies do about it?

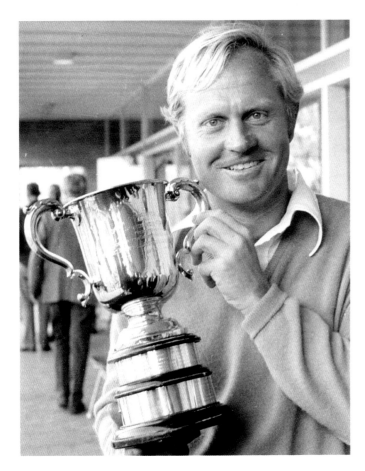

photo: Jack Nicklaus with the Stonehaven Cup 1971, played at Royal Hobart. Courtesy of the Jack Nicklaus museum.

Graham Marsh: 'When I was chairman of the PGA tour in Australia we had 19 tournaments and close to $400,000–$500,000 per tournament in prize money. We were not in control of all the tournaments; we had Daikyo running one of them, Mayne Nickless was running the PGA, Kerry Packer was running the Australian Open and we had Coca Cola. Six or seven of them were around the million-dollar mark and in Australia we were playing for much more money in the '80s than we are today. A large tournament in America at that time was about $1.6 or $1.8 million dollars.'

'What changed the whole dynamic was a contract that the US PGA Tour was able to write with television. This provided a quantum leap in prize money from the $1.5s and $1.6s up to the $3 million and $4 million mark [now the $6 million dollar mark]. With this massive leap in prizemoney everybody else in the world was simply left in the dust.'

'Today look at what is on offer for the average player on the US Tour. Events like the Tournament Players Championship, total purse $9.5 million, US open $8.0 million and the $10 million bonus at the end of the year if you win the Fed Ex Championship. First prize over a $1 million every week and if you run one-hundred on the money rankings you make a minimum of $1 million in prizemoney alone. It is a long hard season and quite sensibly the best players in the world have little appetite for flying down to Australia to play in a million dollar golf tournament late in the year, unless of course they are being paid handsomely. It was a problem back in the '70s; now it is an even bigger problem. How many of these top calibre players can we afford? We have a small economy, and we have a massive number of professional sports. The available

Australian marketing dollars will only go so far. Personally, I just don't see the Australian Open recovering in the short term; we will occasionally draw one superstar if someone has deep pockets and wants to have them here, like a Tiger Woods. The only other reason a player would come down and play is if it is on their bucket list and their wives want to visit and see another part of the world. Apart from that, from a financial point of view and a status point of view it means little to them because it doesn't count for very much any more. It just doesn't count in the same way that is used to count.'

'The only way it could receive a huge shot in the arm would be if we became part of a genuine world tour. The Peter Thomson vision. Realistically I only see that happening is if the US falls on very hard economic times and they have to take tournaments for their players into other countries to keep their tour growing. If there was one or more big tournaments in every major golfing region, including Australia, then the Australian Open could improve.'

'If you have been competing all year in Europe or somewhere else in the world, and you are a top player from Australia, I don't see how many times you can come back at the end of the year and put your heart and soul into competing back home. For many Australians it is no longer their primary source of golf business. A great number, and I truly admire them, do come back and support golf in this country. They could be playing elsewhere for far more lucrative rewards or legitimately resting for the long and arduous season ahead. We are lucky they support our major events and I respect their efforts because they are genuinely putting back into the game.'

Photo: Bruce Devlin 1960 Australian Open at Lake Kurringyup copyright the West Australian.
In the 1960 Australian Open there were 8 amateurs in the top ten, including the winner
Bruce Devlin. Kel Nagle was the best placed pro tied for 4th. Bruce Devlin had 16 top
ten finishes in the major championships.

'What we need in Australia is a truly international golf event.' Peter Thomson

Australia **had** a truly International event in the Australian Open, but the lack of synergy between the governing bodies and administration of golf in Australia has seen the tournament fade from the international radar since Kerry Packer ceased his association in 1979. Since 1979 the energy of the governing bodies and tournament promoters has been dissipated between the Australian Open, Masters and PGA championships with several other events that have been created to try and maintain the Australian 'tour'.

The Australian Masters was founded the same year the Australian Open lost Kerry Packer, 1979. The International Management Group (IMG), a powerhouse in sports management has a vested financial interest in the ongoing operations and success of The Australian Masters. IMG with its proven commercial successes in the past and possessing unmatched leverage with the elite players, as evidenced by securing Tiger Woods to play (and win) 'their tournament' in 2009, looks to continue moving the Australian Masters into the future.

IMG owns the Australian Masters, while the other golfing bodies, Golf Australia and the Australian PGA have a vested financial interest in the success of the Australian Open and the Australian PGA tournaments. There are three entities all pushing in different directions, hoping for the same outcome, a truly international golfing event in Australia.

Aside from Australians, the only truly international stars who have won the **Australian PGA** are **Gary Player** (1957), **Hale Irwin** (1978) and **Seve Ballesteros** (1981).

Unknowingly, the battle for supremacy comes down to the two tournaments that boast the finest list of champions,

the Australian Open and the Australian Masters. Into the future it will be one of these two tournaments that will be known internationally and can attract an international field. For now, however, there seems to be three different million-dollar tournaments in the Australian summer of golf, with all three of them vying for International attention.

The confusion spreads even further when the politics between the two premier golfing states of Victoria and New South Wales enter the fray. Both Victoria and New South Wales boast an extensive golfing resume and sound argument for their lineage as the 'home of golf' in Australia. What is perplexing, however, is that Australia is known internationally for golf in one region, the Melbourne sandbelt. Not only does Australia need its golfing bodies to agree and to focus on their finest tournament, but to have any chance of securing international appeal, Australia also has to manage the political landscape and sporting arm-wrestle between the two major states, New South Wales and Victoria.

The **Australian Open Tennis Tournament** has a home, the Rod Laver Arena, Melbourne. It has the same date every year, January. It is the first 'Major' of the tennis calendar year. The world of tennis casts its eye on Australia every January and it is one of the world's premier tennis events. The success of this tournament has positive ripple effects for the entire game of tennis in Australia.

Geoff Pollard (President of Tennis Australia 1989-2010): 'Virtually all big, successful annual events are held in

the same venue and over the same dates. The Melbourne Cup, the AFL Grand Final, each of the four tennis Grand Slams and the US Masters Golf spring to mind. Cricket learnt this by always scheduling the Boxing Day Test in Melbourne and the New Year Test in Sydney. Only the mighty US Football Super Bowl is an exception. The key reason you stick to the same dates and same city is that it then becomes very much part of the fabric of the city and people plan their activities and holidays around the event ... regardless of who is playing.'

'In the amateur era [1968 and earlier] the Australian Tennis Championships rotated from state to state. Most amateur sports and many quasi-amateur Olympic sports (primarily funded by the National Government) continue in this way today. But when tennis became open to professionals it soon became obvious that Australia would be left behind if it continued this amateur methodology.'

'The first big step forward came when Marlboro agreed to sponsor the Australian Open for five years provided it stayed in Melbourne for those five years. To get support from the other states Marlboro agreed to sponsor the NSW Men's and Women's Opens the week before and the SA Men's and Queensland Women's the week before that.'

Jack Newton: 'When I resigned from the tour as Chairman [2000], I just believed that we needed a body which runs the game and it is a one-stop-shop. Women and men's golf have amalgamated, but I think it needs to go further. I think we need to have probably a commissioner-type idea – not that I am a big fan of all the things America does, but I think we need a commissioner and a board that is represented by amateur golf, professional golf and women's golf. Anything pertaining to golf in Australia, you go to that one-stop site. At the moment we have got the PGA with NSW, Victoria and Queensland, SA and WA – we are just replicating what the amateur bodies have done.'

'NSW, from memory, still represents about 47% of the golfing population in this country, yet small states like Tasmania still get the same vote that NSW and Victoria get. NSW and Victoria equate to something like 75% of the golfers in this country and they get 2 votes and the other 25% gets 5 votes. There are endemic problems.'

'I am suggesting there is a board that sits above all the amateur bodies with representation and all decisions pertaining to golf and policies comes through that board. If you want to ring up about sponsorship you are transferred to the sponsorship department; if you want to ring up about women's golf it goes to that department. Maybe I am dreaming but that is what has got to happen: you cannot have all these different bodies running in different directions.'

History shows us that as soon as the appearance money stopped being paid, the elite golfers ceased competing in Australia, quite simply because it was more financially lucrative to play other tournaments. Golfers do not receive appearance fees to play the four Majors – US Masters, US Open, US PGA and the Open Championship in Britain – and perhaps there was an era where the Australian Open held enough status that it did not need to pay the top players, but that era is over. The Australian Open is one of the oldest Open Championships in world golf but it no longer holds the prestige it once did. The only way the Australian Open is going to get back in the spotlight is with a prize purse that is on par with the World Golf Championship events and other lucrative national Opens.

In 2013, countries with very little golfing heritage at all have international golf events that are attracting the world's best players. The Turkey Open in 2013 has prizemoney of $7 million. Tournaments that Australian pioneers helped to establish like the Hong Kong Open and Singapore Open attract larger prizemoney than the Australian Open.

If Australia is to return to the international spotlight, there needs to be an acceptance that the current model for organising professional events is failing to attract international appeal. Australian golf still seems to be in a state of denial, which means they haven't accepted they have a problem. One solitary person can fix the problem, by speeding past denial, anger and fear and straight into acceptance. Australian golf doesn't have a head-honcho: it has several and it needs one. One person to lead the governing bodies through the 'grieving process' into acceptance and into a bright future for one of the premier sporting countries on Earth. Australia has the history, it has the talent, it has the golf courses and it has the passion. The ingredients are firmly in place; it just needs one chef to put the pie in the oven, an oven that is pre-heated in the Melbourne sandbelt.

Photo: Jack Newton archives 1979 Australian Open champion.

FROM HICKORY TO TITANIUM

WITH PETER THOMSON.

Photo: Getty images. Peter Thomson holes a putt on the 18th green 1953 at St Andrews. Ben Hogan (USA) beat Peter Thomson by four shots with a closing round of 68. 1953 was the only year Hogan played the Open Championship.

PETER THOMSON

This interview transcript is from four interviews with Peter Thomson. Interviews conducted by Andrew Crockett: 29th August 2012 at Thomson Perrett Melbourne; 25th January 2013 phone interview; and 7th May 2013 phone interview. There are some entries from an interview conducted by Marnie Haig Muir via the National Library Oral History and Folklore Collection. Bib ID 4348366 recorded 4 March 2008 in Melbourne, Victoria.

Peter Thomson is Australia's most successful male golfer, winning the Open Championship five times. As a teenager he dropped his handicap from 24 to scratch in one year and burst onto the International golf radar with strong showings in his first three Open Championships finishing 6th, 2nd and 2nd before finally winning his first in 1954 (at the age of 24 - he was winner four times and second three times by the age of 28). Thomson pretty well owned the Claret Jug in the 1950s and went on to win over one hundred professional tournaments all over the world including the Open Championships of Italy, Spain, Germany, Hong Kong, India, The Philippines and New Zealand. He won the NZ Open nine times. Thomson won tournaments in America, Japan, Canada, New Zealand, Britain and Australia. Only his good friend Kel Nagle has more professional wins on Australian soil, with 61 victories to Thomson's 34. Peter Thomson and Kel Nagle won the Canada Cup (now called the World Cup) twice (1954 & 1959) with the victory in 1959 at Royal Melbourne being one of Thomson's finest performances in front of an ever-appreciative home crowd. Thomson shot rounds of 67-69-68-71 to lead the individual scoring for what was then known as a team event.

Peter Thomson played the Open Championship every year that he was fit and able, with an outstanding record that is second to none. He never played in the US PGA tournament. Thomson played the US Open five times – tied 4th his best finish in 1956. He was frequently invited to the US Masters, but only played seven times with his best finish 5th in 1957.

In 1985 Thomson won nine times in one season on the USA Champions tour (9 out of 15 events played to earn US$1.24 million), a tour record. He was President of the Australian PGA from 1962 to 1994 and was the non-playing captain of the victorious International team of the 1998 Presidents Cup. Throughout his career he regularly wrote a column for the Melbourne Age newspaper and other golfing publications and is well respected for his writing ability. Peter Thomson has an immeasurable legacy in world golf, choosing to help grow the game in Australia, Asia and the Middle-East rather than seeking the obvious financial rewards of American pro golf. He has helped to design and re-model hundreds of golf courses in dozens of countries and continues to aid the development of golf around the world.

PETER THOMSON

Your first set of golf clubs.

It is one of those things lost in the midst of time, I can't remember my first clubs, but they were hand me down from someone in the family and made with hickory shaft.

How many clubs would have been in a set in that era?

Well, I don't know if it was a set, but it was the maximum permitted under the rules, of fourteen. So, it was up towards fourteen but not completely. For instance, the lofted clubs ended at number eight. There weren't any such things as 9-irons or wedges. Wedges came in the 1950s.

So the first time you started swinging a golf club you were how old?

Oh, I would have been 13 or 14 and it was the war years between 1942 and 1946 that I started to play.

Royal Park was your first golf club. What was it like on a weekend up at Royal Park in the 1940s?

My first ventures onto the golf course I snuck out onto the course without paying. Fortunately for me, those that saw me from afar recognised that there was a pretty talented kid here playing on our Royal Park course. One of my neighbours spoke to my father about it, that this kid ought to pursue the game of golf because he is going to be good at it. So I suppose things were happening that I had no idea about. Before I got to be playing Saturday competitions I was really just playing after school: 6 holes, perhaps 4 holes depending on the light and the weather. So, I sort of crept up on it.

I guess if the members at Royal Park saw you were hitting it all over the place they would have told you to rack off?

I must have fascinated somebody because, really, no kids of my age played golf. None. It wasn't a young man's game. In fact the golfers were all well-aged people.

So you were obviously very happy with your own company, even as a child?

I wasn't just playing golf, I was playing cricket and football as well. In fact I was neglecting my studies and should have been more of a bookworm, but in later life I am catching up.

So what was a golf ball like then in the 1940s?

There were various golf balls, but I had to find them. During the War golf balls were not made … they were a very precious commodity … because rubber was being used for manufacturing purposes. So, in effect I had to find a golf ball before I could play. Golf balls came in different makes and the covers were very different in some cases. I remember the Bramble ball: instead of having a depression/dimple it had a protrusion in the other direction. That was one of the balls that came my way, which I used, but it wasn't really satisfactory: it was very soft. With the moulded ball, the Haskell ball changed golf; it actually brought the cost down, which was its biggest contribution. Leather balls were very expensive.

The 1940s era with the golf ball you were using: can you remember how many dimples they had?

No, I can't remember the number. Dimples were small, round and there was space between the dimples. I would suspect that the space would have been 50% of the cover. Nobody in the 1940s/50s/60s thought of covering the entire cover with dimples, which is the case now. This is where the control of the ball has been lost. We should never have permitted a fully totally dimpled golf ball. Of course it is made possible by turning the dimples into hexagons and octagons. That is why the modern ball goes through the wind so easily. It is not blown across by a crosswind. That is its worst feature, it has taken out that skill that was required to handle a wind.

I imagine if you found a golf ball you would treasure it and play many holes with it.

Well, I could certainly play one round with one golf ball and I might have stretched that to two or three rounds until it really wore out and the paint would come off, or I might give it a few cuts with a sharp edged 8 iron and have to throw it away.

So, the Saturday competition in that era (1940s): would it always be stroke play?

Oh, no. They had a regular mixture. There was a monthly medal, for instance, which was a stroke play event but stroke play is not that popular in club life. A lot of people I know won't go to the club on a stroke-play day because they can't handle it for one reason and they just don't like it for another. So Stableford and against par was played most often. I think once a month there would be a four-ball-best-ball event, where you would play with a partner. Through the year there was the club championships for the individuals and the pairs/foursomes. So it was a mixture of events that one could play in on Saturdays. It hasn't changed that much over the years. It hasn't changed at all.

As a junior were you allowed in the clubhouse?

Yes, but I didn't really want to be in the clubhouse: I wanted to be out playing. So I wasn't in the clubhouse much. I must confess that my very first shot off the first tee, as a member, playing in a four-ball-best-ball with a partner, an elderly man … the first ball I hit went out of bounds onto the railway line. So, it wasn't a very good start, was it?

Were you a bit nervous?

I think so.

I am trying to imagine what Melbourne was like in the late 1940s.
It was a great place, I will tell you that now. I don't think it has got better. [Laughs] The Royal Park, for example, was full of sporting arenas and the 9-hole golf course was one. But there were plenty of cricket pitches and football posts and other sports to play. Also, a lot of the territory was left as nature. The girls of our age used to make daisy chains out of the flowers that grew in the rough. We used to make our own kites and fly the kites in the wind with a sixpenny ball of string.

I am imagining plenty of trams and lovely old cars.
Of course. Public transport was vital and used by my family. We didn't use a car. I was the first member of the family to own a motorcar. So it was trams, trains and buses.

Can you remember the era where amateur golf received more media attention and kudos than professional golf and can you think of a point on the timeline where that balance shifted?
The 1940s here in Melbourne; the best golf was played by the amateur players. That was until Ossie Pickworth, who was a club pro in Sydney, transferred to Royal Melbourne. Prior to that the amateurs played the best golf. They were scratch golfers and genuine ones and they led the field in golf in Melbourne. This changed, I guess, when I changed status which was in 1949 where I suppose I started to play the best golf in Melbourne, as a professional.

Can you remember how many scorecards you had to hand in to get your first handicap?
No, I can't remember how many. I think one was enough. Actually now that you bring it up, I can recall there was in every club an officer of the club, a member of the club

who was the official handicapper. It was his discretion what handicap you had. For instance, if you had a good round and you were under the par, lower than the par, he would probably clip a stroke off your handicap after he had examined your scorecard, because that was his duty.

Your first handicap was?
It was 24. I would have been 14. When I was 14 I could drive the ball 220 yards if I really caught it. The second hole at Royal Park was 220 yards long, par 4. Although it didn't have a par in those days either: it was called 'standard scratch score'. I could drive the ball onto the green occasionally. Since then I have been to the top of Mt Everest and now I am on the slippery slope down the other side and I can see, just ahead of me, my best drive will be 220 yards and my handicap will be 24. That's the life of a golfer.

I was struck by the fact that you are virtually self-taught. That would be pretty rare today, wouldn't it?
Unfortunately that's true. I think children are best left untaught like I was because there is a requirement to ... to find out things for yourself rather than being told what to do. And this ... the end result of that is that you become totally self reliant, which is the essential trait you've got to have to win things. When you're out playing a golf championship there is really no one [who] can help you. So you've got to rely on our own experience ... and the confidence you've probably built up doing it your own way. I keep preaching this but nobody, I think, listens. They all go for coaches. You know it's perfectly ridiculous ... it is even the best player in the world at this moment is ... has got a coach he drags along with him. And I wonder well why doesn't he ... he should be coaching the other guy if he's that good.

Did you ever have a swing coach?
No, I didn't. I don't know anyone that did. Coaches didn't come into the picture until there was money it for the people who didn't play so well.

So Ben Hogan wouldn't have had a swing coach?
No. Not at all. That is preposterous.

'I've always admired the way he's been able to play golf. When he came over to the American Senior Tour he just ran the tables then said 'that's enough. I'll just go back to Australia and St Andrews and enjoy the rest of my life.'
Tom Watson

Photo: Sir Bob Charles, Gary Player, Arnold Palmer, Peter Thomson and Kel Nagle at the 1987 Senior British Open at Turnberry via John W Fischer III archives.

watercolour art by Robert A. Wade of Peter Thomson's home course Victoria Golf Club, the 11th hole.

Can you tell me more about Standard Scratch Score (SSS)?

When I first went to play at Royal Melbourne on the West Course, the 'standard scratch score' was 75. Huntingdale was 77. NSW, for some reason, had adopted the 'par' figure; I don't know whether it was from the United States or from Britain but somebody got the idea of parring holes in that manner and they dumped the 'SSS' and took up 'par'.

Am I correct in saying that you went from a 14-year-old playing off 24 to a 15-year-old playing off scratch?

Yes. I kept winning everything and eventually won the club championships. A group of the members took me to Victoria Golf Club to play there. It was a big strong course for me and I quickly found I needed more strokes than scratch. [Laughs] It took me another year, I think, to get down to scratch at Victoria Golf Club. I played in the 1947 Pennant team at Victoria Golf Club; there were 7 players in the representative team and I played number 7. My handicap at that time was scratch, but the people above me, at that time, on the team were all plus handicaps.

Victoria Golf Club: how did you get to join?

Victoria Golf Club right after the war was pursuing a policy of actually admitting lots and lots of people who were otherwise or had been ineligible. Now, for instance, Catholics were admitted.

What was your first impression of Royal Melbourne?

The greens. None of them were flat. They were all tilted one way or another and to this very day that is its characteristic.

Then came the job at Spalding …

By 1948 I had left school and was employed by Spalding, making golf balls out at the factory at Sunshine, Melbourne. So I would play on the Saturday. Through the summer and early Autumn the clubs had 'open days' and I had a run where I won the Victoria Closed Championship (they had a closed and 'open' championship: the closed one was for Victorians only) at Victoria Golf Club in 36 holes. The next week I played at Croydon Golf Club and I

shot a 64. The next week I played at Northern Golf Club in an 'open invitation' day and I had a 63. Then I played a four-ball tournament at Huntingdale, in the company of Barry West (who was off scratch) and we returned a card of ten up, or ten under. At the end of that run was the Victorian Amateur Championships and I played at Woodlands Golf Club and I won that in the final from Doug Bachli, my clubmate at Victoria Golf Club.

Doug Bachli was obviously an influence on your early career.

I think everyone was an influence by that stage. I often say, in regards to whom was an influence, that everyone I ever played with was an influence whether they were a good or bad player. If you see someone playing with an absurd action, you are inclined to tuck it away and say 'I will NOT do that'. So, you are getting a lesson. I never won the Victoria Golf Club Championship. I finished runner-up to Doug Bachli. I won the Victorian Amateur Championship, but not the club championship; he was too good.

So none of the older golfers tried to take you under their wing and tell you the right and wrong way to swing the club?

I think some might have made suggestions but I was pretty hard to dissuade from my own methods.

If you got a set of clubs off the factory room floor from a manufacturer, would you then spend time modifying each club to your own requirements?

Yes. Early in the piece there were ways of adding some lead. You took the plate off the bottom of the wood, drilled a hole in the wood and you had your little Bunsen burner and when the lead was liquid you would pour it into the head to increase the headweight. Then put the plate back on, let it cool down a bit and go and have a hit with it and see how it feels. A heavier head gives you more whip in the shaft. That was the way we manipulated our driving clubs, particularly.

Was experimenting with putting techniques as prolific in your era as it is today?

Well, I was. I don't know about other people, but I went through dozens of putters looking for the magic wand. I never found it.

Kel Nagle found one, didn't he?

He did. [Laughs] And he has still got it.

Can you remember your first trip outside of Australia to play golf and how did that come about?

It was New Zealand. We had a visit from 4 NZ Amateur champions. The man who was the secretary of the Australian Golf Union was a New Zealander. He had two jobs: one was running the Australian golf Union; and the other was the manager of Commonwealth Golf Club. He married a lady from Royal Melbourne actually. [Laughs] He had organised a match between Australia and New Zealand. There were four very good players from NZ and four Australians lined up against them. I wasn't one of the four Australians. I was a reserve or emergency player. Now, I played a game with the travelling manager of the Kiwi team, George Roberts, at Kingston Heath. He must have been impressed because by August I had an invitation to go and play a tournament there called the 'Wiseman'.

Right after the Victorian Amateur championship (April 1949) I turned professional, so by August I was looking for something to do other than play against Von Nida in exhibition matches. My turning pro was because of the influence of Norman Von Nida and the sheer glamour of it. I thought 'well, if I can play golf I won't have to work'. There were not enough tournaments to sustain a professional player: he would either have to teach golf or exhibit himself playing on all sorts of courses that would have him.

I accepted the invitation and went to Auckland (NZ) in a flying boat which took nine hours. I eventually got to Hamilton on the North Island, where the event took place and I won it. They invited me back the following year in September to play the NZ Open Championship. I accepted that offer and I won that tournament as well.

FROM HICKORY TO TITANIUM
WITH PETER THOMSON

By the early 50s you were heading to Britain, but you also played some exhibition matches in Asia and South Africa.
I went to Manila to play in the Philippines Open in the early 50s and from there, at the invitation of Bobby Locke, I went to South Africa, where he had arranged some exhibition matches. I was Australian Champion by then and he was South African Champion, of course, and British Champion. We played 60 odd times head-to-head at various golf clubs in South Africa. It earned me a lot of money, enabled me to get married and helped my future. I was now a showman, like Bobby Locke was. *[Laughs]*

The trip to Manila: was that aided by Bobby Locke too?
No, that was Norman Von Nida. He had friends in Manila and had told them 'you must get Thomson to come and play'. Which I did and I finished about fourth, I didn't win it. Some Americans came also and they took the top prizes.

What was a young Melburnian's first impression of somewhere like Manila as a young man?
Oh, I was really carried away. It really was a foreign place. It was a bit of a mess really. Manila had a post during the war, of course. It was really foreign.

You took to the travel quite well though, didn't you?
Yes, I did. I went from Manila to Hong Kong and had a look around Hong Kong, which was Chinese of course. From there I went via Pakistan Airlines to Nairobi, via Karachi. From Nairobi down to Johannesburg was another 4- or 5-hour trip. I was met at the airport and away we went.

What was the aeroplane like that you flew to Manila in?
A piston engine. It was a four-engine Lockheed carrying about 50 passengers maximum. All in one cabin. No class distinctions.

Was that the first time you met Bobby Locke?
No. He came to visit Australia, sponsored by Slazenger. Slazenger were a sporting goods company who made a set of golf clubs with his name on it. A match was arranged at Victoria Golf Club with Von Nida, Locke, Ossie Pickworth and me as the fourth. It was after that match that Bobby Locke invited me to come and play in South Africa. We played 63 rounds of exhibition golf in nine weeks. We did pretty well out of it. In fact, the money I earned playing golf against him in South Africa set me off for my whole life.

What was your first impression of Bobby Locke?
Well, I was really taken away with him. He was the big name! I had accepted that he was the world's best player. He had won several times the year before in the United States, even though there were the problems with him playing there, but he finally told them to stick it and he went on and dominated in Britain. To be able to befriend and play these matches and he was giving me money ... not only was this man a great man he was magnanimous as well. I not only played against him and tried to beat him, but I learnt so much from watching him ... watching him beat me. I kept trying hard to beat him, which was the very wrong thing to do. Watching him stay relaxed and beat me instead of the other way around. We had another just two years later and by that time I had learned a few tricks and I was the winner in those matches.

Did you learn much from Bobby Locke about the professionalism in golf? How to travel well and be well presented?
Yes. For instance he always wore white shoes. One day I asked him where he got them from and he said he had them made in Britain. I said 'What's with the white'? He replied, 'You can wear any colour slacks with white shoes, but if you have black shoes you can only wear black slacks.' I thought that made a lot of sense: we travel with a heavy golf bag and you don't want to make it unnecessarily heavy by having a black pair and white pair and a brown pair. They do now, but we didn't in those days.

I am trying to work out where that moment was when the young Peter Thomson who had Bobby Locke, in his mind, as the best player in the world ... then over a course of time you started to beat Bobby Locke and I imagine naturally you would have replaced Bobby Locke with yourself as the best player in your mind.
Eventually I did work out how to beat him. Its wasn't true but I convinced myself that it was. I was arrogant enough to think whatever he can win I can win. In 1952 at Royal Lytham and St Annes I finished second in the Open to him! I nearly won it. In fact, Norman Von Nida yelled to the media that I had won it. There was a new rule brought in that year about slow play and Von Nida was yelling that 'his young Australian friend should really be the winner because Locke had contravened the rules'.

It must have been nice to have Von Nida helping you, pushing you to come with him to England, Bobby Locke taking to around South Africa …
Oh, it was. I was spoilt and didn't have to worry about money.

Photo: Getty images. The Open 1957 at St Andrews. Bobby Locke won beating Thomson by 3 shots and effectively stopping Thomson winning five in succession. A familiar sight at the Open Championship in the 1950s was the Claret jug being held by these two champion golfers. Between 1949 and 1958 Bobby Locke and Peter Thomson won The Open Championship 8 times. The only other golfers to hold the Claret Jug in this time were Max Faulkner OBE in 1951 and Ben Hogan (USA) in 1953.

'You could blow a whistle when Thomson was playing and it wouldn't affect him.'
Norman Von Nida

Photo: During a practice round at the swilken burn, first hole, St Andrews. The other golfer is South African Harold Henning. The photographer 4th from right is local named Cowie.

Can you tell me about your first flight from Australia to England in 1951? Did you fly Melbourne to Darwin to begin the journey?

Yes, Melbourne to Darwin, then a couple of hours to Singapore where we all stayed in Raffles Hotel. The one crew took us all the way to London. They had to have a rest, so it was first night in Singapore in Raffles, second night in Karachi in a hotel called 'Speedbird House'. By the third day we were hopeful of reaching Britain, but it often didn't happen and we would get stuck in Beirut or Cairo and have to wait for an engine to be flown in from somewhere.

On my very first trip to Britain, Norman Von Nida had arranged for us to play in Cairo and we played the Egyptian Matchplay Championship. Von Nida played Hassenian, a black Sudanese man, in the final.

So you touched down in Heathrow full of anticipation, I imagine. Where was the first stop?

From Cairo we went to London and then to Sunningdale where Von Nida had made his headquarters in England. Von Nida had met some wealthy friends and we were staying in a mansion. George Elliott was the name of the fellow we stayed with. He had every set of golf clubs known to man: Spalding, Wilson, Dunlop, John Letters, Ben Sayers. We played practice rounds every day; it was wonderful – I loved the courses. Interestingly enough this was my first trip to Britain (1951) and I didn't get to St Andrews until 1954. There was no event to draw me to St Andrews, but there was in 1954 – the British Matchplay Championship. [Peter Thomson won his first of 4 British matchplay championships in 1954; he beat John Fallon in the final at St Andrews.]

What was you first impression of England like, compared to where you grew up, Melbourne?

Oh, it was very much like Melbourne. Frankly. Melbourne was a British city filled with British emigrants, like my family. It had been so since 1788.

So you felt very comfortable straight away in England?

Yes. It was like home.

Where was the British Open played in 1951?

At Royal Portrush, although it wasn't 'Royal' in those days; it was just Portrush. But I finished in 6th place … so that was just ordinary.

Was Portrush in 1951 different to anything you had seen before?

Well, it was more difficult than anything in Australia at the time.

Even Royal Melbourne?

Even Royal Melbourne, yes.

So would you say that was your first experience of true links golf?

Yes.

Am I correct in thinking it was later at St Andrews that you really got lit up on links golf?

There is not a lot of distinction between heathland golf and seaside golf. Sunningdale you would call a heathland. The first thing you learn about playing in Britain is the hard ground. The ball bounces. After you hit the ball through the air, it lands and it bounces and it is the bounce that you have to prepare for, that you have to guess in order to arrive at the proximity of your target which is the green and the flag. You have to figure out where to drop your flight ball, then allow for the run at the end of it. I got onto that pretty early. I played all over Britain, Yorkshire, Wales and a lot on the West coast and I learned that there wasn't any difference on the heathland courses and the seaside ones. It was the same task you had as far as judging distance – from usually lousy lies, by the way. The turf that they play from nowadays bears no resemblance to what we played on in the 1950s.

The ball was soft; there wasn't a click when you hit it. It was hard to get a feel, for long putts especially. We used to three putt frequently because of that. The turf wasn't helpful. It was too bare, or dry, you would get little lush patches in the bottom of swales and all sorts of unfavourable lies. There was a special skill you had to find in how to handle that. I used to practise different lies by tipping out about ten practice balls on the practice tee and hitting them from wherever they stopped. I learned that according to the lie would affect how far the ball would carry when you hit it. Say you were hitting with a 5-iron: if it was a good lie and sitting up a bit you would probably hit it, say, 185 yards; if it was sat in a little divot or something, no matter how hard you hit it, you couldn't get it to carry more than 175 yards and I knew this because the caddy was down there catching them. It was another skill you had to learn: how to handle poor fairways.

Can you remember who won the Open that year, 1951?

Yes. Max Faulkner. He was a British player. Beautiful, beautiful player but he was sort of scared of his own shadow really. He didn't win again.

How many Australians were at the 1951 Open Championship?

Von Nida and me.

So you have arrived in London and Norman Von Nida has everything prepared for you, somewhere to stay and people to meet. That must have made life a bit easier for a young Peter Thomson on his first visit to Britain?

Oh, yes indeed. There is no doubt about that. He showed me where everything was. He introduced me to people at Sunningdale who loved to play golf, so I would play socially. I had a variety of caddies when I first went over there. The caddies were not keen on me either; they wanted a really good prospect of a bag to carry. I wasn't it. I was unknown. 'Where did he come from?' So I played with a succession of caddies, both good and bad, until I arrived on one, settled on one called Jack Lee and he came from Royal Birkdale. He caddied for me for 17 years in Britain, except for the times I played at St Andrews, where I used a local caddie. Jack didn't altogether agree with that; he thought he knew as much about St Andrews as he did about Birkdale, but of course he didn't.

First Open victory at Birkdale [1954] in the final round you shot 71 with 35 putts in an almost perfect ball striking round … in your mind did you think/feel you needed a perfect round to win The Open Championship?

Playing for a living, the aim was that you didn't make any bad shots. You avoided shots that went in the wrong direction or didn't go far enough. Eliminating bad shots was part and parcel of the professional play. On that day, if I had holed a few putts on the front nine, I would have galloped away. [He won by a single shot from the legendary Bobby Locke who had won the championship in 1949, 1950 and 1952. Peter Thomson finished 6th in his Open Championship debut in 1951 and for the next seven years he finished 2, 2, 1, 1, 1, 2, 1.]

The Open Championships in the 1950s were not big prizes. I think the biggest prize that I won in 1965 I think was pounds of … I think it was 1500 pounds. Which was a lot of money in those times. You could buy a pretty decent house for that. But it wasn't enough money to get you through the whole year. So the Open Champion had to keep playing so it was the Dutch Open the next week or the French or the German, Italian. One went and played in them as I did.

Can you describe what your media commitments were like after you won the Open in 54?

I was earning part of my living by contributing to first of all the Melbourne Herald, then later, the Melbourne Age. They were most anxious to have some report about the British Open from the player himself, but they didn't account for the fact that I may be a winner. The deadline came very quickly after the end of the event. So I had to catch up and write a story, which was the story of winning and Reuters sent it off. So, after I had finished the round and attended the prize giving I didn't go into the media tent, because we didn't have a media tent but

I did go and tap out a story on a typewriter. The Open finished on the Saturday in '54 and we had already booked some exhibitions in Scotland for the Sunday.

So, after winning the first of your major titles in 1954 did product endorsements come flooding in for the next few weeks?

No, it was very disappointing. That was not their habit. So they didn't want to start something that was going to cost them money.

In '54 when you won, were you or any of the players wearing logos on your hats or clothing?

No, of course not; that was considered very poor class.

Did that sponsorship aspect of professional golf all change with Arnold Palmer and Mark McCormack?

Not singularly. They were in the new way of earning money, but I do remember some other people were doing the same thing. The real pros were chasing money for that sort of thing; wearing a cap or a pair of shoes. Prior to that time, I never wanted anything on me like an advertisement. Back in Melbourne I was the last person to play and win a professional event at Yarra Yarra Golf Club [Spring 1954] wearing a white shirt and a tie, with a cardigan. I thought that was the smartest dress you could apply. Anyway, it didn't last long.

In 1960 there was a burst of … enthusiasm for the professional game of golf. Because for one thing it was the advent of colour television. And that made even my Mum, you know, sit up and watch because it really is a beautiful spectacle compared to say a dreary soccer pitch or a basketball stadium. And so suddenly there was an awareness by the sixties. A lot of people watching television and writing and a whole sort of golf industry suddenly sprouted up around Pro golf tournaments. Prior

to that there was very little. There got to be a lot of hangers-on as well – you know, people figured out, 'Hey, I can make some money out of this.' So they became advisors, entrepreneurs, designers of things.

The game of golf just went … through a boom. It coincided with the advent of Arnold Palmer. Now, Arnold in his early years was a tremendous attraction in the way that Tiger Woods is today. First of all he won a lot of events and became a millionaire in a hurry. And really people came to set their eyes on somebody worth a million. That … I mean, that was an attraction in itself. 'Hey, this guy's got a million pounds or a million dollars.' So those things combined made this 1960s totally different to the 1950s.

1954 seems to be perhaps the biggest single year in Australian golf history with your first Open Championship, Peter Toogood was the leading amateur and Doug Bachli winning the British Amateur … You and Kel also won the Canada Cup and you won the British matchplay at St Andrews … How did 1954 seem to you at the time, in relation to its affect on Australian golf?

Well, I was getting busier and growing up I suppose. It went by in the usual sort of way. It wasn't a momentous occasion with a big gun going off. It slowly grew. Things got better and better for the professional golfer: there was more money to be made.

Now, I went to Britain first in 1951. It was 1954 before I went to St Andrews. So I didn't sort of rush there to pay homage or anything like that. In fact I had … as I say, an awe of it from what I … every golf club that I've played at had a photograph of … of the building. The R and A clubhouse … I mean nobody photographed the course because it's not photographable … not photo … not photogenic: you know, it's sort of flat and dull. No picture I've ever seen gives you the real feeling of what it's like to play on it. But nevertheless I was a bit reluctant to go there in case I was disappointed. So in ... in the autumn of 1954 – that's September – I went to play the British Match Play championship. And I had a week ... the week before it was a free week and I went there, whereas all my opponents of course were home in their beds in England or Scotland or somewhere. But I stayed in the Rusacks Hotel there on the 18th fairway. And really got the feel of the place. And as it happened that year, 1954, the R and A every year appoints a new captain. And they're nearly always illustrious people with fine reputations. And this particular year was the year – the only year – when an Australian was actually elected to captaincy. And it was **Lord Bruce of Melbourne, Stanley Bruce**. He was in the Chair of the R and A or the captaincy for 12 months. So that the next year 1955 when the Open Championship was played on the old course he was the captain that handed me the trophy. 1954 was a remarkable year for ... three Australians. One was me who won the Open Championship, one was Lord Bruce who did a year as club captain of the R and A and the third was Doug Bachli from Victoria Golf Club who won the British Amateur Championship. Now, you know that's a remarkable three facts that no other country and certainly no other club can boast about.

Photo: Opening of the extended 18 hole Canberra Golf Course by Rt. Hon S. M. Bruce (prime Minister) ready to drive off 10th December 1927. Bruce's father, J.M. Bruce, was co-founder of Australia's first golf club, the Royal Melbourne Golf Club, in 1891. From the collection of the National Archives of Australia. NAA: A3560, 7546

After you won the '54 Open Championship in Britain, did you have to pre-qualify in 1955?
Yes.

Can you remember when the pre-qualifying was no longer compulsory for all entrants and approximately what year was that?
I can only guess it was about 1967.

The Open Championship changed from 36 holes on the last day to 18 holes on Saturday and 18 holes on Sunday – why do you think they changed that format?
By the time I got to play the event in 1950, it was already 80 years old. They had plenty of time back in those days before 1950 and they could spread the event into the week before. It was the week of golf, so we played one round on Monday and the second qualifying round was Tuesday. Then we were ready to go. One of the rounds, of the two qualifying rounds, was played on the course proper, whether it was Lytham or Birkdale. In the case of Lytham and St Annes in 1958 in the qualifying round on the course proper I shot 63; they don't' call that a record in the Open Championship because it wasn't in the Open Championship – it was qualifying for it. On the Wednesday during the tournament proper I shot 66, so I went backwards.

I assume you used the small ball for all your major victories?
Oh, yes. I played with it up until it was banned and then we had to change to 1.68 inches.

You always used a local caddie when you played St Andrews?
In 1955, the year after I won the British Matchplay at St Andrews, I fronted up for the Open which happened to be played on the Old Course. So I reckon I knew a bit about it by then and my caddie, Wallace Gillespie, who was a little short guy with a colour to his skin, he was the guy who got me through the Matchplay tournament and the next

year, of course, I hired him again. The last day of the tournament, where we played two rounds, he was vomiting. I couldn't work out what was wrong with him and this was halfway through the morning round. The R&A people came over to work out what was wrong with him and they decided it must be something like a burst ulcer. Now, of course, the bag had to come off his shoulder and they had to take him away to an ambulance. I said to the R&A, 'Can I have him not carry the bag, but come with me?'
'No, you can't do that; you can't have two caddies.'
It was an arbitrary rule – it wasn't in the book – but I couldn't have two caddies. [Peter went on to win the tournament]

So you replaced the caddie and still won the Open Championship?
Gillespie found another one of the local caddies that was idle and that was who carried the bag for me in that last round. I can't remember his name.

I guess you didn't need to say too much to him, aside from 'pass me the putter, please'.
No, I didn't want caddies to open their mouth.

When you first experienced America what was your first impression of their courses?
The first course I played on was Pebble Beach in the Bing Crosby Tournament in January 1950 and that was as good a course as we ever played on. The circuit then deteriorated as we went inland. The inland courses were mainly public courses and dreadfully maintained. In San Antonio in Texas we played off rubber mats for tees. They were like front door mats. Pebble Beach, Cypress Point and Monterey Peninsula: they were the three courses when you played the Bing Crosby.

1974 was the first year that the R&A made the big US-sized golf ball compulsory for the Open Championship. It was also the first year you missed out on playing on the weekend ... coincidence?

I doubt it. By that time I was playing a few months of the year in America and was familiar with the ball, but like everybody else that went through the change, we found it easier to play with. Being larger, it sat up a bit higher and you didn't seem to get any bad lies.

You have been labelled as being 'outspoken' in your career as a commentator of the game. You have been very good at pointing out obvious flaws in the system and had the insight to see how these things would affect the future of the game in a negative way. In many cases you have been correct. What is it in you that has given you the courage to be that person, to be a custodian of the traditions, trying to slow down the rampant commercialism of the sport?
It is me and my personality, I think. Intruding into areas where perhaps I shouldn't have. I wanted to do something and I raged at unfairness. I wanted to keep it clean. For instance, appearance money is distorting the whole quality of tournament play. Golf has a great reputation; nowadays there is no suggestion of any drug taking, for instance. We might have had anti inflammatants to swallow for a sore wrist, but that would be the extent of it.

I didn't succeed in everything I wanted to do. I was present when the US Tour, the 'Winter Tour' as it was called, when they made an announcement that they were not going to pay appearance fees any more. Some of the well known scribes said, 'Well, that is the end of the tour. If you don't pay Hogan to play or Snead to play, well, there won't be any people watching.' Well, there was plenty of people watching. Now I thought, if it is good enough for America it should be good enough for little Australia. So I stuck my head out and said we shouldn't pay anybody to tee off. It didn't succeed, but I feel like it pulled the situation a little bit in the right direction.

photos: Peter Thomson with local caddie, Wallace Gillespie. St Andrews in 1954. Photos John W Fischer III archives. 1955 Peter Thomson walking down the first hole at St Andrews with current US Open champion Cary Middlecoff. In the background is Harold Henning from South Africa and Gillespie (PT's caddie). Photos: John W Fischer III archives.

Kel Nagle

AN AUSTRALIAN LEGEND

KEL NAGLE

Kel Nagle climbed to the summit of Australasian golf with the most professional victories, 61. Peter Thomson is second with 33 and Greg Norman third with 31. Kel Nagle also won the centenary British Open in 1960; tied with Gary Player for the US Open in 1965 but lost the playoff; won the NZ Open 7 times, NZ PGA 6 times, the Australian Open, Swiss Open, Hong Kong Open, French Open, Canadian Open, Canada Cup (now called the World Cup) and many other tournaments around the world including Ireland and Scotland. He twice shot 260 for four rounds, once in Ireland, the other in Hong Kong. He also won three PGA Senior championships in Europe and at the age of 50 was still ranked inside the top ten players in the world. In 2007 he was inducted into the World Golf Hall Of Fame. Kel Nagle is one of the most loved golfers ever to come from Australia, coming from very humble beginnings and never losing his way amid the glamour and opulent lifestyle that can consume some at the pinnacle of the game. Kel Nagle never became bigger than the game of golf; quite the contrary: he remains the every man, the humble soldier, devoted father and loyal husband. At the time I interviewed him he was 92 years of age and despite his health problems one thing that struck me about Kel Nagle is what a happy man he really is, content like a Buddhist monk.

'Hi, Kel. It is Andrew Crockett. I am working on a golf book and was hoping to talk to you?'

Kel Nagle: I don't really like books. I have had three offers to do a book this year and I am just not interested. But good luck with what you are doing.

AC: Kel, it is not 'the Kel Nagle' book, it is a book about many of Australia's pioneer golfers and I was hoping to have a chapter about Kel Nagle. You are, after all, one of Australia's finest ever golfers.

Kel Nagle: Oh, a chapter; not a problem. I thought you wanted to do a whole book and be digging around my garage for months. How much time do you need from me?

AC: Oh, just an hour or so.

Kel Nagle: An hour or so. Oh good, not a problem. What are the questions? What do you want to know?

AC: Peter Thomson tells me that you were both in America a few weeks before the 1960 Open championship and he had suggested to you that your golf clubs were doing you a dis-service. PT encouraged you to get a new set of irons. Can you remember what those new golf clubs were?

Kel Nagle: They were Spalding irons. I took a set of PGF irons across and I wasn't handling them too well in America. Bobby McAlister said, 'I have a spare set of Spalding irons in the boot of my car. Do you want to try those?' I said yes and then played pretty well with them in the Pro-Am at Fort Worth, the Colonial National Tournament and I ran second in the tournament. Julius Boros (Hungarian golfer who won 3 majors) beat me by a shot. Then I went across to Portmarnock with Thomson to play the Canada Cup and we finished third and Peter said, 'Geez, you're playing well. I think you can win the Open at St Andrews.' I said, 'Awww, I am 100:1.' Thomson said, 'Look, I know the course well and we will have a practice together', and that is just how it worked out. It was unbelievable really. I got a set of irons that I felt just suited me and Thomson showed me around St Andrews. It was a bit embarrassing because I was tied up with PGF to use their equipment. But Claire Hickson, the general manager of PGF, released me for twelve months to go with Spaldings, but after twelve months I went back to PGF as I had a contract with them, worldwide. It was a bit embarrassing at the time.

AC: I am sure Spalding were happy…

Kel Nagle: They displayed the irons around with the cup and all that sort of stuff. Then I worked it out for myself, I was putting pretty good. We're good friends, Thomson and myself. We played a lot together in Canada Cups and World Cups and travelled a lot together. I think it was fantastic of Thomson to show me around St Andrews and encourage me, because he was one of the favourites to win the tournament. He was the first to congratulate me on the 18th green, or the 72nd green. Spaldings had a flat in Forgons, the white building opposite the 18th green and I had a room there. I couldn't get across to the room to get my jacket because of all the people, so I collected the trophy in Peter's jacket. I didn't leave the cheque in it though! The 1120 pounds, or something, was in my pocket. [Laughs]

AC: What was that like, 1960 at the Open? Did Arnie have his legion of fans?

Kel Nagle: He was hot favourite to win the Open in 1960 in Britain. I unfortunately got in his way. He had won the Masters and the US Open already that year and he was favourite to win.

AC: Were you impressed with Peter Thomson's knowledge of St Andrews during those practice rounds?

Kel Nagle: He showed me a few places, where to go and where not to go. [Laughs] I worked out the rest of it by myself. I was putting pretty good.

photo: National Archives of Australia A1200, L33755. Kel Nagle Canada Cup 1959 with Peter Thomson in the background.

The following quotes are from an interview conducted by Neil Bennetts for the National Library Of Australia's Oral History and Folklore collection. It was conducted on the 27th August 1990.

When I was due to become a member of the PGA the powers-that-be said they had enough members and they'd closed the membership for two years. By this time I was 19 (1939) and the membership was closed, so I was marking time for the next two years, but I was still practising hard [at Pymble under Tom Popplewell] and playing, but not playing in any competitions. Then the war came on and we were called up for National service. I met my wife, Jean Lewis, and I was married at 21. I went to Darwin during the war and served about 20 months, then went to Morotai [Indonesia] and it wasn't long after that they dropped the bomb and I went back to golf at Pymble Golf Club. I never played during the war. If I had leave I would come home and spend it with my family. I didn't play tournaments until I was 25. Thomson had won a couple of British Opens by the time he was 25. I wasn't too good early in the piece – the nervous system wasn't the best, but it got better. I had to start all over again, virtually. I guess that is why I was a late starter.

In 1951 we had a trip to England; there was Eric Cremin and Norman Von Nida. Norman did most of the gathering of the money. We played a few exhibition matches and things like that. Norman had a lot of friends who were bookmakers and jockeys. They donated money and they sort of sponsored Norman, Eric and myself to Britain. I think I played six tournaments and the only one I qualified for was the Open at Portrush in Ireland that Max Faulkner won in 1951. It was cold and miserable, first trip away from home from Jean and the kids; I was homesick. I was a long hitter in those days but I spent more time in the boonies than I did on the golf course. When I came back from Britain I decided to go back to Pymble Golf Club and Mr Popplewell was retiring and the club gave me the job as head pro, so I spent four years as the professional. I was still keen on playing and I consolidated my game and kept on practising.

After I won the McWilliams wines tournament in 1954, you know, it was very difficult to do both jobs properly so I went freelance from then on and played tournaments all over Australia.

In those days we used to play 36 holes on the last day. We'd play in all weathers – thunder and lightning about – you would still finish the game. The only time we would actually stop was if the greens were saturated and under water. When we were over in England for the British Open everyone plays six rounds of golf. You played 36 holes to qualify and then you played 36 holes to qualify for the last 36 holes. Most of the Open Championship courses in Britain you played 36 holes on the last day. Even after I won the Open championship in 1960 I had to qualify in 1961 to play at Birkdale. Arnold Palmer won. I played with him the last 36 holes and he was wild in those days. Arnold is a much better driver today than what he was in those days. He was in places all over the place … I can still vividly in my mind see places where Arnold made pars out of them and if I took you there and showed you where they were you would say 'there is no way you would get a par from there!' That was Arnold's type: he was daredevil; he attacked. At Troon in 1962 we played the same deal – 36 holes the last day – and again I played with Arnold and he shot 68-68 and I shot 70-70 and I think we had the whole of Scotland following us for the last round. I can vividly remember on the 18th green, after I putted out, they sort of picked me up and handed me across the top of all the heads just so I could put my card in. I don't know where Arnold was, I had no idea; but they really went berserk – we had a really tremendous tussle. Normally if you shoot 70-70 in the last two rounds of the Open it is good enough to win but it wasn't this particular time. [It was good enough to finish 2nd, 7 shots ahead of 3rd place.]

After 1962 they changed it to four rounds. The galleries were getting bigger and bigger with more American players coming over and the R&A developed a sort of seeding where some players didn't need to qualify. They went to four rounds then and they finished on the Sunday. So they played Thursday, Friday, Saturday, Sunday. When we played early in the piece we played Wednesday, Thursday and two rounds on Friday … they never played at weekends.

At St Andrews, the wind sort of changes with the tide. You go all the way out, you turn a loop and you go all the way back in. If you are unlucky you can play against the wind for 9 holes and you can turn around and play against the wind for the other 9 holes. Or it can be vice versa, you can be with the wind on the way out and with the wind all the way back. The weather does make a difference there at St Andrews.

My nervous system for the short putts ... there was a period there from about 1959 through 1965–66 where my nervous system was fantastic. I rarely missed those makeable putts and very rarely three-putted a green. I had a sort of 'pop' method and it just sort of suited me and you know I made plenty of putts.

I didn't play a lot in the United States, but we would play a few tournaments on the way to Britain where I would go and play the British Open, the French Open, the Swiss Open and then I would play a few more tournaments in America on my way home to Australia. I never really took on the 'tour' in America – I was a family man: Jean and I had four children and Australia was where I loved to be. I used to go and play wherever I could to help the PGA and get tournaments going. Once the children got a bit older I used to take Jean with me and we had some nice trips together. Unfortunately I lost her in 1980 and she is sure missed.

One of my lasting memories of a golfer was **Sam Snead** who had a fantastic swing. His setup, his waggle and the rhythm of his swing was copybook stuff. A young player trying to emulate what he was doing couldn't go very far wrong. Ben Hogan was a wonderful player. He was one of those players who if you needed to fade it into the hole he would fade it, if you needed to draw it he would draw it. To my mind he was always in position. Norman Von Nida was a fabulous little player. He never won the Open but he won a lot of tournaments. Fantastic bunker player.

My first trip in 1951 I think it took 27 hours from Sydney to San Francisco. So, it was a long haul sitting on top of the clouds with the engines ticking over. Today you hop in a jet and you are there in no time.

I always felt that walking is a great percentage of the game. I felt that I was concentrating when I was walking and as I got near my golf ball something would seem to click in my mind that it was 4-iron or a 5-iron or a 3-wood or whatever the case may be. Nine times out of ten if I switched, I had pulled the wrong rein, I had used the wrong club.

I never used to take a caddie with me, I would just use a local caddie. Today with the prizemoney situation and the amount of money they are making, the caddie flies all over the world with the player and becomes part and parcel of the equipment really. He knows the caddie, the caddie knows his game, he can rely on the caddie to get up early and get out and take the measurements. The caddie doesn't actually tell him what club it is, but he tells him nearly to the exact yard how far it is. I suppose that is good … but I kind of feel that if I ask someone to hit it 157 yards I don't know if he could get it right on that particular spot.

The whole game has been revolutionised really with golf balls and golf clubs and the manicured courses that they have today. In the early days, particularly in America, we used to play public courses that were never in too good a shape. Now that there is bigger money and the clubs are making money out of the tournaments the courses are well groomed, they have gone to better grasses on the fairways and greens, better weather conditions. It really is … golf is big business. It really is.

After I came back from Britain in 1951 I was in those days very long off the tee, but I was wild and I decided I had

to keep the ball in play so I changed my swing to a more or less three-quarter swing and from then on I started to win. I kept the ball in play. I was long enough, but I wouldn't be called a long hitter. I seemed to have found the right approach to myself and the way I wanted to play. I became very straight off the tee and never in a lot of trouble and I became a really good putter. I even changed my style of putting. I was a rap putter instead of a stroker. Instead of having a big long swing with the putter, I would take the putter back, pause and then pop the ball. Billy Casper does the same thing.

I always tried to drive the ball where it would give me the easiest shot into the flag. You might need to hit it down the left side, down the centre or down the right side to give you the best shot into the green.

The wind makes a big difference, you have to allow for wind. Sometimes you might go out and it is bright sunshine and the ball will go a bit further. If it is cold the ball won't go quite so far. Atmosphere makes a difference; if there is heavy atmosphere the ball, again, doesn't go as far. At sea level the ball goes a reasonable distance, but when you get up in the high altitudes, a place like Denver, the ball goes further through the air because the air is lighter. Normally you might hit a 6-iron 155 yards, but in a higher atmosphere you might hit it 165 yards. Once you get on the green you have to look at the 'nap': which way the grass is laying. If it is a dull green it is usually slow, if it is shiny it is quick.

Golf is not an easy game. I think rhythm is the main thing, if you can sort of create a good rhythm, sort of smooth back and a little quicker through the ball and you won't go too far wrong.

Kel Nagle

AC: Do you remember much about your playoff with Gary Player in 1965 for the US Open at Bellerive Missouri?

Kel Nagle: Yeah, a fair bit.

AC: How were you feeling that day?

Kel Nagle: Awww, probably a bit jumpy to start with. I three-putted the first green, then Gary holed two monsters, the 2nd and 3rd. Then I hit the woman on the head on the 5th and that was it.

AC: That would have rattled you a lot, hitting the woman spectator.

Kel Nagle: Oh yeah. Not very nice, is it? This poor lady is lying down in the grass, she hadn't come to and they were fanning her and she had blood all through her hair. I had walked from the tee all the way up there and she was still unconscious. Then Joe Geyer, who was the commissioner at the time, said, 'Kel, I think you'd better go ahead and play on and we will take her up to the clubhouse'. Well, I had a 6-iron in my hand and I didn't hang on long enough and I turned it over and I hit a lady on the leg. So I got two in the one hole. I made a double bogey 6 and that is how we finished, Gary player 3 shots in front. I missed plenty of short putts that day. I remember three-putting on 9 from about ten foot above the hole. Player was a long way from the cup and his approach putt went 12 feet by and he holed his 12 footer coming back, then I three-putted.

(It was the first time in 40 years that a non-American had won the US Open. The victory also ensured Gary Player would become the third player in history, behind Gene Sarazen and Ben Hogan, to win a career Grand Slam. Of the $26,000 Gary Player won, he only kept $1000, choosing to donate the money to the USGA, junior golf and programs that aided disadvantaged children.)

When I think of the great gentlemen of golf I always think of Kel Nagle. Everybody loved Kel Nagle. He was one of the best putters I ever saw.

Gary Player

photos: 1965 – US Open at Bellerive. Below: Gary Player & Kel Nagle crossing clubs. Black Knight International archives.

I first played with Kel Nagle at The Lakes Tournament when I was 17. We were paired with Marlene Hagge and she thought that I was Kel's son. I have so much admiration for Kel that I named my first born son after him. At that time, 1959, Kel was with PGF Golf Company and had the company build my son an exact replica of his 5-iron, scaled down to about 50%. Kel (Devlin) used that 5-iron to teethe with. There is no doubt that he is one of the greatest gentlemen to have ever played the game of golf.

Bruce Devlin

photo: 1968 Kel Nagle. photographer: Gordon Delisle
National Archives of Australia barcode 5981935 series B941

FOLKLORE

The rubber core golf ball replaced the gutta-percha ball around the turn of the century, 1900. After **James Braid** won the 1901 Open Championship using a rubber golf ball, the Haskell ball became the number one choice for golfers. Coburn Haskell is the name associated with the transition. The rubber balls looked quite similar to the 'gutties' (the gutta was created from dried sap of a Malaysian Sapodilla Tree) but gave the average golfer an extra 20 yards from the tee. Just as importantly it made the golf ball affordable, replacing the 'featheries' that cost as much as a golf club.

Haskell had driven to nearby Akron to keep a golf date with Bertram Work, then superintendent of B.F. Goodrich. While he waited for Work at the plant, Haskell idly wound a long rubber thread into a ball. When he bounced the ball, it flew almost to the ceiling. Work suggested Haskell put a cover on the creation, and that was the birth of the 20th century golf ball. In 1905 William Taylor applied a dimple pattern to a Haskell ball, which maximised the lift while minimising drag.

In 1870 **Young Tom Morris** won the Open Championship with the 'gutty' golf ball and a 36-hole score of 149, 12 strokes ahead of the field. His score of 149 would not be matched until 30 years later when the rubber-cored ball was invented. In a team match on 11 September 1875 at North Berwick, with the Morris's facing brothers Willie and Mungo Park, Young Tom received a telegram from home requesting his immediate return; his pregnant wife, Margaret Drinnen, had gone into a difficult labour. Only two holes remained in the match; Old Tom and Young Tom finished the match, winning, and hurried home by ship across the Firth of Forth and up the coast, but when Young Tom got there both his wife and newborn baby were dead. Young Tom was broken-hearted and died almost four months later on Christmas Day. He was still only 24. A heart attack was the official cause of death.

Tom Morris Jr (1851–1875)

Dan Soutar was born in Carmyllie, Scotland on 3 December 1882. In 1888, his family moved to the nearby seaside resort town of Carnoustie where – over the next 15 or so years – he received a thorough grounding in the game of golf. Starting out as a caddie at ninepence per round, he developed a sound swing and game to the point where he won a number of trophies as a member of the Carnoustie Club. He emigrated to Australia in 1903, and made an immediate mark by winning the 1903 Australian Amateur Championship at the old Glenelg course. In 1905, he turned professional and went into partnership with Carnegie Clark making clubs at Rose Bay in Sydney. That same year he won his only Australian Open Championship at Royal Melbourne, beating the defending champion, the **Hon. Michael Scott**, by ten strokes. He founded the PGA in Australia and wrote the first golf book, *The Australian Golfer*, in 1906.
Daniel Gordon ('Dan') Soutar (1882–1937)

Carnegie Clark. Known simply as 'Neg', Carnegie Clark was right there at the birth of professional golf and professional club making in Australia. 'Neg' was fundamental in forming the Australian PGA in 1911 and laying out dozens of golf courses, including the original layout of Royal Sydney, Royal Queensland and Brisbane Golf Club.

With his Scottish ancestry deep in his veins, Clark grew up as a caddie at Carnoustie and later became a professional golfer and clubmaker. In the early 1900s he was part of the 'Carnoustie 300' – professional golfers and clubmakers who ventured to other parts of the world to promote and share the game of golf and ultimately create their own livelihood. The United States was lucky enough to acquire many of the **'Carnoustie 300'**. Clark, instead of going to America, became one of the first professional golfers in Australia. Clark, born in 1881, arrived in Sydney in 1902 to work in a sports store in Sydney. During his tenure here, Clark undertook what was to become known as his 'Northern Tour'. Visiting Tamworth, Armidale, Glen Innes, Tenterfield, Warwick, Toowoomba, Ipswich, Brisbane, Casino, Grafton, Coffs Harbour, Kempsey, Taree and Newcastle, 'Neg' promoted the game, gave tuition and obtained orders for golf clubs and balls.

As a player, he won three Australian Opens and several Australian PGA titles. Carnegie Clark is credited with introducing the Vardon grip to Australia and being a fine teacher of the game.

Leaving Scotland and establishing himself in Australia was a fruitful move for 'Neg' and he eventually brought his whole family out to Australia, including his mother and father, brothers and sisters. When 'Neg' died in 1959 his wife Alice burned all the records of his life and a chapter of Australian golf is now only visible with shades of grey.

'In 1926 **Fred Popplewell**, **Harry Sinclair**, **Tommy Howard** and Carnegie made a pilgrimage to the British Open and his beloved Carnoustie. That was where it all began for young Neg as a wee laddie in the 19th Century and in 1959, nigh to the first green at Royal Sydney, was where it all ended for that Grand Old Man of Golf.' **Al Howard** (Australian golf legend)

Carnegie Clark (1881–1959)

Australian **Walter Travis** held the British and US Amateur trophies in the same year, 1904. A World Golf Hall Of Fame inductee, Walter Travis was born in Maldon, Australia in 1862. He arrived in New York city in 1886, aged 23. He took up golf when he was 34 years of age and won the US Amateur in 1900, 1901 and 1903. He was tied 2nd in the US Open in 1902 and won the British Amateur in 1904. The news of his victory in the British Amateur sparked a surge of interest in the game of golf in America. Golfers from Scotland and England dominated American golf in the late 1800s and early 1900s. It was 1911 before America had its first US-born US Open champion in John McDermott.

Walter Travis competed in six US Opens between 1902 and 1912 and was low amateur five times and tied for third low amateur the other. Beyond his stellar amateur career, Walter Travis was a writer. After writing Practical Golf and having it published in 1901, Travis went on to create the American Golfer magazine, the most influential magazine of its time. After retiring from competitive golf in 1920, Walter Travis became well-known for his golf course designs and putting tutorials.

'Our opinion is that Mr Travis has won more low gross, low net and open tourneys than any other living golfer. He was practically unbeatable for a stretch of six years from 1898 to 1904 during which time he played in double or triple the number of events entered by either **John Ball** or **Chick Evans**. A guess at the number of his trophies would place it over five hundred and perhaps nearer to a thousand. In 1901, Travis was national champion and in 1915 he was again the Metropolitan champion. His southern victories were numerous.'
The American Golfer, January 1922

Walter Travis was inducted into the World Golf Hall Of Fame in 1979, 52 years after his death.

Walter J Travis (1862-1927)

photo: Walter Travis from John W Fischer III archives

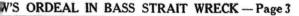

The Sun

NEWS~PICTORIAL
WITH WHICH IS INCORPORATED
THE MORNING POST

WEATHER FORECAST:
Cool, cloudy; chiefly fine.

2776 Registered at the G.P.O. Melbourne for transmission by post as a newspaper.

MELBOURNE : SATURDAY, AUGUST 8, 1931 (28 Pages, with 4-Page Supplement) 1½d.

YOUTH TRIUMPHS IN STATE GOLF CHAMPIONSHIPS

TWO 16-YEARS-OLD STATE AMATEUR GOLF CHAMPIONS will be rivals in the open championship in Sydney this month. They are J. Ferrier of N.S.W. (left) and Harry Williams (right), who yesterday defeated M. J. Ryan, holder of the Victorian title, with four up and three to play. The smiling winner, shown above (left) with the runner-up, is a left-hander. Top: A cinematograph camera record of the new champion's driving style.

THE END OF THE MATCH for the State amateur golf title occurred at the 33rd green on the Victoria links yesterday. Williams (right) is seen receiving the congratulations of the ex-holder of the title, M. J. Ryan.

After the 1936 Australian Open at Metropolitan left-hander Harry Williams was promised huge sums of money by Gene Sarazen to turn pro and play golf in America. Williams said no to the offer, or more accurately he never replied to the verbal offer from **Gene Sarazen**. Williams came second in the Australian Open and Sarazen won it, but it was the left-handed amateur who pushed him all the way.

The enigma of Harry Williams — some myth, some legend — is unparalleled in Australian golf. One story that has been told for years is of the day he played in the bogey event at Victoria and was eight-up after nine holes. He owed shots at both the third and the sixth holes from his plus-two handicap, but eagled them both for wins. At the turn Williams decided that he would go to the races at Caulfield so he marked nine losses on the home side and handed in a card of one-down, which duly won the event.

The character of Harry Williams is one of mystery, a prodigious golfer who could step up to the first tee after not playing for weeks and hit a perfect drive and then go to shoot par figures and beat opponents who were finely tuned. Stories abound of his length in the 1930s, sometimes driving the ball 350 yards.

Five times Victorian Amateur champion (1931, 1934, 1935, 1936, 1939), the youngest ever Australian Amateur Champion (aged 16 in 1931), he won the Australian Amateur again in 1937. Between 1933 and 1939 Williams won the Victoria Golf Club championship four times and in 1936 partnered **Dick Payne** to win the Australian foursomes championship at Metropolitan. In 1937, after winning the Australian Amateur for the second time, Williams was frequently referred to as Australia's greatest golfer; however, he (along with **Jim Ferrier**) was controversially left off the four-man Australian team to tour Britain. Williams retired from competitive golf in 1939 aged 24. He died with his mother by carbon monoxide poisoning in their flat at East Kew on 13th December 1961, citing that they had run out of money in a suicide note.

'There was one Australian amateur by the name of Harry Williams who was a left-hander, I believe the best left-hander that ever lived and possibly the best Australian golf player that ever was. It would be difficult to sort of assess that in relative competitive factors, because **Peter Thomson** has won five British opens and runner-up in another two, but the natural skill of Harry Williams was just something to be seen, or something one had to see to believe — it was really tremendous, and he was about the only amateur that could compete successfully against **Jim Ferrier**. Every time he played Ferrier in an individual match, he beat him. But let me assure you, if Harry Williams had have taken the game up as seriously as what Jim Ferrier or myself did, he would have been a player of equal international renown. From tee to green he was a far superior player to Ferrier. He was probably better than me too, because he was longer. Ferrier from tee to green was what we call a 'nothing player' but he was the best putter that ever lived.'
Norman Von Nida

Harry Llewellyn Williams (1915–1961)

Folklore

'I may have been considered the best bunker player when I was playing, but to consider me the best bunker player who has ever played golf is a fallacy. If you watch the players of today, any one of fifty would be as good a bunker player as what I was. There is so many more people playing golf and the sand irons that they are using today have the 60 degree loft. It was Gene Sarazen who brought in the sand irons around 1932. In those days the lofted club was called a 'niblick' or a 'mashie niblick' and Sarazen got this flanged soul sand iron club manufactured and he was the original wonderful sand iron player. I became a very good sand iron player, Gary Player was a marvellous sand iron player. But I think even better than Gary and I was a Japanese player by the name of Tommy Nakamura. It is just an individual thing, but to become a great bunker player you have to be able to know, as soon as you walk into the sand, the weight of the sand. Through knowing that, through practice, you know exactly what 'bounce' the clubhead will determine when it actually hits the sand. Gary Player was the same, if we were allowed to place the ball in the bunker with firm sand and hitting onto a good green, either one of us would bet we could hole at least three shots out of every ten, into the hole. At least three.'

Norman Von Nida

Folk lore

Francis Ouimet 1923 Walker Cup on the 13th hole at St. Andrews. Not only is it a great photo, it is especially unique for the time. Cameras were big and bulky and the film and lenses slow. Most photographs were posed or taken from a distance. Photographer is unknown

photo: Bobby Locke Golf Australia's Museum Collection, managed by the Golf Society of Australia.

In 1946 after World War II **Bobby Locke** hosted the great **Sam Snead** to 18 exhibition matches in South Africa and won 16 of them. It was all down to his putting.

Bobby Locke, the 'majestic maestro', played 59 events on the US PGA Tour in the late 1940s. He won 11 of them, finished second 10 times, third eight times and fourth five times (34 out of 59 tournaments in the Top 4). He still jointly holds the PGA Tour record for largest margin of victory (16 strokes at the 1948 Chicago Victory Open) with Australia's Joe Kirkwood (1924 Corpus Christi Open) and JD Edgar (1919 Canadian Open).

Locke hit a hook with his driver, hooked his irons, hooked his chips and hooked his putts and in an act of defiance the American tournament organisers set up the course with the pins placed on the far right of every green and Bobby Locke still won. Locke was so good that when he was banned from competing in the US in 1949 some say it was that the Americans were tired of the South African winning all their events/money, while others cite that he had not met his playing commitments in America. At the time of his ban, Locke had just won the 1949 Open Championship and elected to stay in Britain. Once the ban in America was lifted two years later Bobby Locke rarely returned and elected to play his golf in Europe. After serving in the airforce during the World War II, Locke went on to be a true international player, spreading awareness of the game in his home country and winning tournaments in several countries including Australia.

When Australia's **Peter Thomson** was coming through the ranks he believed Bobby Locke to be the best player in the world. Locke would have a lasting effect on the great Peter Thomson's career.

Locke won the Open Championship in 1949, 1950 and 1952 and in 1957 was the man to stop Peter Thomson winning five Opens in succession. Locke also beat Peter Thomson in 1952 by one stroke. Sadly Bobby Locke had a near fatal car accident in 1959 (his car was hit by a train) and he never fully recovered to play tournament golf again. He was elected to the World Golf Hall of Fame in 1977. He died in 1987 as one of the world's truly great players and South Africa's first golfing superstar. He coined the phrase 'you drive for show but putt for dough'.

I played a challenge match against Bobby Locke in 1939 at the NSW golf club and I think I beat him 7 and 6. He hit it in a bunker about 8 times and he couldn't get it out. Then we came up and played at Brisbane Golf Club and in the morning we played 36 holes, he shot 66 and hit the flag with his second shot two or three times, with a 2-iron. He was just unbelievable. He shot 67 in the second round and I think for the day he beat me 3 and 2. What impressed me most about Bobby Locke was his putting and the simplicity factor in his swing. He was skinny at that time and you wouldn't recognise him when he came back all those years later. He was a marvellous personality and a wonderful, wonderful person. He always wore a tie and plus fours. Unfortunately he had that accident and he died prematurely.
Via **Norman Von Nida**

Arthur D'Arcy ('Bobby') Locke (1917–1987)

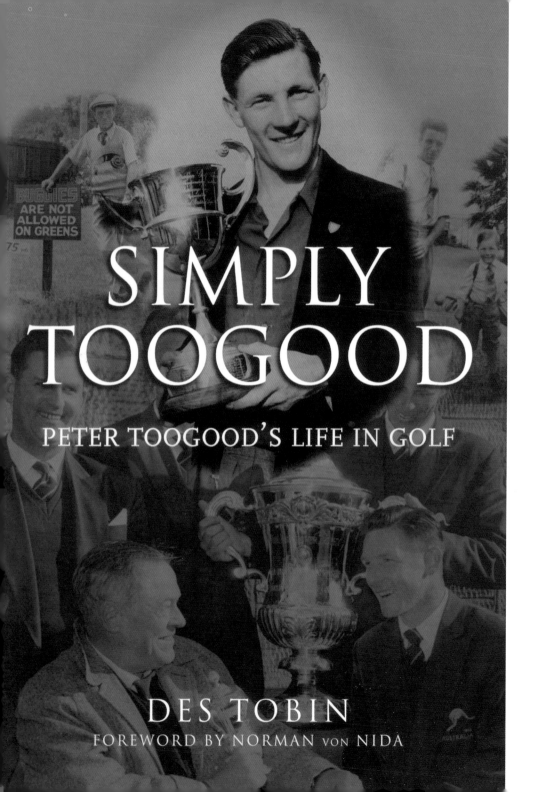

SIMPLY TOOGOOD

PETER TOOGOOD'S LIFE IN GOLF

DES TOBIN

FOREWORD BY NORMAN VON NIDA

Folklore

PETER TOOGOOD is a member of an extraordinary family of golfers.

His grandfather – Alfred Toogood (Senior) – was a prominent English professional in the 1890s and 1900s and finished 4th in the Open Championship at Royal St Georges in 1894. Alfred and his professional golfer cousin Walter Toogood both played representative golf for England against Scotland on several occasions and Alfred Toogood (Jnr) – Peter's father – was a successful Australian professional tour player from the late 1920s until the mid 1950s and a long serving club professional at The Grange GC in South Australia and Kingston Beach in Tasmania.

Peter's brother John was also a celebrated amateur. He won numerous Tasmanian tournaments including two Tasmanian amateur championships and sixteen club championships at Kingston Beach. He was a regular member of the Tasmanian state team and was runner-up to Peter in the 1954 Australian amateur championship at Royal Adelaide.

And Peter's son Anthony – currently the course superintendent at Albury Golf Club – was a successful junior winning the Tasmanian Junior Championship in 1985 and 1986 and representing Tasmania on several occasions before studying in the United States.

Peter Toogood's prodigious golfing talent first came to the public's notice when he made a hole-in-one at the 7th hole at Kingston Beach at the age of 8. His feat put him into the Guinness Book Of Records and remained there for 20 years.

In his teenage years Toogood won the Tasmanian Open and Amateur championships on several occasions and represented Tasmania in the annual interstate series preceding the Australian Amateur championships.

Peter Toogood went on to have a celebrated amateur career during which he played golf all over the world and with many leading amateur and professional players. He won the Australian Amateur championship in 1954 and the New Zealand Amateur championship in 1956. He reached the 6th round of the 1954 British Amateur championship and was leading amateur in the Open championship (won by Peter Thomson) in the same year.

He was a 10-time winner of the Tasmanian Amateur and won the Tasmanian Open championship 8 times. He won 36 club championships at 5 different clubs; was a member of the Australian team that won the inaugural Eisenhower trophy at St Andrews in 1958; and represented Australia on several other occasions. He represented Tasmania in state golf for over 30 years and was state captain from 1952–1980 and won at least one Tasmanian state event in every decade from the 1950s to the 1990s.

On several occasions Toogood considered turning professional and undoubtedly would have done well. For various reasons however he elected to remain an amateur. He completed a degree in physical education and enjoyed a distinguished career in the field of education in Tasmania. He was awarded a MBE (1981) and an Order of Australia (2008) for his services to sport in Education.

When asked to assess Peter's golfing ability and his place in amateur golf, the great Norman Von Nida rated only Jim Ferrier, Harry Williams, Doug Bachli and Bruce Devlin ahead of him. Von Nida praised Toogood for 'his remarkable contribution to Australian golf' and regarded Peter as 'one of the most genuine people I have known and one of the finest golfers I have known and competed against'. High praise indeed coming from one of Australia's finest and, like Toogood, a true legend of Australian golf .

Peter Toogood established the Australasian Golf Museum in Bothwell, Tasmania, close to the famed old links course of Ratho, a course designed by Alexander Reid. Ratho golf links is frequently referred to as the oldest course in Australia and perhaps the oldest in the Southern Hemisphere.

Peter Toogood's complete story is contained in his biography – *Simply Toogood – Peter Toogood's Life in Golf* – written by Des Tobin and published by Killaghy Publishing. It is available by contacting Des Tobin – destobin@killaghy.com

Folklore

In the twentieth century, **Seve Ballesteros** was the youngest winner of the Open Championship. In 1979 Seve won at Royal Lytham & St Annes. He was 22 years, 3 months and 12 days young. He shot a final round 70 to beat Ben Crenshaw and Jack Nicklaus by 3 shots. First prize was 15,000 pounds. 1979 was the same year one of Seve's many errant tee shots ended up in a temporary car park, where he played another stunning recovery shot and made birdie. Three years earlier (1976) a 19-year-old Seve finished second in the Open, after leading by two shots after three rounds. 1976 signalled the arrival of a wonderful new talent. Between 1976 and his first Major victory, Seve won in Europe, America, Japan, New Zealand and even Africa. He went on to be the number one golfer in the World. **Seve Ballesteros** will always be remembered as one of the greats of the game with five Major victories and nearly 100 professional tournament wins. He was inducted into the World Golf Hall Of Fame in 1999, lauded as a pioneer of the European golf tour and acknowledged as one of the most exciting players to ever play the game. (Young **Tom Morris** is the youngest ever winner of the Open Championship (1868) – he was 17 years, 5 months and 8 days young.)

Severiano 'Seve' Ballesteros Sota (9 April 1957–7 May 2011)

Tony Lema won 12 times on the US PGA tour between 1962 and 1966 and also won the Open Championship at St Andrews in 1964 before tragically dying in a light plane crash at the peak of his career in 1966, aged 32.

The twin-engine Beechcraft Bonanza, piloted by Doris Mullen, ran out of fuel and crashed in a water hazard short of the seventh green of Lansing Country Club in Lansing, Illinois, less than a mile from their destination, Lansing Municipal Airport. During the fatal plunge, Mullen swerved left to avoid a group of people standing near the clubhouse.

Lema won the Open at St Andrews with a total of 279 (73-68-68-70). **Jack Nicklaus** was runner-up with closing rounds of 66 and 68 at the Old Course and lost to Lema by 5 shots. It was the first time **Tony Lema** had seen the Old Course of St Andrews and he was tired, having just come off a victory in America in the Cleveland Open by beating **Arnold Palmer** in a playoff and having won three tournaments in the previous 4 weeks. **Tony Lema** had the famed 'Tip' Anderson (a descendant of a past Open champion, Jamie Anderson, 'Tip' had grown up on the Old Course) on the bag at Arnold Palmer's suggestion (Arnold Palmer did not play the 1964 British Open). During the first round Lema credited his caddie for his fine round of 73 in a fifty-mile-an-hour wind – only four players had a better opening round. It was Tony Lema's first full round on the fabled course; he had only played nine holes during his practice round. Lema was a very popular winner with his smooth flowing swing and charming ways. Nicknamed 'Champagne Tony', **Peter Thomson** says, 'He was one of the greatest players I have ever seen.' In the four years that Tony Lema contested the four Major tournaments he had eight top ten finishes including 2nd (by one shot) in the 1963 US Masters, won by **Jack Nicklaus**.

Anthony David 'Tony' Lema (1934–1966)

Harry Kershaw

Bachli

Doug Bachli was the first Australian to win the British Amateur in 1954, at the age of 32. He was a member of the Victoria Golf Club, playing alongside Peter Thomson. Doug played for Australia in the inaugural Commonwealth series, an event which marked the bicentenary of the Royal and Ancient, at St Andrews in 1954 where Australia (**Doug Bachli** (Vic), **Harry Berwick** (NSW), **Peter Heard** (NSW), **Jack Coogan** (Qld), **Bill Shepherd** (SA), **Bob Stevens** (SA) and **Ray Howarth** (Vic)) were unbeaten. Bachli was part of the winning Australian team in the first Eisenhower Cup (with **Peter Toogood**, **Bruce Devlin** and **Bob Stevens**) at St Andrews in 1958. The win boosted Australia's golf image vastly and in 1959, Bachli was made a member of the Royal and Ancient Golf Club at St Andrews.

Bachli also won the Victoria Amateur (1949, 1950, 1953) and Victoria foursomes (1947, 1948, 1949), Queensland Amateur (1948) and Queensland foursomes (1948), Australian Amateur (1948) and Australian foursomes (1948, 1950, 1951). **Doug Bachli** never turned pro; he later founded the Golf Society of Australia, which in turn helped to breathe life into the Australian Golf Museum. He was made a Member of the Order of the British Empire (MBE) in 1996 for his services to golf. The Doug Bachli Trophy is awarded in his memory each year to the player that accrues the highest total of points for stroke performances in designated senior events throughout the year.

Douglas Bachli MBE (1922–2000)

Harry Kershaw never played in golf shoes, he preferred to wear desert boots. He won the NSW Open in 1959 by five shots from a field that included **Norman Von Nida**, **Kel Nagle** and **Bruce Devlin**. As a 15-year-old he shot 61 to win the Marrickville club championship.

'Harry won 19 assistant professional events in a row. He was the assistant to Billy Holder out at The Lakes in Sydney. In 1961 we were all getting ready to get on the plane to go to the Far East Open in the Philippines and Harry wasn't there, so I rang him and said, 'What are you doing? Why are you not coming? You have to come.' He said he had to look after his girlfriend. The next day when I woke up in the Philippines I got the news, 'Harry is dead. He had a car accident.'
Alan Murray

Henry Thomas 'Harry' Kershaw (1940–1961)

photo: This is the only known photo of Harry Kershaw, sourced with the help of Col McGregor and Alan 'Murky' Murray.

FOLKLORE - 1950s

Royal Melbourne was Alex Russell's home course and he began his 1924 Australian Open with a course record 68, which led the field by seven strokes, quite a feat for an amateur. Russell clambered home to win by two strokes from the original professional icon, **Carnegie Clark**. Often in the shadow of his now legendary clubmate, **Ivo Whitton**, Alex Russell also won two Australian foursomes titles, four Victorian foursomes titles, The Victorian Amateur and three club championships at Royal Melbourne.

During the World War I Russell was a battery commander with the British artillery and won the Military Cross. He was also the confidential secretary to Prime Minister Stanley Bruce, a fellow member of Royal Melbourne. It was two years after his Australian Open win that Dr Alister MacKenzie, the famed Scottish architect, arrived in Melbourne having been commissioned to design Royal Melbourne's West Course. Russell was the club captain at the time of Dr MacKenzie's appointment and they became firm friends. Alex Russell's fingerprints are all over Royal Melbourne's East course, Yarra Yarra and several other courses. His design work has been lauded in several publications.
Alex Russell MC (1891–1961)

Bobby Jones retired from golf at the age of 28 having won 13 Major titles. He played a total of 52 tournaments and won 23 of them. He won the US Amateur five times between 1924 and 1930. In 1926 he became the first, and to date the only, amateur to win both the US and the British Open in the same year. In 1930 he won all four Majors in one year by winning the US Amateur, British Amateur, US Open and the Open Championship. From 1923 to 1930 he won 13 of the 21 Majors he entered. He never turned professional. During the US Open Bobby Jones called a one-shot penalty on himself, citing that his ball had slightly moved in the rough. The one-shot penalty cost him the victory by one shot. The US Golf Association sportsmanship award is named the 'Bob Jones Award' and is one of the highest honours in American golf. With University degrees in Mechanical Engineering, English Literature and Law he had a successful career with his Law Practice. Jones also made 18 instructional golf films and helped design Augusta National Golf Club.
Robert Tyre 'Bobby' Jones Jr (1902–1971)

Ben Hogan had a near fatal car accident in 1949, then recovered to win the US Open a year later. Hogan was told by doctors he may never walk again after a head-on crash with a bus on a fog-bound highway in Texas. He suffered a double fracture of his pelvis, fractured collarbone, broken ankle, a chipped ribcage and severe blood clots. Amazingly Ben Hogan, upon seeing the oncoming bus, threw his body in front of his wife, Valerie. They both survived. The car was a write-off. Hogan spent 59 days in hospital and suffered lifelong circulation problems and other physical limitations. A year earlier, in 1948, he won ten times on the US PGA tour.

Ben Hogan is one of only five golfers to have won all four of golfs 'Majors', the others being Gene Sarazen, Gary Player, Jack Nicklaus and Tiger Woods. Hogan only played the Open Championship once (1953) and he duly won it. Hailed as perhaps the best ball striker to ever grace the game of golf, his book Five Lessons: The Modern Fundamentals of Golf is perhaps the most widely-read golf tutorial ever written. The 'Ben Hogan Award' is given annually by the Golf Writers' Association of America to a golfer who has stayed active in golf despite a physical handicap or serious illness; Babe Zaharias first won the award in 1954. In 1953 when Ben Hogan won three majors, he was 39 years old.
William Ben Hogan (1912–1997)

Bill Shankland ...yes, Shank ... played for Australia in Rugby League and also finished 3rd in the Open Championship at St Andrews in 1939, won by Dick Burton. His contribution to golf and charity after the World War II were immense, particularly raising money to help war victims, via his donations to St Dunstan's Hospital.

'When I arrived in Britain I was very lucky to meet Bill Shankland, a former caddie at Royal Sydney who had gone over to play rugby league for Australia and he had stayed on and become a professional golfer. He looked after me. A very good player too – he had a few top-five finishes in The Open. I lived with Bill for about three years; he was wonderful to me, a marvellous person. He used to organise exhibition matches with Bobby Locke, Dai Rees, Max Faulkner, Fred Daly, Jimmy Adams and myself. We used to play these exhibition matches and the proceeds used to go to the St Dunstans (blind veterans military charity). Over a period of two or three years, Bill Shankland himself raised something like one million three hundred and fifty thousand pounds for St Dunstans. Really, a marvellous fellow.' Norman Von Nida
William Shankland (1907–1998)

Roberto de Vincenzo [Argentina] lost his opportunity for a playoff to win the US Masters in 1968 by signing his scorecard for a 66 when he had actually shot a superb 65 at Augusta National. It was his playing partner **Tommy Aaron** who marked his score on the 17th as 4, when de Vincenzo had made a 3. **Bob Goalby** won the title. De Vincenzo's quote afterwards became legendary for its poignancy: 'What a stupid I am!'

De Vincenzo won more than 230 tournaments around the world, 17 top tens in Major golf tournaments between 1948 and 1971 including winning the Open Championship in 1967, aged 44, beating **Jack Nicklaus** by two strokes. He won national opens in Belgium, Brazil, Chile, Colombia, Holland, France, Germany, Jamaica, Mexico, Panama, Peru, Spain, Uruguay, Venezuela and Argentina. He also represented Argentina 17 times in the Canada/World Cup, winning the individual scoring honour twice (1962, 1970) and winning the Canada Cup for Argentina the first year it was contested in 1953 in Montreal, Canada (with **Antonio Cerda**). A brilliant shotmaker who struggled with the putter, a World Golf Hall Of Fame Inductee (1989) and a superstar in his home country inspiring the next generations, including Masters champion **Ángel Cabrera**.

Sir Henry Cotton (1907–1987) was to British golf what **Ben Hogan** was to American golf. He stayed at the top through endless hours of practice. Through his dedicated practice he developed a repeatable swing and very strong hands, two ingredients essential for top-level golf. Cotton placed 17 times in the top ten of the Open Championship and one round of 65 during the 1934 championship is credited with the Dunlop golf company's famous 'Dunlop 65' golf ball thereafter. He served in the Royal Air Force during World War II and raised money for the Red Cross playing exhibition matches. Cotton was awarded MBE for his efforts. During his era he helped raise the profile of golfers. In the British class system, professional golfers were seen as occupying the lower rungs of society. Henry Cotton and Walter Hagen helped articulate the true nature of golfers. Henry Cotton wrote ten books and inspired a generation of golfers to take up the game through his Golf Foundation. Cotton lived the high life with a butler in tow and usually travelled in a Rolls Royce. He was inducted into the World Golf Hall Of Fame in 1980.

photo: Argentina's Roberto de Vincenzo from John W Fischer III archives.

FOLKLORE - AUSSIES

Bill Edgar was called Australia's Bobby Jones in the 1930s. He had a smooth swing that never changed. He played off scratch or better for 39 consecutive years. He won three Victorian and two South Australian amateur titles and 19 club championships at Commonwealth Golf Club. In the 1930s Bill Edgar was one of Australia's top golfers and was chosen to play exhibition matches with golfing greats **Walter Hagen**, **Bobby Locke** and **Gene Sarazen**. In 1977 he was awarded MBE for services to golf.

Gary Player was the first International player to win the North Coast Open in 1956. The North Coast Open was played at Coffs Harbour Golf Club from 1951 and had some famous winners over the years including **Kel Nagle**, **Bruce Crampton**, **Frank Phillips**, **Alan Murray**, **Norman Von Nida**, **Bill Dunk** and **Stuart Ginn**.

Between 1950 and 1971 **Peter Thomson** (9) and **Kel Nagle** (7) won 16 NZ Open tournaments between them.

Tasmanian **Len Nettlefold** (1905–1971) was a left-hander who won two Australian Amateurs and was also a quarter-finalist in the 1927 British Amateur. He won 16 Tasmanian amateur titles and 8 Tasmanian Opens. In 1927 he equalled the amateur record for the Old Course at St Andrews.

In 1973 **Randall Vines** came 5th behind **Johnny Miller**, **Gary Player**, **Mister Lu** and **Jack Nicklaus** in individual scoring at the World Cup in Spain. The Queenslander in the late 1960s also won the Thailand, Hong Kong, Swiss and German Opens. He won two Australian PGA titles in 1972 and 1973 and in 1968 won the Tasmanian Open by a record 17 shots at Royal Hobart.

Australian **George Bell** holds, perhaps, a unique distinction in driving his golf ball an amazing 550 yards onto the par 5 6th hole at Sydney's St Michael's Club and then three putting for birdie.

Mick Ryan – one of only six Australians who have won the Australian Amateur (1929) and the Australian Open (1932). Mick Ryan represented Australia in 1934 and 1938 and also played first-grade Australian Rules and cricket for South Melbourne.

In 1974 **Ted Ball** (1939–1995) won, for the second year in a row, the lucrative Wills Masters at Kensington by beating reigning US Masters and Open champion **Gary Player** by 2 strokes. Ted was Australian Amateur champion in 1960 and won dozens of tournaments including the Indian open, Singapore Open and Queensland, Tasmanian and South Australian Opens.

Bill Bolger won the 1934 Australian Open (beating **Gene Sarazen**) with a record score of 283. A week after his victory his agent, Walter Furlong, had teed up a sponsorship deal with Tooheys (beer) and a large advertisement appeared with Billy Bolger and the caption 'Bolger Trains On Tooheys' Oatmeal Stout'. The endorsement earned Bolger more money than his first place prizemoney from the tournament.

The first year the Wills Masters was played (1960) it was a marathon 162 holes over 9 courses and contested by four players: **Stan Leonard** (Canada), **Peter Thomson** (Australia), **Mike Souchak** (USA) and **Gary Player** (South Africa). Peter Thomson won with scores of 70 at Yeerongpilly, 71 at Tweed Heads, 66 at Orange, 69 at Royal Canberra, 71 at Kooyonga, 71 at Geelong, 74 at Kingston Heath, 72 at Wollongong and 69 at Manly for a total of 633. Gary Player was second with 636.

To tell you how good **Eric Cremin** was as a competitor, he beat me in the final of the Australian PGA championship one year 12 and 10. I played pretty good – I shot 71 in the morning. In the afternoon for the eight holes we played Eric had 7 putts, he holed one chip shot and holed every putt. **Norman Von Nida**

Gary Player and I played with the English cricket captain Ted Dexter one day when the team was out here. We played at Kooyonga (Adelaide) and he shot 66. He outdrove Player by 40 yards every hole and outdrove me by 60–70 yards every hole. We offered him $100,000 to turn pro. If he had have been a golfer instead of a cricketer he would have been the best player Europe ever had.
Norman Von Nida

Tony Gresham OAM is an outstanding amateur golfer from Australia. Born in 1940 he has won dozens of prestigious titles including the Australian Amateur in 1975, NSW Open 1975, South Australian Open 1976, NSW State Champion three times and he also represented Australia in the Eisenhower Trophy from 1968-1980. Tony was also British Amateur semi finalist in 1979 and 1981. Tony spent his life in sport aiding in community activities and in later life has become a prolific winner on the senior amateur circuit prompting some to say he is one of the greatest Australian amateur golfers.

photos courtesy Australasian Golf Museum, Bothwell village, Tasmania.

'Remember where the victory lies – in the struggle not the prize'.

Bob Stevens (Australian Amateur champion 1952)

Tasmania has a firm place in the history of Australian golf, from Alexander Reid clearing land in the mid 1800s to lay out some of the first primitive golf holes in the Southern Hemisphere (Ratho Golf Course) to today, where Barnbougle Dunes golf course is one of the top-ranked public access courses in the world. Tasmania has a legacy with golf. After first appearing in Britain's *Golf Illustrated* in 1906 ('Golf in Tasmania', p. 88, 26 October edition) **Clyde Pearce** was the first to prove that the 'colonial boys' from Australia could beat the best golfers from the 'mother country'; following in the footsteps of fellow Tasmanian Elvie Whitesides, who had won the first ever Australian Ladies Championship just 2 years earlier. After narrow losses to both adversaries in previous years, in 1908 Pearce defeated Carnoustie's **Dan Soutar** in the last round of the Australian Open at the Australian Golf Club, as well as England's **Hon. Michael Scott** in the Australian Amateur Final.

Clyde's younger brother **Bruce Pearce** was also an outstanding golfer. Together they toured Britain in 1911, both winning tournaments and qualifying for the matchplay finals of the British Amateur. Bruce Pearce made it to the quarter-finals, and as a left-hander was considered quite a novelty. The **Toogood brothers, Peter and John**, also from Tasmania, continued the tradition by climbing to the top of Australian Amateur golf by playing each other in the final of the Australian Amateur at Royal Adelaide in 1954. Peter Toogood was victorious, as he was in Australia's inaugural Eisenhower Cup team, four years later in St.Andrews. Today **Mathew Goggin** is the leading golfer from Tasmania.

LOCAL RULES.

1. A ball lying in any rabbit scrape, hoof print, or cart rut, or on, or within two feet of any stone, may be lifted and dropped, not nearer the hole, without penalty.

2. A ball lying in any of the small drains at the first hole, or in either of the two small drains nearest to the second green, may be lifted and dropped, not nearer the hole, without penalty.

3. A ball lying in the garden near the third green shall be lifted and dropped clear of the fence, but not nearer the hole, under penalty of one stroke.

4. "Out of Bounds." Any part of the Great Lake Road, and over the fences to the left of seventh and eighth fairways. Penalty, loss of distance.

29/2678 Mercury, Hobart

BOTHWELL GOLF CLUB

Folklore

photo 1905 Bothwell golf course Tasmania and opposite Bothwell golf course. (Note the tee block adjacent to the green).
Courtesy of the Australasian Golf Museum located in Bothwell village, Tasmania.

FOLKLORE - GOLF CLUB MODIFICATIONS

In your era it was an art form with the tinkering and tweaking of your equipment to get the best results. Can you describe the sort of tweaking you would do for your equipment and for other elite golfers?

That would be a lengthy answer. People have always undermined the incredible skill and feel that the players have, with their ability to be able to decipher whether one shaft is better than the other. They still have the ability today but they have multiple choices today. We never had that. In my era we would have to wait sometimes 2, 3 or 4 weeks to get one set of clubs. We had to adjust the lies, the bounce … we had to weed out the bad shafts that didn't feel like it was a matched set. The search for a persimmon driver was never ending. Players learnt to tinker with their clubs, not necessarily by choice, but by necessity. There wasn't frequencies, there wasn't graphite shafts, no one knew what kick point was, no one knew what a matched set of frequency shafts were. Players would basically order two or three sets of clubs and pick out the ones they liked out of the three sets to get the best selection they could. We had leather grips, but no one could really wrap on a leather grip to a player's liking. It was very complicated.

If you had a set of clubs that you liked, but there was one club that wasn't quite right, would you try and tweak it a bit to make it work or just throw it away?

You would either try and tweak it or get a replacement that felt the same. It was uncanny ... the ability of every top player to say 'my favourite club is the 6-iron and my least favourite club is the 4-iron, they just don't feel the same'. They didn't look the same, because most of the clubs were ground by grinders, so if two people ground one set of clubs you would get a little bit of variation in looks. In those days we would even go to somewhere like PGF and you would stand there, guys like **Kel Nagle** and all these other pros would stand there and watch these guys grind the clubs and they would request, a little bit off here and little bit off there. Then you would have to wait three or four days for them to get chromed.

You're known as one of the best club modification pros of that era – you even helped golfers like _Jack Nicklaus_. Did you have a workshop at home with scales and specialised tools?

Sure. I had a workshop everywhere I travelled. If I wasn't at home, I had a workshop in a hotel room. I'd be at hardware stores. I would always travel with grips and glue and you would always find a club repair shop somewhere – it might be twenty miles away, but you would drive down there. I used to do most of it myself and I knew how to do it. When epoxy came into the business it made it even easier because you could re-shaft clubs and you didn't have to worry about putting pins down them and the heads flying off. We were always fiddling with stuff.

Can you think of a time when you came up with a new technique to modify a club and you went to hit it and it felt pure … then the next week you went out refreshed and won a tournament with it?

I tweaked my clubs every week no matter how I played. You would always find a different wedge with a little bit of a different bounce, or a different weight. It was very common in those days for players to be searching with their equipment, but they did it by feel – they didn't do it like they do now. They have these trailers at the tournaments and they can get a full brand new set of clubs in about 30 minutes. We never had that luxury. They don't have to spend time tinkering with their clubs any more … they have people, lots of people. [Laughs.]

I swung a club with several pounds of weight in the head since the day **Gary Player** told me to do it.

Folklore

The stymie was removed from the rules of golf in 1952. A stymie was possible only in matches involving one ball per side. On the putting green, if two players' balls were more than six inches apart, there was no provision for the ball nearer the hole to be lifted. If that ball lay directly in the way to the hole of the ball to be played then the player was 'stymied'.

He could try to play around or over the interfering ball, but if the nearer ball was struck, no penalty ensued. However, the opponent had the option of playing the ball as it lay or replacing it. If the nearer ball had been knocked into the hole the opponent was considered to have holed out with his previous stroke.

By 1956 on the putting green the rules indicated that the ball 'should' be marked with a small coin or similar recommended item. The rule was changed to 'shall be marked' in 1976.

The 1952 elimination of the stymie from the Rules of Golf was so unpopular in Britain that it was bemoaned on the front pages of several newspapers. In America, **Bob Jones** was so disappointed by the stymie's elimination that he commented, 'The only place where I think a real mistake was made [in the 1952 unification of the Rules] came with the elimination of the stymie.' An entire chapter of Jones' book Golf Is My Game is devoted to the stymie's removal.

In 1974, the R&A outlawed the small ball in Open Championship, but it wasn't until 1990 that the R&A adopted the USGA's 1.68-inch (42.67 mm)minimum diameter rule, relegating the small ball to history. The 'British Ball' was smaller, at 1.62 inches (41.15 mm). That may seem like too tiny a difference to mean anything tangible. But that 3.7% difference in diameter translates into 7.5% less wind that the ball must cut through during flight.

Today a player is required to stand erect, hold the ball at shoulder height and drop it at arm's length (Rule 20-2a); however, prior to 1984 the player was required to drop the ball over his shoulder.

Dr Frank Barney Gorton Stableford's scoring system was first used in competition at Wallasey Golf Club in England in 1932. His unique system has been widely acknowledged for helping speed up the pace of play in club golf competitions.

Gene Sarazen introduced the sand iron in 1932. He used his new design for the first time in the 1932 Open Championship, which he duly won. He was quite a poor bunker player prior to 1932.

The average 18-hole score for the average golfer remains at about 100, as it has for decades, according to the National Golf Foundation, an industry research-and-consulting service. Among more serious recreational golfers who register their scores with the US Golf Association, the average handicap index, a scoring tool, has dropped 0.5 strokes since 2000. On the PGA Tour this year, the average score of players has risen, by 0.28 strokes, compared with 10 years ago.

The driver swing speed of an average lady golfer is 62 mph (100 kph); 96 mph (154 kph) for an average LPGA professional; 84 mph (135 kph) for an average male golfer; 108 mph (174 kph) for an average PGA Tour player; 148-152 mph (238-245 kph) for a national long drive champion.

José Maria Olazábal was the first player to win a Major golf tournament using a metal-headed wood: the 1994 US Masters.

Dai Rees is best remembered as the captain of the Great Britain Ryder Cup team which defeated the United States at Lindrick Golf Club in Yorkshire, England in 1957. It was the only defeat which the United States suffered in the competition between 1933 and 1985.

World Golf Hall Of Fame inductee (2013) **Colin Montgomerie** (Scotland) never won a US PGA tour event. 'Monty' won seven consecutive European Order Of Merit titles from 1993 to 1999 and finished runner up five times in Majors. He holds one of the finest Ryder Cup records (for Europe) having never been beaten in singles and amassed 23.5 points for Europe.

During the final round of the 1978 US Masters, **Gary Player** came from seven shots behind 54-hole leader **Hubert Green** by birdying seven of the last ten holes to win the green jacket. It was his third green jacket. His final round was 64. Hubert Green shot even par 72 to finish one stroke behind Player, tied second with **Rod Funseth** and **Tom Watson**.

In 1945 **Byron Nelson** won eleven tournaments in succession on the US PGA tour. He won a total of 18 tournaments in 1945 and his stroke average was 68.33. Through his peak he had 113 consecutive top 20 finishes. He won the US Masters (1937 & 1942), the US Open (1939) and the US PGA (1940 & 1945). He contested The Open Championship once in his prime, finishing 5th to **Henry Cotton** in 1937. Nelson gained 5 strokes on **Ben Hogan** in 8 holes to win the US Masters in 1942 by one stroke in an 18-hole playoff. He retired when he was 34 years old to become a rancher, though continued his work with golf commentary and endorsements.

The inaugural Los Angeles Open (1926), won by **Harry Cooper**, was the first tournament to offer $10,000 to the winner.

The US Open was first shown on television in 1954. Won by **Ed Furgol** (USA) with 284 (+4). By 1977 the final two rounds were broadcast live. In 1982 all four rounds were broadcast live.

Sam Snead had 48 top ten finishes in the Majors, but only played The Open Championship three times, winning in 1946 at St Andrews. In the 1949–1950 season **Samuel Jackson Snead** became the first player in the history of the game to pass $200,000 in official winnings.

There are approximately 32,000 golf courses on planet Earth with more than half of them in America.

Jack Nicklaus is the most prolific winner of the four Major golf championships with 18 victories. Few remember that he came second 19 times.

Shigeki Maruyama (Japan) shot 58 at Woodmont Country Club in Rockville, Maryland while qualifying for the US Open in 2000. In recognition of this achievement, his father renamed a golf course he owned in Tochigi Prefecture to the '58 Golf Course'. **Ryo Ishikawa** shot an amazing 12 under par (58) in the final round of The Crowns event on the Japan Golf Tour in 2010.

Arnold Palmer came to Australia to play tournament golf seven times; 1961, '63, '64, '66, '68, '70 and 1977. He notched his first Australian victory in 1963 at the Wills Masters at The Lakes in Sydney and he also won the Australian Open in 1966 at Royal Queensland with rounds of 67-70-66-73.

Babe Didrikson Zaharias was an outstanding female athlete who won two gold medals at the 1932 Olympic Games for the 80-metre hurdles and the Javelin throw. She also won a silver medal for the high jump. She turned to professional golf in 1947, aged 36, and in her first year on the ladies' PGA tour of America she won ten times and went on to win all the ladies Major golf tournaments of her era. She died of bowel cancer aged 45.

Charles Sifford is the first black man to be inducted into the World Golf Hall Of Fame. He was an outstanding golfer who was not allowed to join the US PGA tour (in the 1950s) because he was black. He finally became a tour member in 1961 and won two tour events and achieved 21 professional victories. **Charles Sifford**'s legacy will forever be his efforts to desegregate the PGA of America.

photo: 1964 Peter Thomson watches Hara Sumitomo National Archives of Australia B942, Sport (13)

photo of Jim Ferrier courtesy of Golf Australia.

Jim Ferrier

Jim Ferrier was a pioneer of Australian golf and a wonderful putter. He won 18 tour events in America including the US PGA in 1947 which pronounced him as Australia's first major golf champion, even though he had become a US citizen by 1944. A big man, Ferrier was known to be wild off the tee, but with incredible putting ability. In the final match for the US PGA title his opponent, **Chick Harbert**, never made Ferrier hit a second putt on any of the greens – they were all conceded.

Born into a golfing family, Ferrier's grandfather was a scratch golfer at Carnoustie in Scotland, who later settled in China and designed one of the first Chinese golf courses. Ferrier's father, born in China, was five times club champion of Shanghai and later became the secretary of Manly Golf Club when the family relocated to Australia. By the age of 15 big Jim Ferrier was club champion of Manly Golf Club and a year later won the first of what would become four NSW Amateur titles.

Ferrier's matches/rivalry against Victorian prodigy **Harry Williams** are the thing of folklore, Ferrier from Sydney versus Williams from Melbourne. Williams prevailed with a decisive winning record in their matchplay encounters. In 1935 Ferrier shot 67-65-70-64 at Killara to win the NSW Closed championship by 16 shots. As the Australian Amateur champion (1935, 1936, 1938, 1939) Ferrier went to Britain to play the British Amateur Championship (1936) where he made it past nearly 300 players to reach the final against noted **Scot Hector Thomson**, but he lost on the final hole. A year later Ferrier (and Williams) was controversially left off the Australian team that toured Britain. Ferrier and his wife set off for America in 1940 and he turned professional.

Ferrier served as a Sergeant in the US Army from 1944 to 1945. He also won the Australian Amateur and Australian Open in the same year twice – in 1938 and 1939. In 1946 he had two hole-in-ones during the San Francisco Open. Ferrier won nearly 20 times on the US tour, including 5 wins in 1951. He won the Canadian Open in 1950 and 1951. In 1950 he had a scoring average of 70.27 and was second on the US tours money list to the great **Sam Snead**. Ferrier had 14 top tens in Major tournaments including second in the 1950 Masters tournament where Ferrier led a field that included **Sam Snead**, **Ben Hogan**, **Byron Nelson** and **Gene Sarazen** by 4 shots after three rounds. Ferrier's final round 75 left him two behind winner Jimmy Demaret in outright second place. Sam Snead finished 3rd, Ben Hogan and Byron Nelson tied 4th. Ferrier also tied fifth in the 1950 US Open.

In 1947 Ferrier shot 263 (66-67-65-65) to win the Grand Rapids tournament in Michigan, USA and break the world record low score for four rounds. One of the giants of Australian golf, Jim Ferrier is not in the World Golf Hall of Fame.

James Bennett Elliott Ferrier (1915–1986)

Joe Kirkwood

Born in Sydney, Australia in 1897, Joe Kirkwood grew up on a sheep station. He went on to become a true pioneer for World golf by travelling the world doing golf and trick shot exhibitions with the flamboyant Hall Of Fame golfer, Walter Hagen. Joe Kirkwood became the first Australian to win on the US PGA tour by winning the 1923 Houston Invitational. Joe has never been given the respect or recognition he deserved. His wonderful mastery of the game was legendary. His ability to play all the shots, left- or right-handed, high and low, probably led to his downfall as a player. It was said that he could not decide which type of shot to hit. One thing he did do was turn people on to golf, travelling all over the world with Walter Hagen.

In April 1917 he went around Riversdale (Melbourne) in 65 and Royal Melbourne in 68. A Riversdale member then challenged him to a match in which the member used a full set of clubs and Kirkwood only his putter. Using a straight-faced goose-necked putter Kirkwood shot 74 off the stick and won by 14 shots.

In 1921 Kirkwood went to America and Britain, famously beating the legendary Harry Vardon in his first match in Britain. After nearly winning the British Open in 1921 (6th) and 1923 (4th), Joe Kirkwood did manage to come tied third in the British Open (1927) won by the legendary Bobby Jones. In 1922 he beat the best professionals in Britain by an astonishing thirteen strokes in a tournament at Lossiemouth.

After settling in America and winning five events in 1923 alone, Kirkwood determined there was more money in trick shot exhibitions and this became his focus. He later teamed up with the great Walter Hagen, travelling the world together, Kirkwood doing the trick shots and Hagen wooing the crowds/women with his convivial nature. He says that he learned to hit trick shots with the use of just one arm or leg to offer encouragement to injured soldiers who were missing limbs after World War I.

Joe Kirkwood's efforts to popularise the game in Australia have largely gone unrecognised. For it was Joe who attracted American superstars Gene Sarazen and Walter Hagen to tour Australia in the early 1930s which really ignited interest in the game. Joe continued to travel the world spreading interest in the game with his exceptional trick shot routine. Kirkwood was quite a celebrity in his day and did exhibitions for the Prime Minister of Australia, the Emperor of Japan in the Imperial Garden and for the Duke and Duchess of Windsor.

Joe Kirkwood claims to have played over 6000 golf courses in his travels and says his finest round was 62 on a par 72 course at the age of 63. He twice shot rounds of 62 when he was 63 years of age. Kirkwood is credited with scoring twenty-nine holes-in-one, two of which came in the same round and one of them off the face of a watch during a trick-shot exhibition. He popularised the use of wooden tees instead of placing the ball on small mounds of sand or dirt. He returned to Australia in 1928, 1930, 1934, 1937 and 1954; in the 1930s, with Hagen and Sarazen, he attracted large crowds.

The Stowe Country Club in Vermont (USA), where Joe was the first club professional, has held the Joe Kirkwood Memorial Golf Tournament annually since 1967. In his honour, the annual winner of the Australian PGA Championship receives the Kirkwood Cup. His autobiography, as told to Barbara Fey, was published posthumously in 1973 under the title Links of Life and is endorsed by both Richard Nixon and Dwight Eisenhower. Joe Kirkwood is in the American golf Hall Of Fame.

'I first saw Joe Kirkwood when he came out with Walter Hagen. The trick shots that Joe did – he had so much command, or control, over what he did. Hitting shots off someone's toe, a knee, off a watch face … hitting two balls with the one club, hitting with two clubs in his hands, hitting two shots hooking one, slicing the other. He was unbelievable. Many people think he was only a trick shot player, but he was better than that. He won the Australian Open, the Canadian Open ... he won several tournaments in the US as well.'
Norman Von Nida

Joseph Henry Kirkwood (1897-1970)

Folklore

photo: opposite 1925 Joe Kirkwood at Troon for Open Championship qualifier via John W Fischer III, this page photo courtesy of Stowe Golf Club Vermont USA

Joe Kirkwood

photos: left and above courtesy of Stowe Golf Club Vermont USA. Opposite Joe Kirkwood by Sam Hood (1872-1953) NSW State Library - Home and Away 2623

Travels

I've had my laughs where tall giraffes
laid stymies from the tee.
I've missed my two's where kangaroos
were standing close by me.

From Burma to the Golden Gate,
from Maine to Singapore,
from Sydney to the Great Divide,
I've stood and hollered, 'Fore.'

The Seven Seas have known my tees,
beneath an all-world sky.
I've carried ruts and missed my putts
where cobras slithered by.

From Palm Beach to the Chinese Wall,
by Durban's Tropic Loam,
I've slashed my drives along the route,
from California up to Nome.

I've made my score in old Jahore,
cheered by Sultanic queens,
where tigers glared and rhinos stared,
and pythons trapped the greens.

From Shanghai to the Rio Grande,
by Amazon and Nile,
I haven't tried Moscow yet,
but that can wait awhile.

JOE KIRKWOOD
(*Links of Life* by Joe Kirkwood as told to Barbara Fey;
privately published, Oklahoma City, OK, 1973; p. 133)

CANADA CUP 1959 AT ROYAL MELBOURNE

Kel and I had won the Canada Cup in 1954 in Montreal Canada, but it was particularly nice to win it again in 1959 in front of our supportive home crowd at Royal Melbourne. The local support no doubt had a part to play in our success.

Peter Thomson

photos: Opposite, National Archives of Australia A1200, L33764 Canada Cup Wales 1959 crowds. Right, Kel Nagle Canada Cup 1959 with his partner Peter Thomson standing in the background photographer Neil Murray National Archives of Australia A1200, L33757. Above, courtesy of Golf Australia's archives.

Billy Dunk

Course records are only one round, they are not a golf tournament.

You've got to practise those bunker shots, wear out a few sand irons.

Well, I suppose it gets you that way, if you start to miss a couple.

You've got to be a madman to play the bloody game.

The only thing I can think of that doesn't change is the size of the bloody hole.

I don't follow sports these days; I stick in my garden and watch the view out of my back door and that is about it. I sometimes watch the last six holes of a golf tournament.

Arnold Palmer had an aura about him. He could walk into a room anywhere and he was the man! A charisma you couldn't believe.

Nagle is the nicest man you will ever see.

Charlie Sifford [African-American professional golfer who helped desegregate the PGA of America] was a great player who never got the chance in the US because he was black. He was a big man, big feet, big hands, could hit it everywhere … when I was in the US in the '60s in any town you went you could draw a line down the middle of the street and you couldn't go on 'that' side of the line – you went on 'this' side. If you went on 'that' side you were in the wrong part of town.

Up until the mid '80s I used the small ball. I never liked the bigger ball.

I think it is an easy game as it is. All you've got to do is hit it from here to there and put it in the hole. That is not hard. Most people make it hard because they think hard. All of a sudden they think 'I can't do this' and 'What if I slice it? What if I hook it? What if I top it?' and all of a sudden they are not thinking about what they are doing. The more you play, the more you practise, you know you are not going to top it. You've got a fair chance of hitting the middle of the bloody green anyway, so it is not all that hard to do. It is more mental than anything else.

I played better when I was uptight. I used to have to get mad.

Tommy Bolt smashing up a dustbin to get the crowd to come and watch his group – all the crowd was two holes in front, watching Nicklaus.

I don't believe the golf clubs ever made much difference to me. I just believe you've got to hit it in the middle of the club to hit a good shot. Doesn't matter what club you use.

photos: Right, courtesy of Bill Dunk's personal collection. Opposite, John W Fischer III archives.

Timeless Peter Thomson Quotes

In the future, we may get around to
having championships where the greens
have different speeds.

If you hit the centre of the green
with your iron shot, you're never far
from the flag, no matter where
they put it.

Once a carpenter has mastered all
his tools, he can make anything.

Technology means that now, in my mid 70s,
I can drive almost as far as in my youth.

Golf arrived before anyone knew what it was.

I played 30 Open Championships and
I kept saying that I lost 25. So it
wasn't that big a strike rate but it was.

photo: Black Knight International Archives

Question: I found it fascinating reading your thoughts on traditional links golf where the objective is to run the ball onto the green and the difference between that traditional style and the modern American style of golf - flying the golf ball to the target. Given the dominance of American golf around the world, do you think that style of golf of amateurs being able to run the ball in, is a dying style of golf?

Tom Watson: No. I don't think so. You still see a lot of courses that are designed that way, for instance the greens are open where the balls can run on the green. I think that is an integral part of the game. I don't think every shot into the green that you should be able to run it on with the full width of the green, but I think most of the holes should offer that option to run it on somewhere. That is the way I like to design golf courses, I don't like the 'forced carries' that they are making golfers play so many times now. The most important shot in golf is the straight shot and if you hit a straight shot you should be rewarded with that. If you are a little off in your distance you shouldn't be penalised for that. The wayward shots, left and right, those are the ones you should be penalised for and that is where the hazards should be.

Tom Watson

Above: Bobby Locke putting at the Goodall Tournament USA. John W Fischer III archives.

Left: Tom Watson courtesy of Golf Australia archives.

QUOTES

How did I make a twelve on a par five hole? It's simple.
I missed a four-foot putt for an eleven.
Arnold Palmer

You don't know what pressure is until you play for
five bucks with only two bucks in your pocket.
Lee Trevino

For this game you need, above all things,
to be in a tranquil frame of mind.
Harry Vardon

Don't play too much golf.
Two rounds a day are plenty.
Harry Vardon

Golf is about how well you accept, respond to, and score
with your misses much more so than it is a game of your
perfect shots.
Dr Bob Rotella

Why am I using a new putter?
Because the last one didn't float too well.
Craig Stadler

I don't say my golf game is bad,
but if I grew tomatoes they'd come
up sliced.
Author Unknown

Have you ever noticed what
golf spells backwards?
Al Boliska

Be decisive.
A wrong decision is generally less
disastrous than indecision.
Bernhard Langer

Golf is a compromise between what your ego wants you to do,
what experience tells you to do, and what your nerves let you do.
Bruce Crampton

I just try to put it on the fairway,
then the green and not three putt.
Peter Thomson

If you stop and say 'why me' you will fail.
You will create roadblocks for yourself.
Tom Watson

The proper score for a businessman golfer is 90. If he is better than that he is neglecting his business. If he's worse, he's neglecting his golf.

St Andrews Rotary Club Member

Reverse every natural instinct and do the opposite of what you are inclined to do, and you will probably come very close to having a perfect golf swing.

Ben Hogan

They call it golf because all the other four-letter words were taken.

Raymond Floyd

Hitting the ball is the fun part of it, but the fewer times you hit the ball the more fun you have.

Lou Graham

There is an old saying: *if a man comes home with sand in his cuffs and cockleburs in his pants, don't ask him what he shot.*

Sam Snead

The only time my prayers are never answered is on the golf course.

Craig Stadler

I've spent most of my life golfing. The rest I've just wasted.

Author Unknown

If you think it's hard to meet new people, try picking up the wrong golf ball.

Jack Lemmon

Golf is like a chain. You always have to work on the weakest links.

George Archer

It's good sportsmanship to not pick up lost golf balls while they are still rolling.

Mark Twain

Golf and sex are the only things you can enjoy without being good at them.

Jimmy DeMaret

When I die, bury me on the golf course, so my husband will visit.

Author Unknown

If I hit it right, it's a slice. If I hit it left, it's a hook. If I hit it straight, it's a miracle.

Author Unknown

AUTHOR'S PERSPECTIVE AND GRATITUDE

One thing that has struck me from all the interviews and all the interactions I have had with golf's champions is that they are all content within themselves, they all seem happy and there is not much that can ruffle their feathers. Imagine taking an attitude like that onto the golf course, an attitude that ensures the inevitable inequity you are dealt on the course, via a poor lie or a gross injustice, does not upset you, at all. You are calm, you are balanced, contented and you are ready for whatever is around the corner, good or bad. That, to me, seems like one of the vital ingredients for top-level golf.

This book would never have happened if it wasn't for the serendipity of my life crossing paths with Ross Perrett on an international flight from Los Angeles to New Zealand in 1999. The magic man – that is, Perrett – sat next to me on a flight I should never have been able to board … fate has an interesting way. I couldn't quite believe it when he told me he was working with the legend that is Peter Thomson. Without that connection, I would be lost in no-man's land in the golf industry. Ross Perrett saw the light in me and he encouraged me, as he does to many young upstarts. I was 23 at the time.

Peter Thomson is a book all to himself.

Some readers will look at this book and ask questions, the most obvious of which is, 'Where is Greg Norman?' Having come from a background of publishing surfing books I truly thought that Greg Norman, a former surfer, would see the surfing books and want to contribute to this book. I can assure the readers that I did offer Mr Norman the opportunity to contribute – but his manager, Bart Collins, politely declined. Beyond Greg Norman there are so many names missing if this book was a 'history of Australian golf'. As stated in the introduction, it is not a history and I apologise to any elder gents of the game that are not enshrined in these pages and feel they should be.

From all the research that this book has demanded of me there have come some interesting insights and lessons for me, the golfer. It is my hope that those insights and lessons do present themselves to the reader in a subtle way. After talking to Gary Player for forty-five minutes I went to my home course and shot three under for nine holes and holed two bunker shots. For the next four weeks I woke up and went to sleep doing push-ups … these great players have an effect on people around them, there is nothing surer. It is my hope that their fine words have a positive impact on all golfers who read this book.

For those interested in my previous books, they too were entirely independent and self-published. *Switch-foot: Surfing, Art & Music* was published in 2005 and won several awards in the surfing industry. More importantly it was a successful first book that afforded me to keep going. *Switch-Foot II* was published in 2009 and is currently still available. *Acumen: Inspiring Answers To Life's Big Questions* is also still available through my online shop at switch-foot.com

Over the last two years, the most helpful people to me in compiling this book were, in order: my wife Felicity Taylor-Crockett and daughter Lola Taylor Crockett for allowing me to be so inattentive while my mind was filled with golf, John W Fischer III (USA) for foraging through his archives and knowledge to support the book, Ross Perrett for providing me with encouragement to start the book in the first place, Bruce Crampton for allowing me to tell his story, Frank Phillips for the putting lesson, Sam Arthur (*Inside Golf* Magazine) for being such a good man behind the scenes in Australian Golf, Moira Drew (Golf Australia museum) for aiding in the gathering of images, Nicolle Powell (Australian PGA) for connecting me to Bruce Devlin and assisting in image research, Robert A. Wade for being the happiest older gent I have ever met and painting truly wonderful watercolours, Harry Daily for illustrating the book with his handwriting and sketches, Mike Orloff (Gary Player Golf Course Design) for connecting me to the 'Black Knight', Steve Taylor (Cornwall, UK) for always being supportive and proud, Peter Thomson for being so gracious with his time and wisdom, Tom Moore (Golf Heritage Society) for his knowledge of the history, Bruce Young Media for connecting me to Sir Bob Charles, Hamish Jones (Golf Australia) for aiding discussions with Tom Watson, Jamie Kasdaglis for his beautiful art and Andy Sibley at Gemini Tiger creative for knowing how to make this book look timeless. Thanks Tim Learner for being so professional with his proofreading.

I also want to thank, in no particular order but with immense gratitude: Debbie Longenecker and Grace Lipscomb from the Gary Player Group, Jon Perrett from the Best In Golf group for aiding in the connection to Gary Player, Norman Von Nida's daughter Kerri Easdown, John Hay for his passionate work towards Norman Von Nida's legacy, Ian Stanley for teaching me how to read the grain, Bob Shearer for letting me drive his V8, Annette Dunk for the lovely photos of Bill, Helen Perrett for being a supermum and some, Mary Thomson for being a wonderful lady, Kel Nagle for being so humble and content, Matthew Murray (Singapore), Alan 'Murky' Murray, Bill Dunk for his laconic statements, Frank Williams, Richard Marts at PGA in America for helping connect me with Bruce Crampton, Eamonn Taylor (Scotland) for digging through the Mitchell Library archives and finding the Bruce Crampton newspaper clippings from 1957, Bruce Devlin for believing in me and connecting me to David Graham, David Graham for giving me the time of day, Sir Bob Charles for his hand-written letter, Jack and Jackie Newton for being so giving, Tom Watson for speaking with me at the 2012 Australian Open, Mal Chalmers for teeing up the game with Peter Senior at Hope Island.

The Mitchell Library in Glasgow, Almaz Berhe Copyright and Production Services at The National Museum of Australia, Sam Hood (1872-1953) - photographer who took many of the archival photos published from the State Library of NSW, Mark Vivian Picture Research Manager at The Mary Evans Picture Library UK, Lynn Altadonna at Stowe Golf Club for the help with the Joe Kirkwood images, Steven Cable at The National Archives Britain, Simon Wilson World Sport Group for the photo of Adam Scott, Nick Wilson, Andrew Cunningham from Studio Pazzo, Davyd Reeves at Mt Broughton Golf Club, Alex Cleave at Lake Karringyup Golf Club, Jim Wallace in NZ for the early photo of Sir Bob Charles, Sarah Hall-Kearins Imaging and Photographic Services National Archives of Australia, Elise Edmonds Head of Pictures State Library of New South Wales, Jo Millington and Phil Scott at The Adam Scott Company, Cara Downes at the National Archives of Australia, Rebecca Corbett at the National Archives of Australia, Ben Sibson Funding Manager Regional Arts NSW.

Scott Tolley Vice President, Corporate Communications at Jack Nicklaus and the Nicklaus Companies, Jim Mandeville, Director of Photography at The Nicklaus Companies, The Jack Nicklaus Museum, Lee Bradsell at Royal Sydney Golf Club, Bernie Hogan at Thomson & Perrett for assistance with images and for helping me around Melbourne, Jan Rowsell at New Zealand Golf for the assistance with the Sir Bob Charles image from Photosport, Ryan Heywood at Procasual Studio Byron Bay, Graeme Ryan at Ryan Publishing for the Harry Williams image, Norm from the Australian Golf Heritage Society, Emma Williams curator at The Australian Golf Heritage Society, Geoff Gough for the Norman Von Nida interview, Henry Epstein for assistance in communicating with Adam Scott, James Crockett (brother) for aiding with cheap flights, Carl Stevens (Royal Sydney) for the fine hospitality, Ben Robertson (author) for his encouragement, Des Tobin (author) for the Peter Toogood words, Terry Smith (author) for creating wonderful golf books that inspired me, Jack Pollard (author) for creating wonderful factual sporting books, Graham Marsh for his fine contribution and well-rounded approach to the game, Jan Tellstrom for his timeless hickory golf photos, Lionel Freedman Chairman World Hickory Open Championship, James Davis from the Hickory Golf Society (USA) for being a passionate and generous fellow and helping to connect me to the rest of the hickory golf world, Alan Grieve for showing me how to play with hickories, Helen Joseph at The Australian Golf Club, Michael Court for the Norman Von Nida tape, George Greenough, Craig Coster at Graham Marsh Golf Design for aiding with the connection to Graham Marsh, Greg Ramsey in Tasmania for the education on the Pearce brothers, John J Marsh at Secession Golf Club (USA), Scott Hend for being an inspiring golfer from my junior days who went on to the top level showing us it could be done, Nigel Arnison for the insights into the Ben Hogan swing, Chris Graham PGA Professional at Ocean Shores golf club who said to me 'you have to do a book for the simple reason that half the people I teach don't even know who Bill Dunk is, the guy is a legend.'

Thank you, Bruce Green, for showing me around Royal Melbourne's composite course, an experience I will never forget.

My gratitude towards Jack Nicklaus and Gary Player will forever be permanent. I cannot state highly enough how appreciative I am for their kind-hearted nature, given how busy they both are. I wish I had more time to try and communicate with Arnold Palmer and Lee Trevino, two giants of the game. For those who are interested, you do not get to interview these great men without a track record, references, persistence, patience and good timing.

A special thanks to Tom Berndt (PGA Professional) who taught me as a teenager and helped me solidify the foundations my grandfather had given me with the golf swing, foundations that have enabled me to stay close to a scratch handicap for twenty years. Thank you to my golfing friends at Karana Downs Country Club, Indooroopilly Golf Club, Middle Ridge Golf Club, Ocean Shores Golf Club, Cape Cornwall Golf Club and The Moonah Links Legends.

Thank you to Adam Scott for writing the foreword to this book and being a younger Australian golfer who appreciates the history of the game. In my opinion he has the finest golf swing of the modern era. Beyond that he conducts himself like a true gentleman off the course and is a fine ambassador for Australian golf, following in the footsteps of Joe Kirkwood, Norman Von Nida, Peter Thomson and Greg Norman.

Finally I want to thank my parents Sue and Toby Crockett who helped me pay some bills while this book was being compiled. Without their financial support this book may never have been completed. The book had been on my mind since 2005. Beginning in 2011 it took two years of fulltime work to complete. In that period and with very little time to play golf my handicap dropped from 6 to 3, playing on average once a month. I hope the words of the masters improves your game like it has mine.

Andrew J Crockett, July 2013

photo: Glenna Collett Vare 1928 Pebble Beach

MAJOR GOLF CHAMPIONS FROM AUSTRALIA

Men's	Jim Ferrier	1947 US PGA Championship
	Peter Thomson	1954, 1955, 1956, 1958, 1965 The Open Championship
	Kel Nagle	1960 British Open Championship
	David Graham	1979 US PGA Championship, 1981 US Open Championship
	Greg Norman	1986, 1993 The Open Championship
	Wayne Grady	1990 US PGA Championship
	Ian Baker-Finch	1991 The Open Championship
	Steve Elkington	1995 US PGA Championship
	Geoff Ogilvy	2006 US Open Championship
	Adam Scott	2013 US Masters Championship
Women's	Karrie Webb	2000, 2006 Kraft Nabisco Championship, 2001 LPGA Championship, 2000, 2001 US Women's Open Championship, 1999 du Maurier Classic and 2002 Women's British Open Championship.
	Jan Stephenson	1982 LPGA Championship, 1983 US Women's Open Championship, 1981 du Maurier Classic.

BIBLIOGRAPHY

Adams, Matthew E. *Fairways Of Life – Golf Wisdom of the Legends*. New York: Morgan James Publishing, 2011.

Campbell, Bailey. *Golf Lessons From Sam Snead*. London: Frederick Muller, 1965.

Cousins, Geoffrey & Scott, Tom. *A Century Of Opens*. Sydney: Shakespeare Head Press, 1971.

Feinstein, John. *A Good Walk Spoiled – Days and Nights on the PGA Tour*. London: Warner Books, 1996.

James, Russell. *David Graham – From Ridicule to Acclaim*. Melbourne: Ryan Publishing, 2012.

Kel Nagle interviewed by Neil Bennetts, 27th August 1990. TRC 2628.

MacLaren, Muir. *The Australian Golfer's Handbook*. Fourth Edition. Sydney: Langside, 1968.

Macpherson, Scott. *St Andrews – The Evolution Of The Old Course. The Impact on golf of Time, Tradition & Technology*. Christchurch, New Zealand: Hazard Press, 2007.

Mitchell, Peter. *The Complete Golfer – Peter Thomson*. Melbourne: Lothian, 1991.

Moloney, Brendan & Thomson, Peter. *Moonah Links – Home Of Australian Golf*. Sydney: Playright Publishing, 2007.

Nagle, Kel, Von Nida, Norman, Ferrier, Jim & Thomson, Peter. *The Secrets Of Australia's Golfing Success*. Melbourne: Lansdowne Press, 1961.

National Library Of Australia. Oral History and Folklore Collection.

Norman Von Nida interviewed by Neil Bennetts, 1980. TRC 391/47.

Perkin, Steve. *Lessons I have Learned – Peter Thomson – Inspirations and Insights from Australia's Greatest Golfer*. Melbourne: Geoff Slattery Publishing, 2005.

Perrett, Ross & Baker, Kimbal. *Golf Courses Of The Mornington Peninsula*. Edited by Paul Daley. Melbourne: Eagles Nest Publishing, 2005.

Peter Thomson interviewed by Marnie Haig Muir, 4th March 2008. Bid ID 4348366.

Player, Gary. *Play Golf with Gary Player*. London: Collins, 1962.

Pollard, Jack. *Australian Golf – The Game and The Players*. Sydney: Collins/Angus & Robertson, 1990.

Pollard, Jack. *Golf – The Australian Way*. Melbourne: Lansdowne Press, 1970.

Ramsey, Tom. *25 Great Australian Golf Courses – and How To Play Them*. Adelaide: Rigby Publishers, 1981.

Ramsey, Tom. *Golfer's Gift Book*. Adelaide: Rigby, 1983.

Robertson, Ben. *The Von – Stories and Suggestions from Australian Golf's Little Master*. Brisbane: University of Queensland Press, 1999.

Rotella, Robert. *Golf is not a Game Of Perfect*. London: Pocket Books, 2004.

Senyard, June. *Harry Williams – An Australian Golfing Tragedy*. Melbourne: Ryan Publishing, 1998.

Smith, Terry. *Australian Golf – The First 100 Years*. Sydney: Lester-Townsend Publishing, 1982.

Smith, Terry. *The Champions and The Courses They Played – Celebrating the Centenary of the Australian Open*. Melbourne: Geoff Slattery Publishing, 2004.

Smith, Terry. *The Complete Book Of Australian Golf*. Ultimo, NSW: Murray Books, 1975.

Snead, Sam. *Natural Golf*. London: Burke Publishing, 1954.

Sommers, Robert & Brown, Cal. *Great Shots*. Sydney: Pan Books, 1989.

Sowell, David. *The Masters – A hole-by-hole History of America's Classic*. Dulles, Virginia: Brassey's Inc, 2003.

Thomson, Peter. *Peter Thomson's Classic Golf Holes of Australia*. Melbourne: Lothian, 1988.

Tobin, Des. *Simply Toogood – Peter Toogood's Life In Golf*. Melbourne: Killaghy Publishing, 2003.

Von Nida, Norman. *Golf Is My Business*. London: Shakespeare Head Press, 1956.

Wade, Robert. *The Art Of Golf*. Melbourne: Wade Publishing, 2011.

White, John. *The Golf Miscellany – Second Edition*. London: Carlton Books, 2007.

Worley, David. *Bill Edgar – A Legend In Amateur Golf*. Brighton, Victoria: David Worley, 1995.

National Library Of Australia. Oral History and Folklore Collection.

- - -

Peter Thomson interviewed by Marnie Haig Muir, 4th March 2008. Bid ID 4348366.

Kel Nagle interviewed by Neil Bennetts, 27th August 1990. TRC 2628.

Norman Von Nida interviewed by Neil Bennetts, 1980. TRC

PHOTO CREDITS

All hand drawn fonts are by Harry Daily. All hand drawn illustration line drawings are by Harry Daily.
Dedication page, photo of Mickey Heald and author Andrew Crockett by Sue Crockett Photography.
Page 7 People walking St Andrews Scotland (circa 1950) from John W Fischer III archives
Page 132 photo of Norman Von Nida courtesy of the Australian PGA.
Page 150, 151 and 154 by Andrew Crockett
Page 171 Jack Nicklaus game fishing images courtesy of the Jack Nicklaus Museum. Artwork 1908 Clyde Pearce courtesy of the Australian Golf Club.

Artwork on page 28, 30 and 31 is by Robert A. Wade

At The Feet Of The Masters Collage (pages 26–27)

Bill Dunk image from Bill Dunk's private collection

Bruce Crampton image from Bruce Crampton's private collection

Bruce Devlin from the National Archives of Australia (A1200, L58266)

David Graham portrait by artist Darren Love.

Frank Phillips image from Frank Phillip's private collection

Gary Player image from Black Knight International archives

Graham Marsh, Ian Stanley, Bob Shearer images from courtesy of Golf Australia's Museum Collection, managed by the Golf Society of Australia.

Jack Newton image from Jack Newton's private collection

Jack Nicklaus image from Jim Mandeville/the Nicklaus Companies

Jan Stephenson image from The National Archives of Australia (A1500, K28400)

Kel Nagle image from The National Archives of Australia (A1200, L33755) 1959 Canada Cup @ Royal Melbourne with Peter Thomson

Norman Von Nida image courtesy of the PGA of Australia.

Peter Thomson image from John W Fischer III's archives.

Peter Toogood image from Peter Toogood's private collection

Sir Bob Charles image courtesy of Photosport and NZ Golf

Other books by this author:

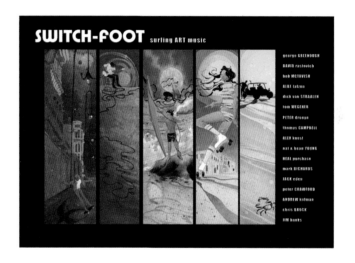

This book was assisted by:

Harry Whitton

Bruce Devlin

Doug Bachli   Kerry Packer   Bump & Run   Design   Canada

Fred   Nyana Nyana   Bump and Run   Bump & Run

Popplewell   Japan

Karrie Webb   Russell   Randall Vines   Fred

Russell   Doug   Bach Li

Peter Alliss   Tom Moore

Royal Melbourne   Ossie Pickworth   Victoria

Russell   Kong Hong   Malaysia   Victoria

Dan Soutar   Peter Thomson